Mysteries of the Inner Self

Great Mysteries

Mysteries of the Inner Self

by Stuart Holroyd

Aldus Books London

Editorial Consultants:
COLIN WILSON
DR. CHRISTOPHER EVANS

Series Coordinator: John Mason
Design Director: Günter Radtke
Picture Editor: Peter Cook
Editor: Eleanor Van Zandt
Copy Editor: Mitzi Bales
Research: Frances Vargo
General Consultant: Beppie Harrison

Printed and bound in Yugoslavia by
Mladinska Knjiga, Ljubljana

Introduction

What is the strange relationship between
the reality of the outside world and our
experience of it? Much of the time we
choose to act as if the world runs on wholly
rational lines, and we who inhabit it are
equally and predictably logical. Yet the
evidence of completely irrational aspects of
our existence lies all around us. Is our
physical form itself merely a temporary
casing for our inner being? The reports of
many ordinary people who have suddenly
been aware of their own bodies as an
outside spectator would be suggests that
the self and the body may not be an
unbreakable unity. The experience of many
who come close to death but recover
suggests that there may well be a point at
which the personality and the body
consciously part company—and the
personality continues. Then too there is
the fascinating and ambiguous world of
dreams which each of us visits nightly.
What do our nonsensical dreams have to
do with the sensible outside world—and
how do we account for the chilling
frequency of dreams which foretell the
"real" future? Is there some mysterious
link between our inner worlds and the
outer reality? Our inner selves—like our
dreams—are puzzling, enigmatic,
mysterious. But the quest to discover their
secrets is intriguing.

Contents

Chapter 1
Other Places, Other Times, Other Lives

Are space, time, and mortality really as limiting as most people believe them to be? Can people leave their bodies to visit another plane of existence, and then reenter the physical self they know? Here are some fascinating cases of astral experiences: a ship passenger who arrived more than three hours after he has been seen on board . . . a famous medium who looks over a doctor's shoulder in Iceland while her body is in New York . . . a modern artist who paints what he has seen on travels out of his body. This evidence points to the possibility of different levels of reality, which scientists today are investigating.

One day in 1828 Robert Bruce, the first mate on a ship trading between Liverpool, England and Canada, saw a complete stranger seated in the captain's cabin, writing on a slate. The man turned and gazed at him with such a fixed grave expression that Bruce took alarm and rushed up on deck to report what he had seen to the captain.

"You must be going crazy, Mr. Bruce," said the captain. "A stranger and we are nearly six weeks out! Go down and see who it is."

"I never was a believer in ghosts," said Bruce, "but, if the truth must be told, sir, I'd rather not face it alone." So the captain and mate went down together to the cabin, only to find it empty. When they examined the slate, however, they found written on it the words, "Steer to the Nor'west."

"Have you been trifling with me, sir?" said the captain sternly. Bruce swore that he had told the exact truth. The captain sat at his desk and pondered deeply for some minutes. Then he turned the slate over and asked Bruce to write "Steer to the Nor'west" on it. Satisfied that the writing on the two sides of the slate was completely different, he sent for the second mate and the steward in turn, and had them write the words. In this way he tested the entire crew. Not one of them had handwriting remotely resembling that on the slate. The ship was thoroughly searched from stem to stern, but no sign of a stowaway was found. "Mr. Bruce, what the devil do you make of all this?" the captain finally asked.

Opposite: this vision of one universe suspended inside another, entitled *Universes No. 2*, was painted by the psychic Ingo Swann, who claims to have explored space while traveling out of the body. Many of his paintings portray the dazzling wonders of the universe as he has experienced them. In this painting, the clouds and hills represent the physical universe, and the stars the psychic universes. His goal in painting, he said in an interview for *Psychic*, is "to recreate in the minds of others certain conditions of existence or awareness that I have experienced."

Experiences of "Soul Travel"

Below: Paul Twitchell is one of the many people who have claimed the ability to project the astral body, which he calls "Eckankar" or "soul travel." His writings have won him a large following in Europe and America, and many of his adherents claim that he has visited them astrally and cured them of illness or saved them from danger. Twitchell sees himself as standing at the hub of a spiritual wheel, sending cosmic power to his pupils at the rim of the wheel via "spiritual lines" represented by spokes.

"Can't tell, sir," said Bruce. "*I* saw the man write; *you* see the writing. There must be something in it."

Because the wind was favorable and a detour would only lose them a few hours, the captain gave orders to change course to the northwest. After some three hours of sailing, the lookout reported an iceberg ahead with a ship close to it. When they drew closer, the captain saw through his glass that the ship, with many people aboard, was virtually a wreck and frozen fast in the ice. He sent out boats to rescue the survivors. When the third rescue boat returned and its occupants were ascending the ship's side, the mate was astonished to see among them the man he had seen in the captain's cabin some hours before.

"Upon my word, Mr. Bruce, this gets more and more singular," said the captain when the mate identified their new passenger. "Let us go and see this man."

At the captain's request, the man wrote the words, "Steer to the Nor'west," on the blank side of the slate, and he was as astonished as anyone when the slate was turned over and the same words in the same handwriting were found on the other side.

"I only wrote one of these. Who wrote the other?" he said, turning the slate over and over. He had no recollection of the event that had so alarmed Bruce, but he remembered an incident that could have been connected. That day at about noon he had fallen into a deep sleep of exhaustion, and when he awakened he had announced that he was sure they would all be saved that day, because he had dreamed he was aboard a ship that was coming to their rescue. The captain of the wrecked ship confirmed this story. "He described her appearance and rig," the captain said, "and, to our utter astonishment, when your vessel hove in sight she corresponded exactly to his description of her."

This story, published in Robert Dale Owen's *Footfalls on the Boundary of Another World* in 1860, was related to that author by Captain Clarke, a close friend of Robert Bruce's. He described Bruce as "as truthful and straightforward a man as ever I met in all my life," and told Owen, "I'd stake my life upon it that he told me no lie." It is certainly an extraordinary story, but it is typical of thousands that collectively add up to substantial evidence for one of the strangest and most incomprehensible of human abilities: the ability to travel out of the body to distant locations. The evidence comes from all over the world and from all periods of human history. Some cultures have accepted out-of-the-body, or astral, projection and have found explanations for its occurrence, but until recently the West had generally dismissed the phenomenon as hallucination, or shrugged it off as fantasy or superstition.

It seems that people of all ages and from all walks of life have had out-of-the-body experiences. In fact, statistical surveys suggest that out-of-the-body experiences, or OOBEs as they are generally referred to in writings about them, occur to as many as one person in five. Usually the phenomenon comes at a time of crisis, but sometimes it happens spontaneously and for no apparent reason. Such experiences cannot be dismissed as mere hallucination or fantasy because in some cases the person is seen by others while he or she is out of the body, or is able to offer some verifiable evidence of the astral journey.

Below: in this painting a Tartar shaman dances around a fire to induce ecstasy. Among the peoples of central Asia shamanism is widespread. The shaman is believed to be capable of leaving his body at will. He does this for one or more of these purposes: to meet God face to face and bring Him an offering from the people; to increase his knowledge through contact with higher beings; to seek the soul of a sick person—it being believed that illness is caused by the "rape of the soul"; and to guide the soul of a dead person to its new abode. Shamans are also credited with other powers, such as turning themselves into animals and foretelling the future.

A woman who lived in Ireland, for example, and was in the habit of projecting out of her body, located the house of her dreams on one of her trips. Over a period of a year she returned to it many times, and each time it pleased her more. She and her husband were planning to move, and she thought the house would suit them ideally if only she knew where it was. They went house-hunting in London—on the ordinary physical plane—and to her delight one advertisement they answered took them to the house she knew so well. Everything down to the furniture and the decorations was as she had seen it on her out-of-the-body trips. Furthermore, the place was remarkably cheap because it was said to be haunted. When the prospective buyer met the owner,

Right: an American Indian shaman or magician-priest-doctor, in a 16th-century view. Human longing to escape the confines of the earthbound physical body is often expressed subconsciously in dreams of flying. The shaman deliberately induces a trancelike state in which he seems to leave his body. He dons a feathered costume and imitates the movements of birds in an attempt to become, in spirit, like a bird and to free his soul from physical limitations.

the latter stared at her and screamed, "You're the ghost!"

Most OOBEs are simple experiences of what is known as *autoscopy*—that is, seeing oneself from a distance. The view is normally from above and usually occurs during sleep, frequently after childbirth or an operation. Those who experience it are always firmly convinced that they have seen themselves as never before, clearly, distinctly, vividly, and in detail from outside. Traveling OOBEs are rarer, but a considerable number of psychically gifted people have developed in themselves the facility to practice astral projection. The OOBE, whether it occurs only once and spontaneously or frequently and deliberately, always leaves those who have it with the conviction that they possess a second body or double that is not subject to the limitations of the physical body. Most become convinced that some kind of personal identity or consciousness survives death.

Space, time, and mortality are the fundamental limiting principles of physical existence. Basing our idea of reality on the testimony of our senses, we have come to believe that we can only be in one place at a time and can obtain first-hand information only about the present moment. We also think that the physical body is like a machine that gradually runs down and finally stops functioning altogether. Religions and esoteric philosophies of mankind have always held that there are planes of reality beyond the physical where the limiting principles of space, time, and mortality do not apply. But common sense has generally scoffed at this view as wishful thinking. Strangely enough, modern developments in physics, psychology, and philosophy have tended to lend support to the religious and esoteric view, and to oust common sense from its position as supreme arbiter of what is real. Some experts say today that our senses were not evolved to give us knowledge of the Universe, but to enable us to exist within our environment. Their main function is to reduce the amount of confusing miscellaneous information that surrounds us, and to enable us to select what we need for practical survival.

If we accept the possibility of nonphysical planes of existence, the question then arises as to how we can gain information that would provide the proof about it. There have always been people claiming that they have special access to these nonphysical planes: shamans, witch doctors, mediums, mystics, psychics, and sensitives, for example. They have been regarded at different times and by different cultures either as demigods or frauds. Western scientists have recently begun to investigate their claims more seriously, and one of the areas of systematic and intensive scrutiny has been out-of-the-body experience. If people can really transcend the limitations of space, time, and mortality the implications for science, for philosophy, and for life are immense.

Some years ago a famous experiment was conducted with Mrs. Eileen Garrett, a medium who was highly respected by scientists because she took a serious approach to the study of her paranormal abilities. Eileen Garrett was able to project out of her body at will in a trance state, and to report on what she saw. In this particular experiment she was in an apartment in New York with a secretary and a psychiatrist. The target point for her projection was the office of a doctor in Reykjavik, Iceland. The

What are OOBEs?

Below: the late Eileen Garrett, one of the foremost mediums of this century, who experienced astral projection on several occasions.

Below: during an experiment for the American Society for Psychical Research (ASPR), Ingo Swann sits beneath a suspended platform on which two target pictures have been placed. He is attempting to project his consciousness up to the ceiling and so view the pictures lying on the platform. Electrodes stuck to his head measure his brain activity.

doctor had assembled a number of objects on a table in his office, which the medium was to attempt to describe. She not only described the objects correctly, but also repeated word for word a passage from a book that he was reading at the moment, and reported that the doctor's head was bandaged. Both the passage from the book and the fact that he had a head injury just before the experiment took place were later confirmed by the doctor, who also said that he had sensed the presence of Mrs. Garrett in his office during the experiment.

A present-day psychic who both projects out of his body at will and at the same time reports on his experience is the New York artist Ingo Swann. Swann has demonstrated OOB perception over both long and short distances. Under controlled laboratory conditions he has projected out of the body to the ceiling and correctly identified objects and geometrical shapes placed on a platform well above his head. In his autobiography *To Kiss Earth Good-Bye*, he gives some examples of a type of astral projection experiment he devised himself. The target was not a physical object but a location on the earth's surface identified by its latitudinal and longitudinal coordinates. Swann would sit in a chair smoking a cigar, and an experimenter would give him a randomly chosen coordinate that he would attempt to probe psychically. For instance, given the coordinate 32°E and 30°N, he responded: "Ah, looks dry, like Italy, no, not Italy, what are those things in the far distance, ah, they look like Pyramids, is that Cairo?" The coordinate was, in fact, of a situation near Cairo.

In another experiment Swann was given the coordinate 49°20′S and 70°14′E, and he responded: "I see what seems to be a mountain sticking up through some clouds, no, not just a mountain, it must be an island." The experimenter said he was wrong and that the location was right in the middle of the southern Indian Ocean. Further checking revealed, however, that there was an island at the indicated location, with mountains rising at its Eastern end. Swann continued his psychic probe, and drew a sketch of a part of the island showing a small landing field, some buildings, and some boats docked at a single jetty that had a lighthouse at its farther end. His sketch was later found to correspond with the features of the part of the island indicated by the coordinate, where a meteorological station was situated. This type of OOBE is called "remote viewing."

In 100 such experiments Swann gave 43 exactly correct descriptions of the location, and 32 descriptions that were nearly correct. He had 19 failures, and the remaining 6 were unverifiable. The tests were conducted under the supervision of Dr. H. Put-

Experiments in "Remote Viewing"

Below: response drawings by Ingo Swann from the ASPR experiment shown opposite. Bottom: target pictures from the test. They are marked S (south) and N (north) to indicate their placement on the platform and so suggest the point of view from which Swann saw them. This was one of a series of such experiments which indicated that Swann could see, psychically, the target drawings—by either clairvoyance, telepathy, or out-of-body vision. By signaling when he had returned to the body, Swann helped experimenters detect changes in brain activity during the event.

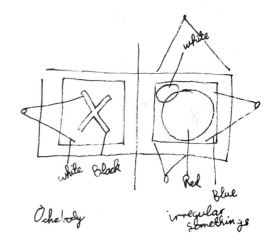

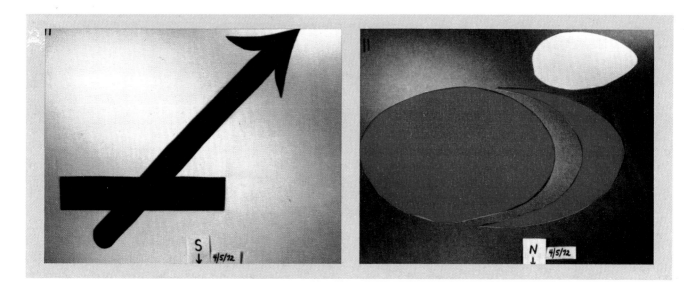

The Scientists Investigate

Right: Russell Targ, a physicist associated with the Stanford Research Institute. He has conducted many experiments on the possibility of out-of-the-body perception, or "remote viewing," by artist Ingo Swann and others.

Far right: Dr. Harold Puthoff, another scientist who has worked on the investigation of psychic phenomena at the Stanford Institute.

hoff, a physicist of the Stanford Research Institute in California. He is typical of the new generation of scientists who are studying paranormal phenomena seriously, and believe they may provide the key for a future scientific revolution as radical as the revolutions that stemmed from the discoveries and theories of Copernicus, Newton, and Einstein. Puthoff has carried out a number of OOB tests with several psychically gifted subjects, among them a former police commissioner, Pat Price. In one series of tests with Price as the subject, a group of experimenters drove to a randomly selected location in the San Francisco area and remained there for half an hour. Price attempted to project himself to the place they had gone, and to describe the location. When independent judges were given his and the experimenters' separate descriptions, they were able to match six out of nine of them correctly. Price was also successful in projecting to an island in the Indian Ocean, reporting that while there in his second body he had heard people speaking French.

Thousands of accounts of OOBEs have been collected and analyzed by the English researcher Dr. Robert Crookall. Over several decades he has carefully investigated, checked, and collated accounts from correspondents from all over the world. Here is a typical case from his records.

A young Englishwoman had just gotten married and was traveling with her husband on a transatlantic liner to the United States, where they were going to live. She was terribly seasick during the first day of the voyage. Her mother, sitting in her kitchen in England, was thinking about her daughter at the time. Suddenly she felt that she was out of her body and flying over the ocean. Finding the ship and the right cabin, she went in, took her daughter's hand, and told her that she would feel better if she washed, dressed, and went on deck. Then she flew back home. She noticed that only five minutes had elapsed since she had had the sensation of leaving her body. A few days later she received a letter from her daughter that confirmed every detail of the strange meeting: the time it had occurred, the condition the daughter had been in, and the exact words the mother had spoken to her.

Tales like this generally bring forth a polite smile, an unbelieving shrug, or an exclamation of "Incredible!" But the systematic and controlled research that parapsychologists and physicists are devoting to OOBEs today is steadily reducing their improbability. If just for the sake of an experiment a man can leave his physical body, project to a distant island he didn't know existed, and come back with an accurate description of it and its inhabitants, it is not at all improbable that a mother, strongly motivated by love and anxiety, might go out of the body to give comfort and help to her daughter at a time of distress.

Space is reportedly the limitation most easily and commonly transcended in OOBEs, and most accounts of such experiences record perception of events remote from where the physical body is situated. There is evidence, however, that the limitations of time can also be transcended in the OOBE. The following is an account of an experience by one of the best-known of all astral projectors, Sylvan Muldoon:

"In the spring of 1927, I awakened one night in the astral and found myself in a strange place—an unusually attractive park. I looked about me, observed its characteristics, and noted many special features, as well as its general aspect. I noted particularly a high rocky wall, and two small bridges crossing a stream. I had no memory of ever having visited this particular place, nor did I know where the place was. . . . It was two months later when, on a trip with a friend, I accidentally entered a park in a town about 50 miles from my home, and discovered it was the same place I had formerly visited in the astral!"

OOB time travel is a specialty of Alex Tanous, a present-day psychic who has on several occasions helped the police solve crimes and find missing persons, supposedly by projecting back in time and picking up a trail of events from the place where a person was last seen. At a meeting of psychologists, he once projected back to Russia at the time of the Revolution, and gave a vivid description of scenes and events details of which were later verified. On another occasion he told an anxious young woman whose mother was in the hospital for an operation exactly what was going to happen. By projecting into the future and observing events in the hospital, he told the woman that her mother's ailment would turn out not to be cancer, that a small section of the right lobe of her lung would be removed, that the operation would last one hour and 45 minutes, and that she would be out of the hospital within 10 days. These details later proved right.

So-called "false arrival cases" afford curious evidence that someone's double can be ahead of his or her physical body in time. The great novelist Leo Tolstoy vouched for the reality of this phenomenon. When the famous medium Daniel Dunglas Home was visiting Russia, Tolstoy and his wife went to meet him at Saint Petersburg railroad station. They saw Home get off the

Below: results from one series of remote viewing experiments conducted by Targ and Puthoff at SRI. The targets used were a group of machines located within the institute, and the one chosen for a given experiment was unknown to the experimenter sitting with the subject. The other experimenter would use the machine during a specified 15-minute interval while the subject attempted to reproduce it in a drawing and describe it on a tape recording. The psychically gifted artist, Ingo Swann achieved a close match.

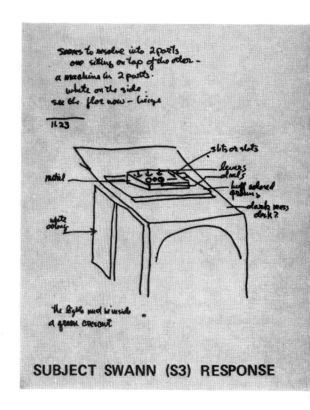

SUBJECT SWANN (S3) RESPONSE

Below: Alex Tanous, an American of Lebanese parentage, apparently possesses a great many psychic gifts, including the ability to leave the physical body and travel not only in space but also in time. Occasionally people have claimed to have seen him and even talked with him while he was physically in another place. While under observation in a laboratory he has projected himself into another room and moved an object inside that room.

train and walk rapidly away, totally ignoring them. Tolstoy's wife sent a note to his hotel expressing their disappointment at his strange conduct. The note was awaiting Home when he arrived by a train that came in three hours later than the one his double had arrived on.

False arrival cases are said to be particularly common in Norway, where apparently the appearance of a double some time before the person shows up in the flesh is so normal that it is often taken as a signal to start making coffee. Whatever the reason for the prevalence of this phenomenon in Norway—Crookall has suggested that "the high altitude . . . with diminished supply of oxygen favors the release of the double"—it is not confined to natives of that country. In 1955 an American business-man, Erkson Gorique, landed at Oslo airport and asked a taxi driver to take him to the best hotel. He had never been in Norway before and knew no one there. Imagine his surprise when the reception clerk at the hotel he was taken to said, "I'm glad to see you again, Mr. Gorique. It's so good to have you back." Wherever he went he was recognized and greeted, and everyone was under the impression that he had been there some months before. A wholesaler he visited on business welcomed him warmly by name and said, "You were in such a hurry the last time that we were not able to conclude the final details of our business." When Gorique protested that he had never been to the country before, the wholesaler told him about the common Norwegian experience of the "*Vardøger*," or forerunner. He assured Gorique that his experience wasn't such a rare thing, and he shouldn't let it disturb him unduly.

Gorique had been contemplating his journey some months before, and it seemed that in doing so he had unwittingly projected his double.

All the evidence for the reality of OOBEs points to the fact that the physical body is but a container, an "envelope" as some have called it, and that the essential self is not necessarily identified with it. There are many accounts by people who have been close to death of leaving the shell of the body and looking down on it with total indifference—even with a sense of relief at being finally freed of its limitations. If we make the assumption that human personality and the physical body do not constitute an integral unit, but are two separable entities, it is theoretically possible that there might be circumstances in which a body might be a host to more than one personality. Furthermore, if human personality survives death it is conceivable that it might return to inhabit another physical shell after one has served its temporary purpose.

Take the case of the Brazilian girl Silvia, born in São Paulo in March 1963. She began to introduce Italian words into her speech at an early age, but although she had Italian ancestry three generations back, nobody in her family or environment spoke Italian. It was her grandmother who first noticed Silvia's strange tendency, and from early in the child's life she kept a diary in which she noted the foreign words that Silvia came out with from time to time. She noted other things too. From the age of one month, Silvia manifested fear whenever an airplane flew overhead. Later when she was talking she referred to friends with

Italian names, particularly one called Affonsa Dinari. One day when she was nearing her fourth birthday she happened to see a color photograph of Rome, and she said excitedly, "That's the Capitol. That's the house I used to live in, and that's the school, and those are the rocks I used to jump about on." The caption under the picture was simply "Rome, Italy," with no mention of the Capitol. When her family investigated further they found that what she had pointed out was indeed so named. On another occasion she told how she had died in her previous existence. A friend had run toward her carrying a bomb that looked like a fountain pen. The bomb had suddenly exploded. "My friend and me, we went up and up . . ." she said. When her grandmother asked her what had happened next, Silvia said, "Then I came here."

This is one of many cases that have been collected by the Brazilian Institute for Psycho-Biophysical Research, and seem to provide evidence for reincarnation. The staff of the Institute, headed by an electronics engineer, Hernani Andrade, have carefully checked out hundreds of cases of young children having knowledge that they could not have obtained by normal means. Investigating Silvia's story, for instance, they found that the Allies had in fact dropped bombs of a fountain pen type on Rome during World War II. A prominent member of the Institute writes: "Allowing for the creativity of childish imaginations, we consider that we have gathered good evidence showing that reincarnation is a probability worthy of very serious consideration."

The very idea of reincarnation may be distasteful to the modern rationalist view of reality, but it is a fundamental belief in most of the world's religions, and one that the great Western philosophers of the ancient world—Pythagoras, Socrates, and Plato—all believed in. The idea that humans have a second immortal body is also basic to the beliefs of Christianity. In rejecting the idea of reincarnation, rationalism is rejecting not only the beliefs of many of the great thinkers and leaders of mankind throughout history, but also those of a steadily increasing number of present-day scientists. When the great accumulation of evidence from a wide variety of sources is seriously investigated, a philosophy that holds space, time and mortality as absolute limiting principles begins to look questionable.

"False Arrivals" as Phenomena

Below: the Russian writer Leo Tolstoy who, along with his wife, saw the "false arrival" of the British medium D. D. Home at St. Petersburg railroad station. Although born an aristocrat, with great wealth and property, Tolstoy turned in later years to a life of asceticism in keeping with his radical moral and religious thinking.

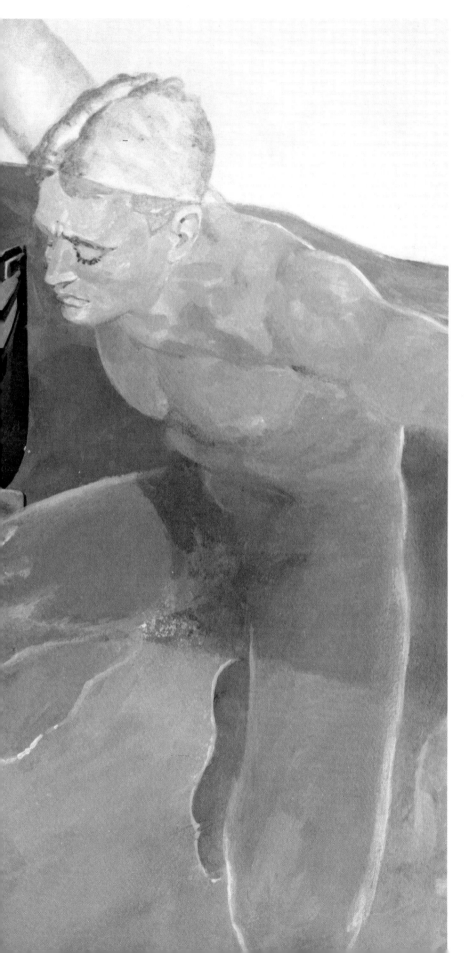

The Sublime Vision of a Drowning Man

One gray windy day in 1929 a man named Robert went for a swim in the ocean with a friend named Mildred. He had an extraordinary experience, which he related some years later.

The sea was rough that day and the current extremely strong. He was about to head for shore when he heard a faint cry from a frightened youngster clinging desperately to a board. Robert managed to reach him and hoist him onto the board just before he himself was overcome by a mountainous wave. He felt himself sinking. Suddenly, he found himself high above the water and looking down upon it. The sky which had been gray and menacing, glowed with a glorious light. Waves of color and music vibrated around him, and he felt an indescribable peace.

Then below him he saw his friend Mildred in a rowboat with two men. Floating near them was a limp and ungainly object that he recognized as his own body. He felt a great sense of relief that he no longer needed it. The men pulled the body out of the water and lifted it into the boat.

The next thing he knew, he was lying on the beach, cold and aching. He later learned that it had taken two hours to revive him. His help had saved the boy from drowning.

Chapter 2
Theories From the Past

Was the experience of the soul leaving the body familiar to the ancient world? The venerable *Tibetan Book of the Dead* places the dying man's soul at the moment of death in the summit of the skull—the neuroscientists now believe that consciousness in a dying patient gradually retreats to the fourth ventricle of the brain. Did the Tibetan shamans know as much about death as the most sophisticated medical men of today do? Is there a mysterious shamanic tradition of psychic travel in the form of a "double" which is still alive today? What can we learn from the ancient traditions about the relationship of the body and the soul?

Reports suggest that United States and Soviet government agencies have been vying with each other for years to develop methods of psychic espionage. The idea of using astral projection to discover the enemy's closely guarded secrets may sound like something out of futuristic fiction but, according to some interpretations, it can actually be traced back to the Bible. The prophet Elisha in the Second Book of Kings is supposed to have used his psychic powers for just such a purpose.

Syria and Israel were at war. Time and again the Syrian king had selected a point to launch a surprise attack, only to find that the Israelites had moved their army to that very place and were well-prepared to defend it. The king's plans were made in the seclusion of his own bedchamber, so he began to suspect that one of his trusted advisers was passing secret information to the enemy. He called them together for questioning. One, bolder than the rest, stepped forward. He denied that any of them had been responsible for betraying the king, and he offered a new theory to account for the leakage of information. He told them of the strange psychic powers of the Israelite prophet Elisha. "Elisha the prophet that is in Israel telleth the king of Israel the words that thou speakest in thy bedchamber," he suggested.

The Syrian king seems to have accepted the idea that a man many miles away could, through some mysterious or magical power, discover the secret plans of his innermost council. He determined to capture the prophet, and sent a large expeditionary

Opposite: this early 19th-century miniature from the *Bhagavata Purana*, written around the 10th century, depicts a scene from the legend of Usha's dream flight. In the story the young woman has a spontaneous out-of-the-body experience, in which she visits a distant place and returns with information about it that can be objectively verified. A modern Indian religious teacher, Bhagwan Shree Rajneesh, believes that humans are composed of seven bodies, ranging from the physical body up to the Nirvanic, each capable of having its own dreams. Dreams of the more spiritual bodies are more likely to contain elements of reality, Rajneesh maintains, than are the familiar dreams of the physical body.

Evidence from the Ancients

force to surround the town where he was living. However, once more he proved to be no match for Elisha. The prophet prayed to God, and the Syrian soldiers were struck blind. Elisha led them to the King of Israel, restored their sight, gave them food and drink, and sent them home. Not surprisingly, perhaps, they troubled Israel no more.

The story of Elisha suggests the interesting possibility that psychic powers had an early use in espionage. But not all such accounts that have come down to us from the Ancient World have had such a happy outcome. The story of Hermotimus of Clazomene, a Greek mystic of the 6th century B.C., is a cautionary tale. All psychic travelers in particular should bear it in mind.

Hermotimus was in the habit of spending days out of his body, roaming around the material and astral worlds. He would leave his physical body in the care of his wife, and when he returned to it he would tell her all about his adventures. His wife became rather bored with his tales and resentful of his long absences, and she decided to give him a shock. He had always stressed before his departures that if his physical body were moved at all he might have difficulty getting back into it. So she recruited two helpers, supposed friends of her husband's, to move his body to another room. Hermotimus' wife didn't doubt that he would be able to reenter his body, but she thought that if it were difficult this time, he might think twice before embarking on another excursion. What she didn't know was that the two supposed friends were in fact her husband's rivals in sorcery. They simply cremated his body. Hermotimus' ghost, it was said, hung about his home for years afterwards, wailing for restoration of the physical body he had been cheated of.

There is a belief found in many different parts of the world that in sleep a person travels out of his body. It is therefore thought to be dangerous to awaken a person too abruptly, because his traveling body may not have had time to get back into the physical one, and the two may be permanently separated.

The notion that man has more than one body, and that the

Right: a painting of the prophet Elisha raising the son of the Shunammite woman from the dead. Elisha was credited with the ability to travel astrally.

physical is only one of several forms of existence, can be found in ancient cultures and religions all over the world. Long before Christianity people believed in the resurrection of the body after death, and in mystic journeys of the spirit during life. The Church Fathers waged a campaign against all forms of pagan superstition and magic, but the ancient belief in astral travel was not regarded as a superstition. Saint Augustine tells a story that involves the acquisition of verifiable information during an out-of-the-body experience.

A senator by the name of Curma was near death, and after several days in a coma, his spirit separated from his body. He heard his name being called, and thought that he was being sum-

Below: a painting by Botticelli of St. Augustine (A.D. 354–430). A profound thinker and author of many books, including the *Confessions* and *The City of God*, Augustine believed in the possibility of out-of-the-body experiences and told a story of an OOBE yielding verifiable information.

Animism and Soul Rebirth

Right: a representation of a tree spirit
carved on fhe branch of a sacred tree in
India. Animism, the belief that everything
in nature has a spirit, is believed to be the
first form of religion that primitive people
develop.

Below: an 18th-century Jain icon in brass
representing the spirit liberated from matter.
Like Hinduism, the Jain religion teaches the
transmigration of souls and the belief that
eventually the soul can be freed from the
cycle of rebirths. Appropriately, the
liberated spirit—called the Jina or Victor in
Jainism—is suggested in this icon by
empty space.

moned for posthumous judgment. But he learned from other spirits that he was still alive and that it was another Curma, a goldsmith who had just died, who was being called. He noticed that not all the beings around him were spirits of the dead, because some were of people he knew to be still alive. If he himself were not dead, then, he and they must be on a visit to some limbo region. Finally he returned to his physical body, came out of his coma, and immediately sent someone to the house of Curma the goldsmith. The messenger returned with the news that the artisan had recently died.

The idea that humans have a second body that coexists with the physical one but can separate from it during life, particularly in conditions of trance or sleep, and survives it after death, arose very early and is widespread. It rests on the belief that everything has another reality apart from the reality it presents to our senses. According to this belief, there is another world, invisible and intangible but no less real, lying beyond the world we can see and touch. Nothing is what it seems. Trees, mountains, stones, plants, rivers, lakes—all have spirits. The stars and planets are living entities that influence life on earth, and the world is full of hidden mysterious forces and interactions. The essence of this belief, which we now call *animism*, was expressed as far back as the 6th century B.C. by one of the earliest Greek philosophers, Thales of Miletus. In his words, "All things are full of gods."

To the Western scientific mind of the 19th century, such a statement seemed to be pure nonsense. Modern science was founded on the idea of the existence of an objective physical world that would yield its secrets to investigation by analysis and dissection, and on the belief that man, with his trained intellect and sophisticated tools, was equipped to discover ultimate truths. Its criteria of reality were clear. Everything existed in three-dimensional space; all matter was an aggregate of invisible atomic particles possessing mass and controlled by mechanical forces that obeyed fixed laws; every event must be causally linked with a prior one. Anything that failed to meet these criteria could not possibly be real. The ancient animist view of the world was rejected by 19th-century science as childish and ignorant.

In the present century, however, new scientific discoveries have reversed many of the notions of the 19th century, and the early animist ideas no longer appear entirely ridiculous. To the three dimensions of space Einstein has added time as a fourth dimension, and modern quantum theory postulates a multi-dimensional Universe. Mass has been shown to be a property of matter only at the macroscopic level, and even then to be convertible to energy. At the microscopic level mass disappears completely, and particles becomes waves. Other particles appear possessing illogical properties like negative mass or the ability to move backward in time. At this microscopic level, uncaused events constantly occur, effects sometimes precede causes, and mechanical laws break down and have to be replaced by mathematical laws of probability. Strange as it may seem, 20th-century physics has moved away from the scientific philosophy of the 19th century, and in many ways appears closer to the old animist view. Scientists examining the hierarchy of living organisms find it increasingly difficult to draw a line below which they can

Above: this wooden Eskimo salmon mask, worn at a spring festival, depicts not only the physical form of the fish but also the frightening spirit that lurks within it. The Eskimo religion is animistic, and contains many elements of fear. The spirits that inhabit all creatures are potentially menacing, and the spirits of humans that have died must be placated and guarded against by a host of taboos and special precautions.

The Aura of the Second Body

Below: the ancient and widespread belief that all living things have a nonmaterial essence has received some scientific backing in recent years with the development of Kirlian photography. This process, the work of Soviet scientists, reveals a glowing aura given off by animals and even plants, such as this daisy. Even when part of a leaf is cut away, the aura of the removed section will remain visible in the photograph.

confidently assert that consciousness does not exist. Nothing is just what it seems. There appear to be other dimensions of reality not accessible to human senses.

Soviet scientists have in recent years been investigating the energy fields, or auras, that surround and emanate from living organisms. Mystics and sensitives throughout the ages have claimed to be able to distinguish an aura surrounding the physical body. Modern techniques of electrophotography have confirmed these claims. Photographs have established that a second body, often called a bioplasmic or energy body by scientists, does in fact surround the physical one. Even more, they confirm ancient theories about this aura. In the 2nd century A.D. the Greek writer Plutarch described how different kinds of human auras corresponded with different physical and psychological states. The Soviets have found that the light emitted by a living body is bright, dull, colorful, or colorless depending on the state of the person.

Another unexpected result of recent research into the aura is that the human body emits strange shafts of light from certain points, and these points seem to correspond exactly with the

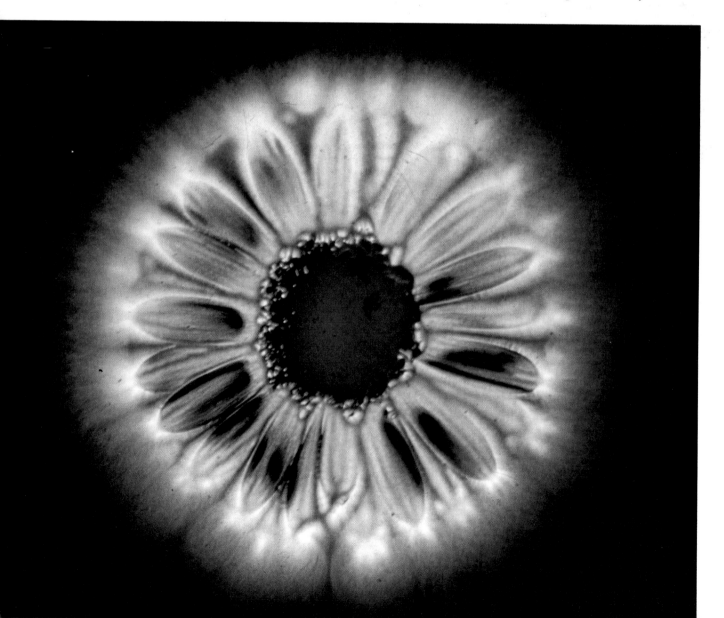

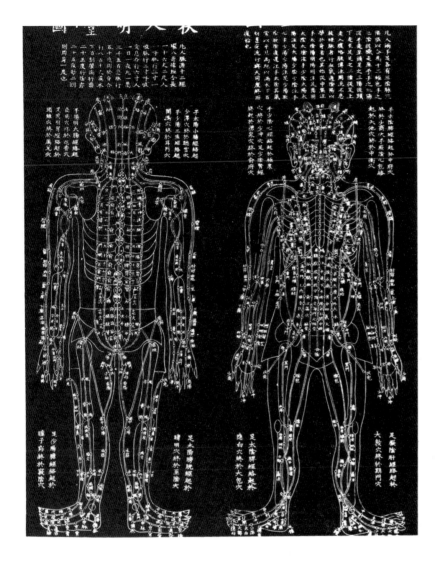

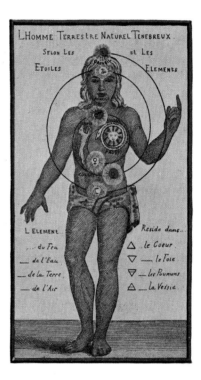

Left: an ancient Chinese chart showing the points for acupuncture, each associated with an organ of the body. The points are located along 12 lines, or meridians, through which the life force is believed to flow. Research into the aura shows that shafts of light are emitted from points corresponding to acupuncture points.

points used in the ancient Chinese technique of acupuncture. Acupuncturists believe that the body is traversed by a system of invisible meridian lines which carry the life force essential to the body's health. The insertion of needles at certain points along a meridian line will help cure discomfort or pain at other points along the line. Great skill is needed in order to select these points. Acupuncture is puzzling to those trained in Western medicine because the meridian lines and points do not correspond to any physical system in the body. They cannot be located by eye. The discovery that the points correspond to shafts of light in the human aura does, however, lend more credence to the suggestion that the acupuncturist may be operating on the subtle, or astral, body to cure the physical body.

The idea of the subtle body is widespread, but it is found especially in Eastern religions and occult beliefs. It is thought to be the ethereal and invisible counterpart, or double, of the physical body. It is said to be composed of semifluid matter and a network of ganglia, and is supposed to be separate from the physical body but meeting it at certain points. In yoga, the points at which the physical and subtle bodies meet are known as the

Above: this illustration from *Theosophica Practica*, a book by the 17th-century German mystic Johann Georg Gichtel, shows the seven chakras, which—according to Hindu belief—are located at points where the subtle body and the physical body are connected. The chakras are thought to be centers of psychic energy. Like the acupuncture points, they seem to correspond to the points where light is released in the aura.

Right: Filipino "psychic surgeon" Tony Agpaoa, who performs what appear to be operations using only his bare hands to open the body. His 40-bed clinic receives patients from many countries.

 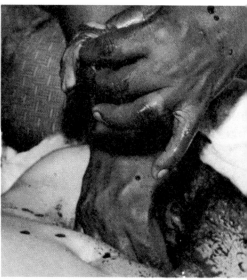

Far right: an abdominal "operation" being performed by Agpaoa. Some observers have suggested that the blood and diseased tissue are produced by sleight of hand and that perhaps the healing reported by patients results from his having really operated on the subtle body.

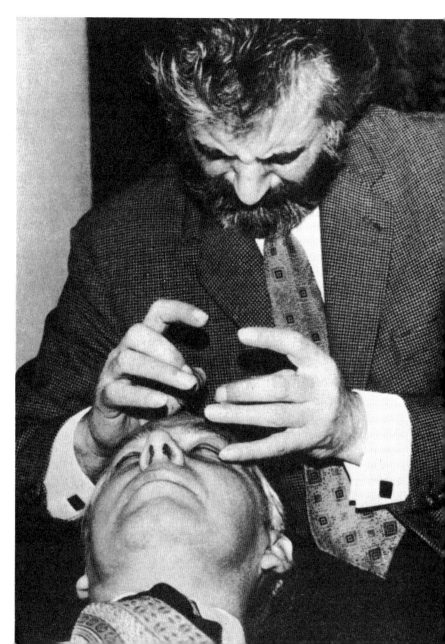

Right: medium George Chapman doing a psychic eye operation while controlled by the spirit of Dr. William Lang. Chapman remains in a trance during the treatment and does not touch the patient. He maintains that illness results from the spirit self not being in harmony with the physical self. The spirit body, he says, supplies energy to the physical body. He admits that not all of the operations have been successful, but startling and apparently spontaneous cures are reported by many of the people who visit his clinic in England.

chakras or wheels. They are thought to be psychic centers of superhuman energy. It has been found that the points at which the chakras are said to be located also correspond with shafts of light in the human aura.

In Brazilian Spiritist healing, operations are sometimes performed on the physical body and sometimes on the subtle body, also known as the perispirit. In the operations on the perispirit, the physical body is not touched. Guy Playfair, a present-day English psychic researcher who has lived in Brazil for many years, has witnessed operations of both kinds. In his recent book *The Flying Cow*, he describes the work of Edivaldo Silva, a school-teacher who in his spare time as a spirit healer has treated about 65,000 patients in 10 years. Edivaldo told Playfair that when he operated he was in a trance state, and never remembered any of his patients later. He was controlled by a number of spirit doctors, but mainly by a Spanish-speaking one called Dr. Calazans.

When Playfair watched Edivaldo, controlled by Calazans, in action, he noticed that his voice and manner was different from when he was out of trance. Edivaldo was usually gentle and soft-spoken, but under Calazans' control was authoritative and brusque. In one operation witnessed by Playfair, the patient was a man aged about 30. He lay on a table with his shirt unbuttoned to expose his chest and stomach. Edivaldo-Calazans moved his hands about in the air above the man's stomach, keeping up a commentary as if for a class of medical students while he worked. At first Playfair caught only odd phrases such as ". . . separate the etheric double . . . fourth dimension . . . remove the plasma from the red corpuscles." Edivaldo-Calazans kept waving his hands about. "Now he's feeling it open," he said. "Not in the mind, but in the body itself, above the stomach. . . . Now we are putting in a drain, to serve as tubing."

When the operation was over Edivaldo gave instructions that the patient rest completely for 48 hours; but it turned out that the man had brought nobody with him and had intended to drive himself home. Edivaldo was immensely amused at this and sent him to lie on another bed while he attended to the next patient. Playfair reports: "The man climbed stiffly off the bed and slumped onto the other bed. He looked dazed and weak. The whole operation had been entirely invisible to my eyes, but he had certainly felt something. He began to moan. . . ." He continued moaning and muttering incoherently to himself for a long time, and in an interval between operations Edivaldo drew the onlookers' attention to him. "See the effect of the anesthetic?" he said. "Know what that is called? No? Shock, that's what. Anaphylactic, or postoperative shock." He ordered the man to sit up and drink some coffee, and told him he would shortly be well enough to go home by taxi.

Operations on the second body that cure the physical body are also regularly performed today by the English healer George Chapman. His control is Dr. William Lang, an eminent eye specialist who died in 1937. Bernard Hutton, a journalist who was cured of polio and incipient blindness by Chapman, has written a remarkable book, *Healing Hands*. He tells of numerous healings allegedly performed by Lang through Chapman, which have involved no contact between the healer and the patient's

The Mystery of Spiritual Healing

Below: William Lang, a British ophthalmologist and Fellow of the Royal College of Surgeons who died in 1937 but who—according to many people—is said to be still operating on patients today, via the medium George Chapman. The spirit of Dr. Lang is reported to have successfully treated a great variety of ailments by operating on the patient's spiritual body.

What is Shamanism?

Below: an Eskimo shaman beats his drum during a Christmas celebration that still retains elements of the pagan festival it supplanted. The drum is one of the aids used by a shaman in his process of inducing a state of ecstasy so as to leave his physical body. In Eskimo belief, the shaman plays a vital role in placating the important spirits that control the natural world, for he can fly to their dwelling places and there perform the required rituals.

physical body. Evidence for the reality of second-body healing may not be conclusive, but it is certainly abundant.

Healing is also one of the chief functions of shamans, the magician-priests who still survive today in tribal communities from Australia to the Arctic. Shamans are believed to be able to leave their body at will, and to travel throughout the material world or the regions of the dead. They claim that there are spirits, gods, and demons that are responsive only to their powers. Besides curing sickness, the shaman directs communal sacrifices and escorts the souls of the dead to the other world. According to Professor Mircea Eliade, who has written a scholarly book entitled *Shamanism*, the shaman is able to do these things because he has mastered the techniques of ecstasy: "that is, because his

soul can safely abandon his body and roam at vast distances, can penetrate the underworld and rise to the sky. Through his own ecstatic experience he knows the roads of the extraterrestrial regions. He can go below and above because he has already been there. The danger of losing the way in these forbidden regions is still great; but sanctified by his initiation and furnished with his guardian spirits, the shaman is the only human being able to challenge the danger and venture into a mystical geography."

The "techniques of ecstasy" are in fact the techniques of out-of-the-body projection. The word "ecstasy" means literally "standing outside," and the shaman achieves this trancelike state through dance, music, fasting, meditation, drug-taking, or self-hypnosis. In some tribal societies the shaman not only accomplishes the healing of ailments believed to be caused by "loss of soul," but also practices divination and clairvoyance, and can travel out of his body to locate lost objects, people, or animals. Shamans are reputed to be able to cover vast distances in an instant, to be in two places at the same time, and to visit places inaccessible to ordinary mortals. Buddhist legend tells of the miraculous lake Anavatapa, and Hindu legend of the mysterious northern land Svetadvipa. Both are places that can only be reached by those capable of magical flight. Legends of visits to the underworld, which are common in Nordic and Greek mythologies, are expressions of the shamanic tradition. Eskimo shamans claim to undertake fantastic journeys, remain out of the body for days, and return to tell of adventures in the depths of the sea or among the stars. During their flight their physical bodies remain in a state of suspended animation, motionless and apparently lifeless. Eliade says, "they always take the precaution of having themselves bound with ropes, so that they will journey only 'in spirit;' otherwise they would be carried into the sky and would vanish for good."

One of the chief functions of the shaman is the guidance of the souls of the dead. This role is particularly emphasized in Lamaism, the Tibetan form of Buddhism. The famous *Tibetan Book of the Dead* is a kind of guidebook to the afterworld, directing the departed soul as to which routes to travel and which to avoid. The "science of death" is a complex science in Tibetan tradition, and a dying man needs the assistance of highly trained priests in order to accomplish the right manner of separation of the soul from the physical body. The priest supervises the retreat

Below: this 17th-century engraving shows a shaman of central Asia wearing a coat decorated with embroidery and a fringe of bones. In the young shaman's initiatory dream, he is dismembered by demonic beings, who scrape the flesh from his bones. The bones are then put back together and covered with new flesh. In Siberia it is believed that he is given the same number of spirits as there are bones left over after he has been reconstituted.

Below: spirits of an Eskimo shaman, drawn by the shaman himself. Some Eskimos believe that a person's soul is a kind of miniature of him that lives somewhere in his body. Others think that many of these souls are scattered around the body—particularly at the joints.

Right: Pluto and Persephone pictured on a Greek amphora. According to mythology, Pluto—also known as Hades—abducted his niece Persephone and carried her down to the shadowy underworld in which he lived. This underworld was conceived of as a gloomy and marshy place crossed by several rivers, to which the souls of the deceased would travel.

Below: a photo taken in the 1920s showing a Tibetan lama wearing an apron made of human bones. A Jesuit missionary to Tibet in the 18th century reported that the Tibetans did not bury their dead, but fed the bodies to birds and other animals. This was an expression of their belief in the passage of souls from one creature to another and an affirmation of man's oneness with all of nature.

of consciousness in the dying man, making him focus attention on each of his bodily functions and senses in turn and deliberately relinquish them. He guides the departing soul into the summit of the skull, and at the moment of death shouts the magic syllable "Hik!" in order to open a hole in the skull through which the soul can depart. When the separation has been properly accomplished, the priests chant ritual texts to guide the soul on its way.

Strangely enough, neuroscientists studying the process of dying have discovered that consciousness gradually deserts the physical body, finally retreating into the fourth ventricle of the brain. This ventricle forms part of a complex that is the first internal body structure to appear in an embryo. It is as if the soul retreats by the way it came. Moreover, at the moment that consciousness finally deserts the fourth ventricle, the body loses about one-half to three-quarters of an ounce of weight. This is a phenomenon that has been known for 60 years but has never been explained in terms of loss of physical matter. Perhaps the Tibetan shamans know certain things about death that surpass the scientific knowledge of the West.

In four books published since 1968, Carlos Castaneda, an American anthropologist who became apprenticed to a Mexican Indian sorcerer, shows that the shamanic tradition is still very much alive today. Even if his books were fictitious, as some critics have suggested, they would still constitute a brilliantly imaginative evocation of shamanism, and it does not seem too highly improbable that in Don Juan and Don Genaro the young anthropologist had the good fortune to meet and be taken into the confidence of two genuine modern shamans.

Toward the end of his first book, *The Teachings of Don Juan*, Castaneda describes an OOBE, and a subsequent discussion of it that he had with Don Juan. Don Juan had told him that a sorcerer can soar through the air for hundreds of miles to see what is happening or to strike a fatal blow to an enemy. After drinking a potion concocted by Don Juan from the root of datura, or devil's weed, Castaneda took off. He pushed up with both feet, sprang backward, and glided on his back. "I saw the dark sky above me, and the clouds going by me. I jerked my body so I could look down. I saw the dark mass of the mountains. My speed was extraordinary. My arms were fixed folded against my sides. My head was the directional unit. If I kept it bent backward, I made vertical circles. I changed direction by turning my head to the side. I enjoyed such freedom and swiftness as I had never known before. . . ." He finally descended and landed amid landscape he recognized as being about half a mile from Don Juan's

The Nature of the Human Soul

Left: a scene from the Indian epic *Mahabharata*, which tells of a war between two related royal families. One of the combatants, Drona, lays aside his armor and regrets that he, a Brahmin, has taken up arms and shed blood. He sits yogi-fashion under a tree and begins to collect his soul together from his limbs. As his head is cut off by the brother of a man he has killed, his soul rises up like a red flame. The story recalls the symbolic assistance given to the dying by Tibetan priests, who shout the magic syllable "Hik!" at the point of death in order to open the skull and enable the soul to pass through it.

Castaneda and the Other Self

Below: the elusive anthropologist and best-selling author Carlos Castaneda photographed in the research room of the UCLA library. His books about a Mexican Indian sorcerer called Don Juan, who initiated him into the world of drugs and magic, has sold hundreds of thousands of copies.

house. He was completely naked and it was nearly dawn. He tried to run but hurt his feet on the stones of the road. He hid behind bushes when he saw someone approaching along the road, but when the figure drew closer he saw that it was Don Juan and that he was bringing his clothes.

The experience was unusually real and vivid, but was it an hallucination? "Did I really fly, Don Juan? . . . I mean, did my body fly? Did I take off like a bird?" Castaneda asked. Don Juan replied that the purpose of the devil's weed was for flying, so of course he had flown, and as he took more of it he would learn to fly perfectly. Castaneda wasn't satisfied. He asked if a friend would have been able to see him fly. That depended on the friend, Don Juan said. Exasperated, Castaneda asked what would have happened if he had been tied to a rock with a heavy chain. Don Juan was puzzled by his insistent questions, and answered that he would have to fly holding the rock with the heavy chain. He didn't understand Castaneda's problem, and his insistence on the word "really." The sorcerer's world was one of multileveled reality. "The trouble with you," he told his apprentice, "is that you understand things in only one way."

Castaneda gave up his apprenticeship after some frightening experiences that made him fear for his sanity and his life, but he couldn't stay away for long from the strange world of adventure and knowledge that Don Juan had introduced him to. He later met Don Juan's friend and fellow-sorcerer Don Genaro, an ebullient old man full of clownish humor in whose presence he always "experienced the most outlandish sensory distortions." At the beginning of his fourth book, *Tales of Power*, Castaneda relates one of his weirdest experiences. Don Juan was supervising him in some exercises in intense visualization. He called up before his mind's eye images of 32 persons in succession. Don Juan told him that to conclude he should try to call up Don Genaro. Castaneda went through the prescribed procedure, and suddenly Don Genaro was standing in front of him, large as life. "You called me, didn't you?" he said "Where were you?" Castaneda asked. He was sure that the two old men must have contrived an elaborate trick just to astonish him. But Don Genaro replied that he had been in his home in central Mexico several hundred miles away when Castaneda had called him. Don Juan explained in a matter-of-fact manner that, "Genaro is a man of knowledge. . . . And being a man of knowledge, he's perfectly capable of transporting himself over great distances." He went on to say that consummate sorcerers were capable of being in two places at once. "For a warrior like Genaro," he said, "to produce the other was not such a far-fetched enterprise."

Castaneda was full of questions, which Don Juan answered patiently.

"Is the other like the self?"

"The other is the self."

"What's the other made of?"

"There's no way of knowing that."

"Is it real or just an illusion?"

"It's real of course."

"Would it be possible to say that it is made of flesh and blood?"

"No. It would not be possible."

"But you have to admit, Don Juan, that there must be a way to know."

"The double is the self; that explanation should suffice. If you would *see*, however, you'd know that there is a great difference between Genaro and his double. For a sorcerer who *sees*, the double is brighter."

Don Juan said that in all the years Castaneda had known Don Genaro, he had only been with the original Genaro twice, and every other time he had been with his double.

"But this is preposterous," Castaneda said.

Don Juan said, "I've told you time and time again that the world is unfathomable. And so are we, and so is every being that exists in this world. It is impossible, therefore, to reason out the double. You've been allowed to witness it, though, and that should be more than enough."

Castaneda was understandably astonished by his experience of calling up Don Genaro's palpable and physical double, and bewildered by Don Juan's explanation. His readers no doubt share his bewilderment and incredulity. But tales of the appearance of a person's double in solid corporeal form are so common the world over, and in many cases so well authenticated, that the phenomenon, inexplicable though it is, has to be taken seriously. Such tales are even found in the annals of governments. For example, a member of the British House of Commons, Dr. Mark Macdonell, appeared in the House in his double and cast a vote on an important measure when his other body was confined to his bed because of a serious illness. Another member of the august assembly, Sir Carne Rasch, was seen in the House by other members during an important discussion in 1908, although at the time he was laid up with influenza. A member of the Legislative Council of British Columbia, Charles Good, was not only seen by other members but also photographed with them in January 1865, though he was gravely ill at home and possibly in a coma. Politicians are not normally accomplished in the art of sorcery—at least in the strict meaning of the term—and one would not look among their number for adepts of second-body projection. Evidence for the reality of the human double among them, then, is most unexpected.

The Catholic Church has always accepted that bilocation, or being in two places at once, and astral travel are possible, though with the reservation that only individuals of great sanctity are capable of achieving these powers. Such a man was Saint Anthony of Padua. According to tradition, while he was preaching in a church in Limoges in 1226, he suddenly remembered that he was supposed to be present at that moment at a service in a church on the other side of town. He interrupted his sermon, knelt down, and drew his hood over his head. For several minutes the congregation waited patiently for him to resume, assuming that he was praying. Meanwhile, in the other church, monks saw the saint appear among them, heard him read an appointed passage in the service, and then witnessed his sudden disappearance. His double returned to his original body, and the first sermon was resumed.

Saint Alphonsus Liguori came round from a five-day fast and trance one autumn day in 1774, and told the friars assembled

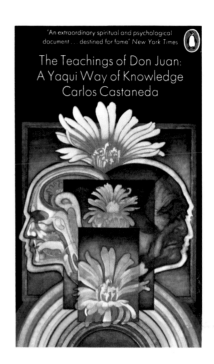

Above: the cover of Castaneda's first book, in which he describes meeting the Yaqui sorcerer and his own apprenticeship with him.

Below: his third book tells how Castaneda learned to "see" without drugs, through meditation and exercises in perception.

The Devil's Weed

For more than two years, the young anthropology student had been apprenticed to the old Indian and had learned from him many strange secrets about the desert. Then one day the Indian, Don Juan, told him that it was time to test the Devil's weed. The student, Carlos, gathered the plants. Under the Indian's direction he laboriously concocted a paste from the roots of the plants and finely ground seeds and insects. Don Juan then prepared a potion, which he told Carlos to drink. It made the young man's heart pound. Don Juan ordered him to smear the paste over his naked body. The smell suffocated him, but he obeyed. When he tried to walk he discovered that his legs were "rubbery and . . . extremely long." He moved forward and then soared into the air. He glided effortlessly among the clouds. "The marvelous darkness gave me a feeling of sadness, of longing . . . as if I had found a place where I belonged . . ." Suddenly he knew that it was time to come down. He descended with slow, jerky motions that nauseated him, and he lost consciousness. When he came to, he was lying naked, about half a mile from Don Juan's house. He saw a man coming toward him, carrying clothes. It was Don Juan.

The OOBEs of Padre Pio

Right: *St. Anthony of Padua and the Christ Child*, painted by Tiepolo. St. Anthony is reported to have traveled out of the body once in order to assist at a service in a church other than the one in which he was physically present at that moment.

Below: one of the stigmata that appeared on the hand of Padre Pio, an Italian priest reported to have traveled out of the body to help others. It appeared when he was 31 years old. He was praying when suddenly he cried out and collapsed, unconscious. His fellow friars ran to his aid and found him bleeding from his hands, feet, and body. Shortly after this he began to perform miracles. He reportedly healed hundreds of people before he died in 1960.

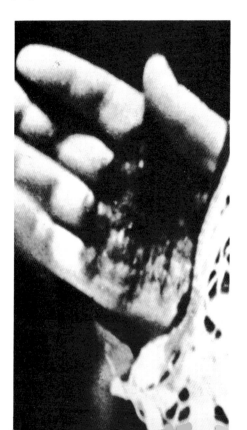

around him that he had been out of his body and had attended at the deathbed of Pope Clement XIV. News of the Pope's death had not reached the monastery at the time, because Rome was four days' journey away. His statement was later confirmed by people who had been at the bedside of the dying pope. They said they had seen him there, kneeling in prayer.

The tales of Saints Anthony and Alphonsus may be no more than legends, but there are people living today who can testify to the ability of the Capuchin monk Padre Pio to materialize from nowhere, and help people in trouble. Padre Pio hardly ever left his monastery near Poggia, Italy, but his busy double was out healing and helping all over the place. During World War I an Italian general, after a series of defeats, was on the point of committing suicide when a monk entered his tent and said, "Such an action is foolish," and promptly left. The general didn't hear of the existence of Padre Pio until some time later, but when he visited the monastery near Poggia, he identified him as the monk who had appeared at a crucial moment and saved his life.

During World War II an Italian pilot baled out of a blazing plane. His parachute failed to open but he miraculously fell to the ground without injury, and he returned to his base with a strange story to tell. When he had been falling to the ground, a

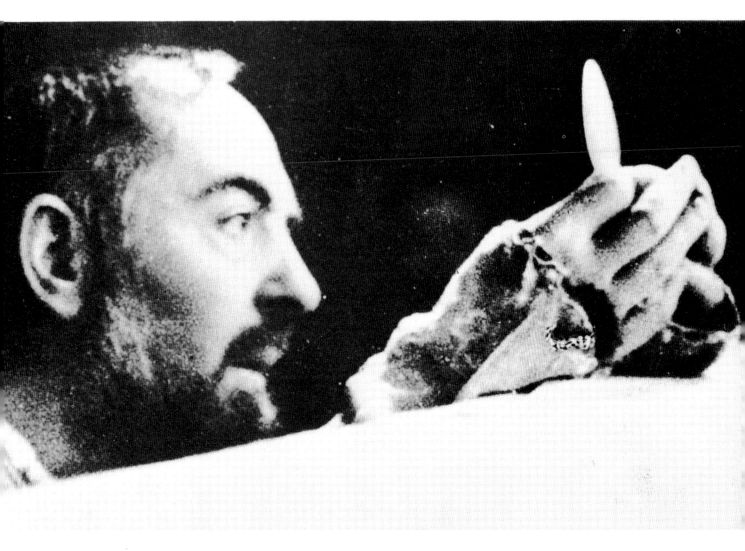

Above: Padre Pio celebrating Mass. He was widely loved and venerated, and many people have told stories of his out-of-the-body visits to people who were suffering or in danger when he appeared to them.

friar had caught him in his arms and carried him gently down to earth. His Commanding Officer said he was obviously suffering from shock, and sent him home on leave. When he told his mother the tale of his escape she said. "That was Padre Pio. I prayed to him so hard for you." Then she showed him a picture of the Padre. "That is the same man!" said the young pilot. He later went to Poggia to thank the padre for his intervention. "That is not the only time I have saved you," said Padre Pio. "At Monastir, when your plane was hit, I made it glide safely to earth." The pilot was astounded because the event the Padre referred to had happened some time before, and there was no normal way he could have known about it.

There are numerous other tales of the amazing bilocations of Padre Pio, a man of our century who, motivated by his vocation as helper and healer, exercised a paranormal faculty whose reality is attested to throughout all ages and cultures of the world. The evidence, taken together, adds up to a substantial case for the reality of the human double—the astral, the etheric, the bioplasmic, the subtle, or the energy body as it has been variously called. It is certainly a strange phenomenon but it has been well attested, and as Don Juan said, "The world is unfathomable. And so are we. . . ."

Chapter 3
The Projection of
the Astral Body

What are the elements of an out-of-the-body projection which seem to be common to many accounts? Is there indeed a pattern for these extraordinary experiences? What have scientific observers learned in their attempts to study the phenomenon? Some detractors suggest that reports of OOBEs are in fact particularly vivid hallucinations—and certainly many of those experiencing them are suffering from abnormal conditions. But what about the perfectly ordinary stable people who have found themselves observing their own bodies . . . from a distance? And what about those who have encountered an astral body on its perambulations? Are they hallucinating as well?

Imagine that you were to wake up from a dream, reach out to switch on a bedside lamp, and find yourself grasping at a void. Coming fully awake, you realize that you are suspended in mid-air. You are in command of all your sensory faculties, and can see all the familiar features of your room including your own physical body lying peacefully asleep in the bed below. It is difficult for anyone to imagine how he or she would initially react to such an experience. William Gerhardie, the English novelist whose first astral projection occurred in this way, was neither alarmed nor frightened. He said to himself, "Now this *is* something to tell. And this is *not* a dream." Gerhardie's account of his first astral projection appears in his partly autobiographical novel *Resurrection*, which was published in 1934. Gerhardie is certain of the authenticity of the experience, and his description is a useful one on which to base an examination of out-of-the-body experiences. The author had no prior knowledge of the phenomenon before it happened to him, and he was able to observe it with the professional writer's curiosity, detachment, and eye for detail. The most convincing evidence for the reality of astral projection for a person who has not experienced it is the fact that many of the same characteristics can be found in accounts from widely different sources. Several of these characteristics are to be found in Gerhardie's narrative.

He remained suspended in the air for several minutes, then felt himself pushed forward and placed on his feet. He staggered to

Opposite: the projection of the astral body as imagined by a modern artist. Nearly all accounts of such experiences include a reference to the cord—usually described as silver in color—that links the astral body to the physical body. People who have researched the subject of astral travel believe that about one person in 100 has had an out-of-the-body experience.

Vivid Accounts of Extraordinary Experiences

Below: British novelist and playwright William Gerhardie, who described his out-of-the-body experience in a semi-autobiographical novel, *Resurrection*, published in 1934. After coming back to his body, he checked all the rooms through which he had traveled and was able to verify details he had noticed during his experience.

the door but was unable to turn the handle because he had no grip in his hand. He became aware of a strange appendage. At his back was a coil of light that resembled "the strong broad ray of dusty light at the back of a dark cinema projecting onto the screen in front." To Gerhardie's astonishment he found that the cable of light "illumined the face on the pillow, as if attached to the brow of the sleeper. The sleeper was myself, not dead, but breathing peacefully, my mouth slightly open." He saw an aspect of his face he had never seen before, because of course he had never seen himself asleep.

"But I was not dead, I consoled myself; my physical body was sleeping under the blankets, while I was apparently on my feet and as good as before. Yet it wasn't my accustomed self, it was as if my mold was walking through a murky heavy space which, however, gave way easily before my emptiness." While wondering how he would get out, he found himself pushed forward so that either he passed through the door, or the door through him. The apartment was in darkness except for a subdued light that seemed to emanate from his own body. He entered the bathroom and from habit tried to switch on the light, but he found he was unable to press the switch. All the time he was aware of the strange tape of light "like an umbilical cord" between his two bodies, "by means of which the body on the bed was kept breathing while its mold wandered about the flat."

Determined to approach the whole matter scientifically, and to prevent himself from later thinking the whole experience had been a dream, he began to make systematic observations. He noted that the bathroom window was open and the curtain drawn, and he registered the existence of a new towel rack. Passing into other rooms, he noted which windows were closed. He attempted to open the linen closet but failed. Then suddenly he was pushed along "like a half-filled balloon." He flew out through the front door and "hovered in the air, feeling an extraordinary lightness of heart." He realized that he could quickly fly anywhere he wished, but he was afraid that something might happen to sever the link with his sleeping body. His new being, registering his anxiety, flew back to his sleeping body. But, Gerhardie writes, when "I felt it hovering over my old body on the bed, drab disappointment came back to me. 'Not yet,' I said. And again I flew off. When I flew thus swiftly, my consciousness seemed to blot out and only returned when again I walked or moved at a reasonable speed . . . Consciousness returned suddenly. I was stepping lightly over an open patch of grass . . . The thought occurred to me: how do I know I am not dreaming this? and the answer: look for the lighted cord behind you. It was there, but it was very thin . . . Then, with a jerk that shook me, I opened my eyes. I was in my bedroom . . . Not a detail of my experience had been lost to my mind and there was quite another quality about it all, that of reality, which removed it from the mere memory of a dream . . . I got up, and went through the rooms, checking the mental notes I had made about which windows were closed or open, which curtains drawn; and the evidence in all cases proved correct."

Gerhardie's narrative is a vivid description of what an out-of-the-body experience is like, and its details are corroborated in other accounts. Dr. Robert Crookall, a leading psychic researcher and authority on astral projection, has collected and compared many such accounts in his various books on the subject. Taking Gerhardie as a starting point, it is illuminating to see how many of the features he describes can be paralleled in the description of other astral projectors.

a) Positions of the astral body after separation. Many people report occupying a horizontal position above the physical body for several minutes after separation, and then having a sensation of being pushed into a vertical position.

b) The "strange appendage." The "silver cord" connecting the physical and astral bodies is mentioned in the biblical *Book of Ecclesiastes*, and has been referred to in accounts of OOBEs by people isolated from outside influences—for example by Basuto tribesmen in South Africa. Gerhardie mentions three characteristics of the cord that tally with numerous other accounts: that it is attached to the brow of the physical body (the pineal gland, or "third eye" of occult physiology is in the middle of the brow); that it is luminous; and that it becomes thinner as the distance traveled from the physical body grows greater.

c) The "murky, heavy space." Numerous accounts speak of the conditions first encountered in the astral in terms of fog, grayness, heaviness, or murkiness. Crookall attributes this to consciousness being "enshrouded by the still-unshed body veil." In other words, consciousness is clouded, confused, and unable at first to adjust to the new conditions.

d) Confusion over relation to physical reality. During their first OOBE many people try to do things that they would do in the physical body, such as open doors or closets or move objects, and find they are unable to do so. Many projectors are also surprised to find that they can move at will through walls or doors. The second body feels so real and substantial that it takes time to realize that it has neither the capacities nor the limitations of the physical.

e) An attitude of alert attention. On adjusting to the new conditions, projectors frequently move around and make mental notes of their environment for later corroboration. Many report a sense of enhanced alertness, of sharper mental functioning than they have on the physical plane. They feel more alive, more real. This ability to focus and control attention is one of the characteristics of the OOBE that makes it totally undreamlike.

f) Conflicting emotions of exaltation and apprehension. Gerhardie's "extraordinary lightness of heart" when he realized that his subtle body enjoys total freedom of movement is typical. So is his worry lest, possessing such freedom and not knowing the laws that govern this unprecedented experience, he might go too far and sever the link with his physical body.

g) The conscious will as a motor force. Projectors *think* themselves into different locations. Gerhardie realized that he could travel anywhere in the world in a flash simply by willing to do so, and when he thought about his physical self his second body "obeyed and flew back." His observation about the blotting out of consciousness temporarily during high-speed astral travel is confirmed by many other experients.

h) The experience of reentry. Gerhardie speaks of returning to

"A Body Stored Away"

"I neither drink nor take drugs and all I brought to my bed was a considerable nervous exhaustion which sleep was required to restore." So begins William Gerhardie's description of his out-of-the-body experience in his semiautobiographical novel *Resurrection*.

When he became conscious in his astral body he was suspended in mid-air, light as a feather. Once on his feet he felt as if he were defying gravity. In appearance he seemed identical to his physical body on the bed, to which he was attached by a luminous cable.

When he tried to open the door, he found he could not turn the handle. Then he discovered that he could pass right through the door, and he moved around the apartment, making observations, lit by his own cord.

His new body responded to his thoughts and floated this way and that according to his whims. Part of him wished to fly to distant places, but part was afraid this might sever the link with the sleeping body.

When he awoke, he found that his earlier ideas of life after death had been shattered. It seemed to him that we already have a body stored away, rather like a diver's suit, in our own everyday bodies, "always at hand in case of death or for special use."

Above: the ancient and enduring theme of the thread or cord of life is portrayed in this painting of the three Fates. According to mythology, the three women, daughters of Zeus and Themis, determined the destiny of every human. Here Clotho (right) spins the thread of life and Lachesis measures its length, while Atropos waits with some scissors to cut the thread when that span of life is ended.

the physical "with a jerk that shook me." The suddenness and shock of the return is an experience reported by many projectors.

Although Gerhardie's account of his first out-of-the-body experience has all the above characteristics in common with the reports of other projectors, it would be misleading to call it a typical case. The list of common characteristics could be considerably extended if we took as points of reference the testimonies of other experients, but OOBEs come in many varieties and no characteristic, however common, necessarily applies to all of them. The commonest are the presence of the silver cord, the sense of enhanced alertness, and the fact that the conscious will can effect transitions in space in a very short time, though not always instantaneously. Different speeds of travel are reported by different projectors.

It is only in recent years that astral projection has been taken seriously by some psychologists, and there remains a great deal of research work to be done to see whether certain physiological and psychological states precede certain types of astral projection. Crookall has noticed differences between enforced, spontaneous, and deliberate projections, and some experienced projectors offer advice on the most suitable conditions for an out-of-the-body experience. But knowledge, at the present time, remains tentative and incomplete. Apart from the work of Crookall, the only substantial contribution to the subject has been made by Celia Green of the Institute of Psychophysical Research in Oxford, England. She published some of the results of her work in 1968 in a book entitled *Out-of-the-Body Experiences*.

Celia Green's study was based on the testimonies of 326 experients who completed a questionnaire sent out by the Institute. Over 60 percent of the group reported having had only one OOBE, 21 percent had had six or more, and the remaining 18 percent had had between two and five experiences. The group consisted of people of all ages, and showed that the incidence of OOBEs diminished in later life, was common in childhood among subjects who had had more than one experience, and tended to cluster between the ages of 15 and 35 for those who had had only one experience. Most of the cases were not as sustained or full of detailed description as Gerhardie's, but were merely momentary projections. Eighty percent of the subjects reported no awareness of being in a second body, but simply of being a "disembodied consciousness" located at a distance from the physical body. About 32 percent reported that their projections had occurred as a result of an accident or under anesthetic; 12 percent reported them occurring during sleep; 25 percent under conditions of psychological stress; and the rest while awake and active and going about their normal routine.

The very fact that many of the subjects of this study had only one or two fleeting experiences of projection is significant. It suggests that though only a few may undergo prolonged and intense astral journeys, there may be many more who have had some sort of relevant experience at a far less intense level. Two such examples are quoted from the study. The first is a young

The Cord of Life

Left: a drawing from *The Projection of the Astral Body* by Sylvan Muldoon and Hereward Carrington. Muldoon described in detail the appearance and apparent function of the astral cord. When the astral body is only slightly separated from the physical body, as in this illustration, the cord's diameter is about one and a half inches. As the astral body moves farther away, the cord narrows until it is only as thick as a thread. According to Muldoon, energy passes through the cord from the astral body to the physical body. A heartbeat would be felt in the astral body and the cord at the same moment it was seen in the physical body.

man who wrote: "During the morning while driving fast along a road the drone of the engine and vibration seemed to lull me into a stupor and I remember I seemed to leave my motorbike like a zoom lens in reverse and was hovering over a hill watching myself and friend tearing along on the road below and I seemed to think 'I shouldn't be here, get back on that bike!' and the next instant I was in the saddle again."

The second subject was a waitress who, after working nonstop for 12 hours, left the restaurant to go home and found that she had missed her last bus. She reported:

"However, I started walking as in those days I lived in Jericho, a 15 minute walk at most. I remember feeling so fatigued that I wondered if I'd make it and resolved to myself that I'd 'got to keep going' . . . The next I registered, was of hearing the sound of my heels very hollowly and I looked down and watched myself walk round the bend of Beaumont St. into Walton St. I—the bit of me that counts—was up on a level with Worcester College

Below: the head of a wooden statue of Tutankhamun, showing the cobra traditionally applied to the foreheads of statues of Egyptian rulers. This symbol of power derives from an ancient legend about how the Egyptian god of creation acquired a third eye, which he placed in the middle of his forehead. This third eye has also been associated with astral projection, and has been described as the point where the astral cord begins.

chapel. I saw myself very clearly—it was a summer evening and I was wearing a sleeveless shantung dress. I remember thinking 'so that's how I look to other people.'"

Both of these reports suggest a slightly altered state of consciousness, precipitated in the one case by the monotony and the vibration of the ride, and in the other by fatigue. Neither mentions a sense of possessing a second body, but as Celia Green remarks, many first-time experients are too preoccupied with the novelty of viewing themselves from an objective viewpoint to pay attention to the attributes of their second self. They nevertheless have a total conviction that the second self, even if it is only a "disembodied consciousness" is, as the waitress wrote, "the bit of me that counts."

All systems of occult physiology maintain that the physical and astral bodies are normally completely merged and coincident, but that certain circumstances can throw them out of coincidence. In some people, too, the bonding between the two is looser than normal, and separation can take place relatively easily. The most common cause of separation is a crisis or accident. An experience recounted by the biologist and writer Lyall Watson in his book *The Romeo Error* is typical of this kind of out-of-the-body projection.

The author was driving with a safari group in Kenya when their bus skidded and rolled over several times. He lost consciousness for a moment, and in that time had a brief out-of-the-body experience. He was projected outside the bus and saw that it was about to roll over again, and that when it did one of the occupants would almost certainly be killed. He came around at that point, and took immediate steps to rescue the trapped passenger.

This is a good example of an OOBE serving a useful purpose by enabling a person to obtain information paranormally, act on it and, in Lyall Watson's case, save a life. There are a number of other reported cases of lives being saved as a result of a projection. The most dramatic is that related by a well-known medium, the Reverend Max Hoffman.

At the age of five Hoffman was a victim of a cholera epidemic in Germany. He was diagnosed as dead, and duly buried. The night after his burial his mother woke up to find the child's double standing at her bedside. He told her he was not dead, and begged her to recover his physical body from the grave. He said they would find him lying on his side with his right hand under his right cheek. The apparition returned on three successive nights. Though the father was reluctant to apply to have the grave opened on the dubious evidence of what was probably an anxiety dream, his wife finally prevailed upon him to do so. When the grave was opened the child was found in exactly the position his projected double had told his mother that he was in. Doctors were able to resuscitate him. The physical body had been in a state of suspended animation, just clinging to life, while the astral body went in search of help.

Where the psychic link is strong, as between mother and child or husband and wife, life-saving astral experiences frequently occur. Dr. Crookall has recorded a case of a woman who passed out while taking a bath and lay for some time face down in the water. She left her body and went downstairs to the living room

A "Disembodied Consciousness"

Below: biologist Lyall Watson has explored many of the unexplained phenomena of the world, and himself underwent an out-of-the-body experience in Africa.

A Vision of Danger

The biologist and author Lyall Watson was
driving with a safari party through the bush
of Kenya when suddenly the little bus
skidded in the dust and overturned. It
rolled over twice and then balanced on the
edge of a gully.

A moment later, Watson found himself
standing outside the bus looking at it. And
yet he could see his own physical body
slumped unconscious in the front seat of
the bus. A more alarming sight was the
head and shoulders of a young boy who had
been pushed through the canvas top of the
vehicle when it had come to a stop. If the
bus fell into the gully—which seemed
likely—the boy would be crushed.

The thought scarcely crossed his mind
when Watson found himself regaining
consciousness in the front of the bus. He
rubbed the red dust from his eyes. The
memory of what he had just seen was
extraordinarily vivid. At once he climbed
through the window of the bus and freed
the boy, moments before the vehicle rolled
over.

Telling the story in his book *The Romeo
Error*, published in 1974, Watson said
"there is no doubt in my own mind that my
vantage point at that moment was detached
from my body," but he was unable to
provide a scientific explanation for his
experience.

Below: the 19th-century French writer Guy de Maupassant sometimes saw his own double—an experience he seems to have found more annoying than frightening.

where her husband was reading. She tapped him on the shoulder. He did not actually see her apparition, but he had a sudden compulsion to hurry to the bathroom. He was just in time to drag his wife out of the water and bring her around by artificial respiration. Meanwhile she hovered above the scene, and was later able to describe his every move.

Helping and healing are other useful functions frequently performed by projectors. There is a Scottish doctor who is said to project regularly in his second body to give his professional help to people who send out psychic calls at times of distress. One of Crookall's correspondents, a Major Pole, relates how once, when he was desperately ill on a houseboat on the Nile River, the doctor materialized before him, diagnosed his condition, and wrote out a prescription. He chatted meanwhile, as doctors will, telling Major Pole in a matter-of-fact manner about his astral errands of mercy, and mentioning that he always took the precaution of locking his office door when he was projecting so that nobody would disturb his physical body. On returning to England, Major Pole managed to track down his strange benefactor through a radio appeal.

The conviction of the astral voyager that his essential self is not identified with his physical body is an aspect of the experience that can itself be of positive and life-preserving value, for example under conditions of torture or extreme physical hardship. A particularly interesting case of this kind is that of Ed Morrell, a man who had many OOBEs while serving a four-year prison sentence in Arizona some 50 years ago. He later wrote about them in his book *The Twenty-Fifth Man*. Morrell used his secret faculty as a weapon in a psychological war with his guards. The guards were incredibly sadistic in attempting to crush his spirit. They beat him brutally and put him in a tight straightjacket that they doused with water so that it would shrink and increase his pain. During one night of intolerable agony, Morrell suddenly experienced a sense of release from his body. He no longer felt pain, and was joyful and elated by his sense of freedom. He found that he could pass through the prison walls and travel at will to any place he thought of. Moreover, when he returned to his physical body he felt refreshed and invigorated. The guards redoubled their efforts to break him, once leaving him in the straightjacket for 126 hours, but the astral travels of Morrell's double continued to sustain and revitalize his spirit and his physical body, and nothing they could devise defeated him.

Of course, such a case could be put down to delusion, or explained as a stratagem of the unconscious to overcome the ravages of pain, but Morrell expresses the conviction, typical of the astral traveler, that his essential conscious self, "the bit that counts," had been able to transcend the limitations of time and space. In addition, during his second-body excursions he witnessed events that he was later able to verify, for example a shipwreck, and he saw people unknown to him at the time whom he later met, including his future wife.

Morrell's astral experiences finished after he was released from prison. When he was happy, healthy, and free from stress he found that he could no longer leave his body. This might suggest that out-of-the-body experiences are compensatory and perform the same function as dreams which, according to the psychologist Carl Jung, help to establish a balance in the psyche and make good certain deficiencies in a person's total life experience. Such a theory might account for some astral experiences, but it clearly does not apply to all cases, and it does not imply that the experience is merely subjective. The fact that Morrell and others have acquired information at a distance during out-of-the-body experiences, information that has later been verified and that could not have been obtained through any of the normal channels of sensory communication, stands as clear evidence that in astral experiences the psyche interacts with the objective physical world.

Other theories try to explain out-of-the-body experiences by suggesting that they occur in people suffering from abnormal or pathological conditions such as epilepsy, brain damage, drug addiction, and chronic alcoholism, or during attacks of migraine, influenza, or typhus. Although this may frequently be the case, there are plenty of examples of astral projection by people whose condition can in no way be classed as abnormal or pathological.

In the same way many nervous and unstable people have had psychic experiences. Their instability does not necessarily make these experiences invalid, nor does it account for the hundreds of experiences undergone by people of stable temperaments.

Various famous writers have written about experiences of the double. Guy de Maupassant's double frequently annoyed him when he was writing, and sometimes sat opposite him at his desk and dictated his stories. Shelley, the English romantic poet, frequently projected his double. Once it was seen walking in the woods by Byron and others when the poet was known to be with other friends elsewhere. On another occasion Shelley reported seeing his double himself, pointing toward the sea where he was later to meet his death. The Swedish dramatist Strindberg, a man

Some OOBEs of Famous Writers

Below: a painting of the English Romantic poet Percy Bysshe Shelley, who is said to have projected his double on several occasions and to have seen it himself, pointing to the place of his death.

"Masters of the Techniques of Ecstasy"

Opposite: this Hindu fakir sits in a yoga position, with his tongue pierced by two wooden sticks and his body pierced by small hooks from which fruits are hung, in an effort to free the soul from its earthly nature. Years of practice are required to achieve the difficult feats of the yogi and the state of spiritual bliss.

Below: this 15th-century Turkish manuscript illumination shows two shamans dancing to induce a state of ecstasy. Most of the recommended methods of deliberately projecting the astral body are less strenuous, emphasizing techniques of concentration and visualizing.

who lived perilously near the edge of insanity, had moved to Paris after the breakdown of his second marriage. Desperately longing to be back with his family, he had an astral experience in which he found himself in his home and saw his mother-in-law playing the piano. Soon afterward he received a letter from her saying that she had seen his double appear, and asking if he were ill.

The corroborating testimonies of others, and the fact that verifiable information is sometimes obtained, indicates that though abnormal conditions may facilitate the projection of the double, the double is nevertheless real, and not an hallucination. Some forms of astral projection may arise as psychic compensation, and some may be due to abnormal or pathological conditions, but the phenomenon is so varied and individual that no theory can be all-inclusive. The hale and hearty have out-of-the-body experiences, as well as the ailing and introspective. They can occur spontaneously and for no apparent reason, they can be precipitated by circumstances such as accidents or psychological crises, or they can be deliberately cultivated and induced. Various authors have examined the conditions and methods that are helpful for deliberate astral projections.

Mircea Eliade in *Shamanism* repeatedly makes the point that shamans are "masters of the techniques of ecstasy," and Dr. Robert Crookall has noticed correspondences between these ancient traditional techniques and the descriptions of modern

astral projectors. A strange document was obtained by the American psychologist Prescott Hall through a medium who herself had no knowledge of or interest in astral projection. It was published in the *Journal of the American Society for Psychical Research* in 1961, and purported to be detailed instructions on astral projection from a nonphysical source. Looked at together these accounts seem to provide some kind of guideline for the would-be astral projector.

The right weather conditions seem to be important. The air should be clear and dry, the temperature between 70° and 80°F. Conditions of humidity and electrical storms are not favorable. The would-be projector should not eat anything for several hours before an attempt, and should try to avoid a high protein intake for a considerable period before. Favorable physiological conditions are also created by breathing exercises. Heavy rhythmical breathing is said to assist the loosening of the double, and the ancient yogic technique of pranayama, or holding the breath in, is practiced by some projectors to wing the astral body on its way.

Shamans often dance and whirl to the point of exhaustion to induce ecstasy and start the second body on its journey, but less strenuous means are generally recommended for the novice. Relaxation, quiet, deliberate reduction of muscle tension, a mental state of reverie or unfocused consciousness, of withdrawal of attention from the physical world, are essential psychological preconditions. Hall's article also offered a number of images for contemplation in the progressive stages of projection exercises, revealed through the medium's informers. To loosen the astral from the physical body they suggest imagining oneself "as a point in space floating, or as a piece of cloud or as steam." To initiate movement in the astral body they suggest contemplation of the image of a twirling star suspended in space, or images of oneself flying, swinging, or rocking. For the final stage of separation and release of the astral body they gave a number of visualization techniques. For example, they suggest concentrating on the image of a whirlpool or going down through a whirlpool. This gives practice in the exercise of contracting to a point and then expanding. A cone is another image used. The projector must visualize passing through a waterspout or hourglass shape, constructing a cone of circles becoming large or smaller, and turning such a cone inside out. Another exercise is to visualize a tank gradually filling with water, with oneself floating on the top as a point of light. The object is to find a small hole in the side of the tank through which one can pass out.

Robert Monroe, an American businessman who has been having astral experiences regularly for more than 15 years and has learned to control them at will, writes in his book of 1971, *Journeys Out of the Body*: "I believe that anyone can experience existence in a Second Body if the desire is great enough." He also recommends a sequence of exercises to help in astral projection, the key feature of which, as in all methods, is visualization.

But the questions still remain. What is the point of astral projection? What rewards are to be expected from it, and what dangers are incurred? The best way to examine these questions is to consider the accounts of those who are experienced in the techniques of astral projection.

"Anyone Can Experience an Existence in a Second Body"

Opposite: This painting by Columba Krebs, *The Dream of the Double on an Astral Trip*, shows the astral body projecting itself in a spiral bath, possibly after concentration on a whirlpoool or cone.

The Tattwa Cards: Aids to Expanding the Consciousness

The Tattwa cards, representing the five elements—(left to right) fire, earth, water, air, and spirit—and 20 subelements formed by combining them, were used by members of the Golden Dawn as aids to expanding the consciousness and experiencing visions. The symbols were derived from Tantra, an Indian method of using sex as a way of attaining higher states of consciousness, and were apparently found by some members of the Golden Dawn in a Theosophical treatise. To use the Tattwas, one selects a card and concentrates on its symbol until no other thought or image is present in the mind. The person imagines the symbol as a kind of door and wills it to open. He then passes through it in his imagination and experiences a vision. The vision is often related in some way to the symbol chosen; for example, if he chooses the water symbol he may find himself swimming in a lake or river.

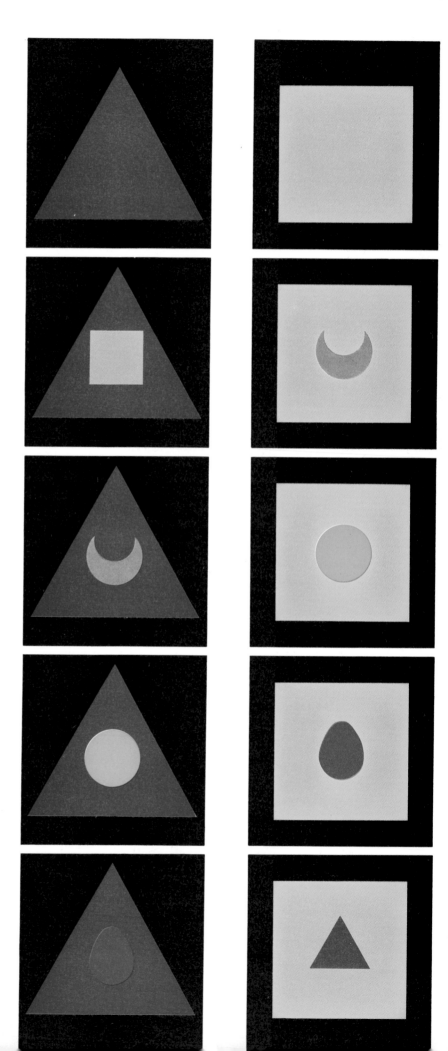

Chapter 4
Virtuosi of Astral Projection

If it is possible to project one's self out of the physical body, is it possible to learn how to do it at will? Here are the reports of several experienced psychic travelers who mastered the skill of conscious projection and have left a record of their techniques. What are the methods they suggest, and what do they tell of finding in the world they inhabit outside the body? Is there any relationship between that world and the world suggested by the theoretical physicists of orthodox science? Is there indeed a rational foundation for the notion of multiple universes?

Sylvan Muldoon had his first experience of spontaneous projection at the age of 12, so when he was 21 and had the experience he later described as "the most unusual I ever had," he was already a seasoned projector. At the time he lived in a small quiet town in Wisconsin. One moonlit summer evening in 1924 he went out for a walk after dinner, and fell into that mood of listlessness, loneliness, and philosophical perplexity that introspective and impressionable young men are prone to. He returned home in disgust, went into his room, locked the door, and flung himself on the bed. When his physical body began to turn numb and his sensory functions deserted him, he recognized the signs of an imminent projection and gave himself over to the experience.

He felt himself rise in the air, then outward and into a vertical position. Gradually the misty atmosphere cleared and he was able to move freely. He walked about indoors for a short time, and then went out into the street. There a bewildering thing happened. He was whipped away at supernormal speed and suddenly found himself in a strange house. There were four people in the room, one of them an attractive girl of about 17, who was sewing a black dress. He found himself propelled without any effort to a position directly in front of the girl, where he remained for a short time watching her. Then he moved around the room, making mental notes of the furniture and various objects. He could see no reason for his being in this place, so he

Opposite: *Rays of Power*, by psychic artist Columba Krebs, portrays a human being receiving the protective powers emitted by the "Grand Central Sun," which is invisible to ordinary sight. Perhaps significantly, the central beam of light strikes the person in the center of the forehead, the location of the "third eye" and of the projecting silver cord that links the astral body to the physical body when parted.

Sylvan Muldoon's Detailed Accounts

Below: Sylvan Muldoon, co-author of *The Projection of the Astral Body*, who had his first out-of-the-body experience at the age of 12. After that, he had numerous such experiences, which he described in detail in his book.

willed himself back to his physical body, taking a last look around before he left and noting from outside that the house was a farmhouse.

Some six weeks later Muldoon was on his way home one afternoon when he saw a girl get out of a car and go into a house. He immediately recognized her as the girl he had seen on his astral excursion, and knowing that she did not live in the house she had entered, he waited for her to come out. When she did he accosted her and asked her bluntly where she lived. The girl said it was none of his business, and would have brushed him off and gone on her way had he not to her amazement started to describe her home, inside and out, in great detail. Muldoon does not record the girl's reaction to his uncanny intelligence, but he states that as a result of this meeting she became a very close friend. He visited her home, which was 15 miles from his own, several times, and recognized all the features and details he had noted on his previous astral visit. He confessed to the girl how he had come by his knowledge, and further convinced her by projecting his visible double into her room. She later participated with him in several experiments.

The thought of disembodied voyeurs hovering around is enough to give any normally modest young women the creeps. Muldoon and Oliver Fox, a British scientist and another experienced projector, are careful to portray themselves as gentlemen of the utmost propriety, both in the body and out of it; but their records are of events of 50 years ago, and in the permissive 1970s it wouldn't be surprising if there were to appear the confessions of a lecherous astral projector. It requires little imagination to conceive how the following experience related by Oliver Fox in his book *Astral Projection* would appear in an updated version.

It was an autumn afternoon in 1913, and Fox lay down in his room "intending to experiment." He was soon able to leave his body and go out into the street. He had walked for about 100 yards when he was "caught up in some strong current and borne away with great velocity." He came to rest in a beautiful small park which he did not recognize. A school party seemed to be in progress, and children dressed in white were playing games and having refreshments under the trees. "Bluish smoke rose from the fires they had lit, and a magnificent amber sunset cast a mellow glow upon the peaceful scene."

Fox walked on till he came to some houses. The front door of one of them was open and he went in, curious to know whether the occupants would become aware of his presence. He mounted a flight of richly carpeted stairs and entered a bedroom on the first landing. "A young lady, dressed in claret-colored velvet, was standing with her back to me, tidying her hair before a mirror. I could see the radiant amber sky through the window by the dressing table, and the girl's rich auburn tresses were gleaming redly in the glamorous light. I noticed that the coverlet of the bed had a crumpled appearance and that there was water in a basin on the washstand. 'Ah, my lady,' I thought, 'you too have been lying down, and now you are making yourself presentable for tea—or is it dinner?' . . ."

Fox moved behind her and stood looking over her shoulder

into the mirror. He could see the reflection of her attractive face, but not a trace of his own was visible. Realizing that she could not see him, he wondered whether she would be able to feel him. "I laid a hand upon her shoulder. I distinctly felt the softness of her velvet dress, and then she gave a violent start—so violent that I in my turn was startled too. Instantly my body drew me back and I was awake. . . . The western sky had been blue when I lay down; but on breaking the trance I saw that it was actually the same glorious amber color that it had been in my out-of-the-body experience. . . ."

Both Muldoon's and Fox's narratives could be dismissed as a young man's romantic fantasies if they stood alone, but in the context of the total work of these two men they are perfectly credible descriptions. Muldoon and Fox independently discovered their ability to project, cultivated and developed it, and gradually learned some of the rules governing this strange experience. They were both well aware that the experiences they reported would appear to others to be nothing more than extremely vivid dreams. They wanted to demonstrate that OOBEs were more than dreams, and to encourage others to experiment for themselves and prove the point.

Muldoon's material was written with the encouragement of the distinguished psychical research Hereward Carrington. Carrington had published a book, *Modern Psychical Phenomena*, in which he had a chapter on astral projection based on the testimony of a French projector Charles Lancelin. Shortly after its publication he received a letter from Muldoon, who was then unknown to him. Muldoon said that, judging from the material in the book, he doubted whether Lancelin was a conscious projector, and that he could write a book on the things that Lancelin did not know. He gave so many details of his intimate knowledge of the subject in his letter that Carrington eagerly followed up the proposal. Two years later in 1929 their book, *The Projection of the Astral Body*, was published. Most of it was written by Muldoon, and it remains to this day the most informative single work on the subject written by someone who had actually experienced the phenomenon of astral projection.

Carrington makes the point in his Introduction that Muldoon's material is convincing because in fact his claims are modest. He does not profess to have visited distant planets, to have projected into the past, the future, or the spirit world, or to have relived his own past incarnations. "He asserts, merely," says Carrington, "that he has been enabled to leave his physical body at will, and travel about in the present, in his immediate vicinity, in some vehicle or other, while fully conscious. This is perfectly rational. . . ." The skeptic may not consider it rational, but it is certainly modest compared with the claims of some other projectors.

Muldoon's first out-of-the-body experience occurred in an environment conducive to the manifestation of paranormal phenomena. His mother was interested in Spiritualism, and one summer she took him and his younger brother to a Spiritualist Association camp in Iowa. They stayed in a rooming house where half a dozen well-known mediums were also staying. In the middle of their first night there the 12-year-old Sylvan awoke

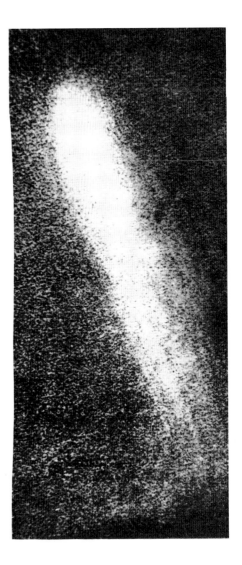

Above: a photograph believed to be that of an astral body swaying, by the French writer on psychic phenomena H. Durville. His book *Phantoms of the Living* tallies in many respects with the discoveries reported by Sylvan Muldoon.

The Path of the Astral Body

Below: Hereward Carrington, British psychical researcher, who wrote the introduction to Muldoon's book on astral projection. His early experience as an amateur conjurer was useful in exposing fraudulent mediums.

after sleeping deeply for several hours. He found himself in a "bewildering stupor," unable either to arouse himself into normal waking consciousness or to fall back to sleep. He couldn't ascertain where he was. He was aware that he was lying somewhere, but when he tried to move he found that he was powerless. He felt as if he were stuck to whatever he was lying on. He was in a condition that he later defined as "astral catalepsy." In medical terms, *catalepsy* is a trancelike condition that sometimes lasts for several weeks. Astral catalepsy, according to Muldoon, is an unpleasant state in which one is fully conscious but completely unable to move.

Other unpleasant sensations followed. He felt that he was floating, that his entire rigid body started vibrating up and down at great speed, and that there was a tremendous pressure at the back of his head which came in spasms. "Amid this pandemonium of bizarre sensations—floating, vibratory, zigzagging, and head-pulling—I began to hear somewhat familiar and seemingly far-distant sounds," he wrote. His senses began to function again, first hearing, then sight. Things seemed hazy at first, then gradually cleared until he saw his surroundings and knew where he was. To his astonishment, however, he found that he was floating toward the ceiling. "It was too unnatural for me to understand, yet too real to deny," he wrote. He had neither experienced nor heard of the existence of the second body at the time, and he assumed that he was in his physical body while mysteriously defying gravity. He was still cataleptic, and remained so for about two minutes after he was "uprighted from the horizontal position to the perpendicular, and placed standing upon the floor of the room."

Suddenly he felt free and able to move. He turned and saw his physical body lying on the bed. An "elastic-like cable" extended between the center of the brow of the physical body and the back of the head of its "astral counterpart." He was swaying from side to side and had difficulty keeping his balance. He was understandably alarmed because he thought that he had died. His first instinct was to go to his mother and awaken her. He went to the door and tried to open it, and was further astonished to find that he just passed through it. He then went around the house trying to shake people and call to them, but his hands passed through them "as though they were but vapors." It was uncanny. All his senses seemed normal except that of touch. He started to cry. He saw an automobile pass the house and heard the clock strike two. He prowled disconsolately about for 15 minutes, then began to feel a pull on the cable. He became cataleptic again, and was drawn back toward his physical body and into a horizontal position above it. With a shock that shuddered painfully through his entire frame his two bodies came together again and he found himself awake—alive and filled with sensations of awe, amazement, and fear.

The correspondences between Muldoon's and Gerhardie's accounts of their first projections will be obvious. Both found themselves cataleptic and suspended in midair for some time before some force moved them into a standing position. Both were unsteady on their feet at first, but when able to move felt the second body to be substantial enough to attempt to open a

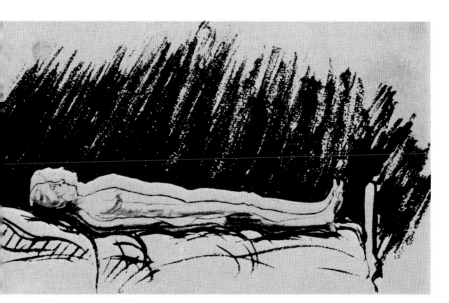

Left: one of a series of drawings from Muldoon's book. It shows the astral body slightly out of coincidence with the physical body. At the beginning of his first OOBE, Muldoon experienced an unpleasant sensation of floating and vibrating slightly above his physical body while at the same time he felt pressure at the back of his head.

Left: in this drawing the arrows show the path usually taken by the astral body in leaving the physical body. Muldoon claimed that dreams of flying are often caused by the astral body floating in this position, and that the pulling of it back into the physical body will produce a dream of falling.

door, and were surprised to find that they could pass through doors and walls. Both saw the cable connecting the two bodies and attached to the brow of the physical one, and on returning to the physical both experienced a sudden jerk or shudder. Gerhardie was more adventurous and inquisitive on his first excursion, and learned more about the potentials of distant projection, but Muldoon was only 12 years old and his reaction of fear, loneliness, and anxiety to contact other people is only to be expected.

When he became accustomed to the experience of astral projection, Muldoon began to investigate the phenomenon in a systematic way and to develop his own theories about it. He came to the conclusion that prolonged projection from a state of sleep, such as he had experienced the first time, was probably rare, but that "instantaneous projection" was not uncommon and might happen to people without their realizing it. He wrote: "When something unusual or unnatural occurs to upset the

The Range and Sensations of Astral Projection

Right: here the astral body is upright and still within the cord activity range. This is the distance within which the cord will transmit energy from the astral body to the physical one. Activity within the cord ceases when it is stretched to its minimum thickness. Muldoon found that the range of cord activity varied according to his state of health at the time. When he was feeling well it was about 15 feet, but when he was in poor health it was considerably less.

Right: the astral body being pulled back into the physical body, or—to use Muldoon's term—*interiorizing*. He claimed that there are three types of interiorization: the spiral fall and straight fall, both of which accompany a dream of falling and are unpleasant sensations, and the slow vibratory fall, the normal method, which is gentle and controlled.

Opposite: this self-portrait by the student of magic Austin Spare shows the artist in what he called the death posture, bent slightly forward, his fingers blocking his nostrils and starving the lungs of oxygen. He is surrounded by creatures of the unconscious and symbols of magic. Under the guidance of a woman named Mrs. Paterson, who practiced witchcraft, Spare claimed to have visited places outside terrestrial reality—"spaces outside space"— into which he would be suddenly precipitated. His paintings and drawings reflect his visions of and voyages into the psychic world.

harmony of the physical—a shock, a jolt, a broken habit, an intense unappeased desire, sickness—in fact, anything which would cause a lack of perfect material coordination—there is always a jar to the astral." Even so commonplace an event as the jolt a person experiences when he descends a staircase in the dark and, at the bottom tries to take an extra step, can momentarily jar the astral body out of coincidence with the physical. In sleep, Muldoon maintained, the astral body always moves slightly out of coincidence, perhaps only a fraction of an inch, but often much more. "If you could hold consciousness up to the very last moment, in the hypnagogic state," Muldoon says, "you could feel this act of discoincidence, as indeed nervous and fatigued people often do."

Muldoon's theory of the purpose of what he calls discoincidence during sleep is interesting, particularly in the light of modern Soviet research into the "energy body" through means of electrophotography. The astral body, he claims, is a "con-

"Dream Control"

Below: this old engraving shows the astral form floating upward from the body of a sleeping girl. According to Muldoon, the most pleasant way to promote astral projection is to construct a dream that involves an upward motion such as flying and to dwell on this just before falling asleep.

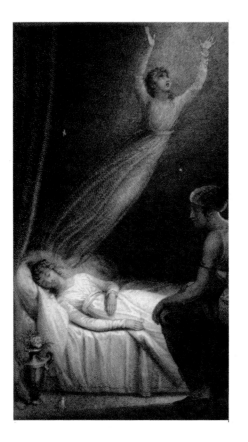

denser" of cosmic energy, and it regularly discoincides from the physical in order to become recharged with energy. So in the person who is fatigued or run down discoincidence will be more pronounced, and will occur more frequently than in people of more robust constitution. This theory has a certain logic and appeal, for it would explain the fact that people who have OOBEs are often frail. Muldoon himself was of delicate health throughout his life. Eliade remarks that shamans are usually recruited from among the delicate and sickly, and a true shaman is "a sick man who has succeeded in curing himself." It would also explain the fact that many projectors, for example Ed Morrell, report that they return from their astral travels feeling refreshed and revitalized.

"If you ask me which is the most pleasant way to promote astral projection," Muldoon wrote, "I should answer by saying 'dream control.'" The astral body may be called the "dream body," he said, "for it is in that body that we dream—even though we may be in coincidence or completely separated from the physical." The first stage of the dream control method of promoting projection involves holding consciousness up to the very moment of falling asleep, or as Muldoon calls it, "rising to sleep." To do this he recommends holding an arm in the air so that it will begin to sway and tend to fall when sleep comes, resulting in a slight awakening. The next stage is to construct an appropriate dream, to dwell on it and hold it clearly in mind so that it continues when the body completely succumbs to sleep. The dream should be one that involves an upward and outward movement of the body, a dream of flying or of going up in an elevator, for example. Muldoon claims that "a properly constructed dream is sure to move the astral body out," and explains that "the astral naturally moves out of coincidence at the moment of sleep; it naturally starts itself, and that is just the moment when you must mentally project yourself into the up-going elevator (or whatever the dream may be) and 'keep going.' . . . In such a dream the astral body acts out exactly whatever the dream may be. . . . If you become *completely* conscious in such a dream, you would usually find yourself in some place corresponding to the place of action which was last seen in the dream."

Oliver Fox also maintained the reality of the dream world and the possibility of projecting the astral body by means of dream control. His own research, he wrote, began with a dream.

"I dreamed that I was standing on the pavement outside my

Right: a painting of *The Prophet Muhammad's Night Journey* showing Muhammad traveling through the seven celestial spheres to approach God. Several people who have experienced astral travel have reported the existence of more than one plane of reality. The French psychic Yram claimed that humans have several bodies, of varying degrees of density, capable of passing through materials of certain densities. Robert Monroe, an American who has written about and experienced OOBEs, believes that there are three planes of reality: Locales I, II, and III. The first is the physical world of ordinary consciousness; the second is the plane of thought; and the third, Locale III, is both physical and mental.

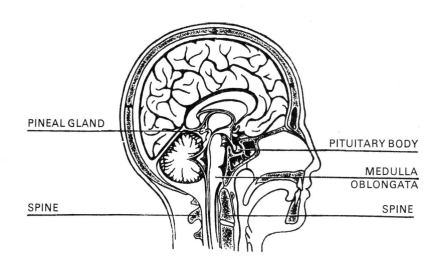

Right: a diagram of the head taken from C. W. Leadbeater's book *The Chakras* showing the pineal gland, located slightly behind the pituitary. Science has not discovered the function, if any, of this gland; many psychics believe it may be the doorway through which the astral body is released. Oliver Fox observed that he felt a distinct click in this part of the head on returning from a "dream of knowledge."

PINEAL GLAND

PITUITARY BODY

MEDULLA OBLONGATA

SPINE

SPINE

Right: another illustration from Leadbeater's book—this one entitled *The Streams of Vitality*. It shows the locations of the seven chakras and the paths along which energy flows from one to another.

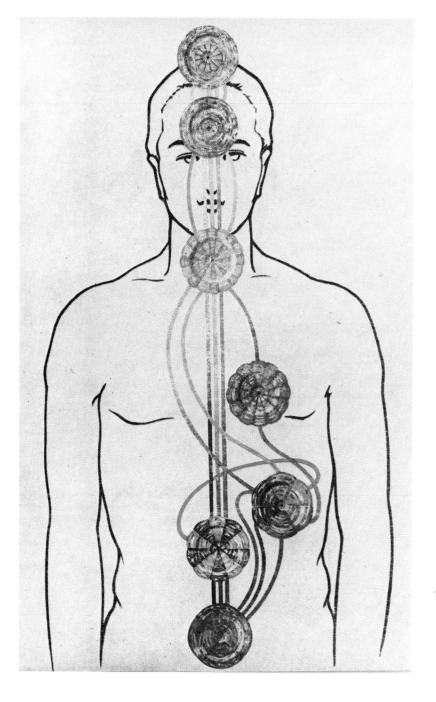

home. The sun was rising behind the Roman wall, and the waters of Bletchingden Bay were sparkling in the morning light. I could see the tall trees at the corner of the road and the top of the old gray tower beyond the Forty Steps. . . . Now the pavement was not of the ordinary type, but consisted of small, bluish-gray rectangular stones, with their long sides at right-angles to the white kerb. I was about to enter the house when, on glancing casually at these stones, my attention became riveted by a passing strange phenomenon so extraordinary that I could not believe my eyes—they had seemingly all changed their position in the night, and the long sides were now parallel to the kerb! Then the solution flashed upon me: though this glorious summer

Chakras and the Pineal Gland

Below: the *Brow Chakra* from Leadbeater's book. This chakra is believed to be the center of psychic visions and, when fully developed, to endow the person with clairvoyance. According to Leadbeater the chakras can actually be seen by "a fairly evolved and intelligent person" who has brought his own chakras "to some extent into working order."

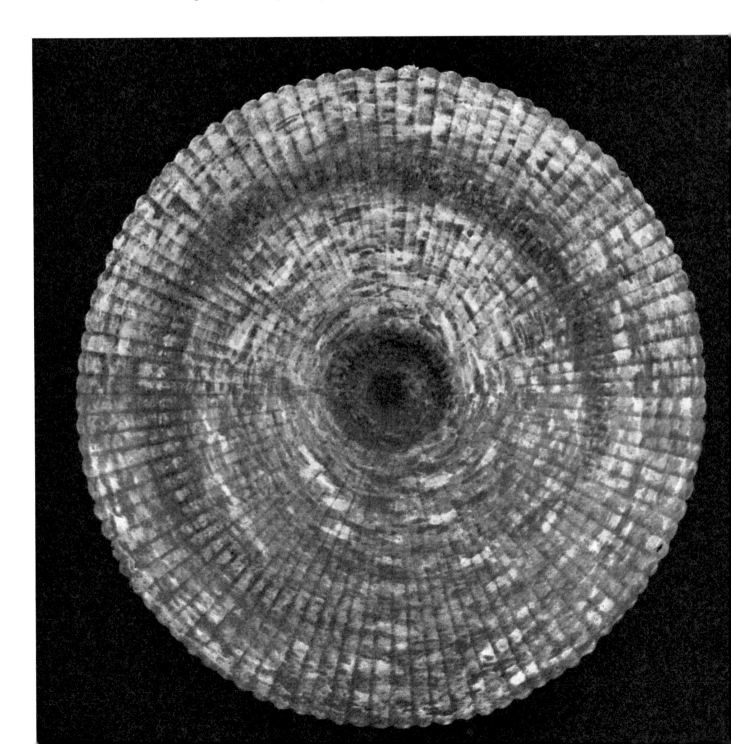

These four drawings from *The Secret of the Golden Flower*, a Chinese "Book of Life," show (above, below, and opposite) four stages of meditation, in which the person transforms himself and releases his primal spirit.

Below: *Gathering the Light*. This phrase is reminiscent of Oliver Fox's gathering up and compressing the "incorporeal self," which could then be astrally projected.

Below: *Origin of a New Being in the Place of Power*. Only by following specific instructions as to posture, breathing, and concentration can the person develop within him the immortal spirit body.

morning seemed as real as could be, I was *dreaming*."

Fox called the kind of dream in which one is conscious of dreaming a "Dream of Knowledge," and he discovered that with practice he could prolong and control such dreams. He also found that in a Dream of Knowledge he could do some curious things. "I could glide along the surface of the ground, passing through seemingly solid walls, etc., at a great speed, or I could levitate to a height of about 100 feet and then glide. . . . I could also do some intriguing little tricks at will, such as moving objects without visible contact, and molding the plastic matter into new forms." He found that the effort of prolonging a Dream of Knowledge produced a pain in the head, which he realized was a warning "to resist no longer the call of my body." As the call of the body grew stronger he experienced a period of dual consciousness, in which he could simultaneously feel himself standing in his dream body and lying on his bed, and see both the dream scenery and his bedroom.

What, he wondered, would happen if he tried to resist the call back to the body and disregarded the pain in his head? He screwed up his courage to make the experiment, and had "a never-to-be-forgotten adventure."

He dreamed that he was walking beside the sea. "It was morning; the sky a light blue; the foam-flecked waves were greenish in the sunshine." He became aware that he was dreaming, and when he felt the pull back to the body he exerted his will to continue in the dream. "A battle ensued; now my bedroom became clearly visible and the shore-line brighter." The pain in his head became increasingly intense and he fought against it, resolutely willing to remain in the dream world. Then suddenly the pain ceased, something seemed to go click in his brain, and he felt delightfully free. He continued his walk, "reveling in the beauty of the morning. . . . It seemed to me that the apparently solid shore and sunlit waves were not the physical land and sea; that my body was lying in bed, half a mile away at Forest View; but I could not feel the *truth* of this. I seemed to be completely severed from that physical body. At this point I became aware of a man and boy approaching. As they passed me they were talking together; they did not seem to see me, but I was not quite sure. A little later, however, when I met another man and asked him the time, he took no notice and was evidently unaware of my presence."

He began to get worried. When he willed to end the dream and wake up nothing happened. He didn't know how much time had elapsed in the physical world. He wondered whether he was dead, and then began to worry lest, if he were alive, he should be prematurely buried. He desperately willed to get back to the physical, but the shore-scene remained vividly before him. He tried to hold down a mounting feeling of panic. He willed and willed, and suddenly something seemed to snap, he felt another click in his brain, and he found that he was awake and in his bedroom—but he was completely paralyzed. After some time he managed to move a little finger, then other fingers, then his hand, and at last he emerged with relief from his state of catalepsy.

Fox attributed the click in the head to the passage of the astral body through what he called the "pineal door." He later found that he could go into a trance state and induce projection by concentrating on the pineal gland and willing to ascend through it. He imagined the process as one of gathering up and compressing the "incorporeal self," rushing it to a point in the pineal gland, and hurling it against a kind of trap door that would briefly be forced open and then click shut after the astral body had passed through. He stressed, however, that though this was what he felt happened in projection, his readers were at liberty to take it as a figurative description.

Fox tended to experience more adventurous and far-flung projections than Muldoon. Once he found himself in an oriental city and saw street bazaars and a huge black sculptured elephant in a kneeling position. On another terrifying occasion he was bound, bleeding and naked, to an X-shaped framework and saw robed figures moving about in the dimness. He roamed through an astral counterpart of London where among all the familiar features there were buildings and monuments that he did not recognize and thought must belong to the past or future of the city. Sometimes he practiced *skrying*, which he described as "like gliding, but in a vertical direction," or as "rising through the planes."

The idea of the existence of several planes or dimensions of the astral world was central in the conceptual scheme of Yram, a mysterious French contemporary of Fox, whose true identity remains unknown. The English version of his book was published in 1900 under the title *Practical Astral Projection*. Yram believed that humans have not merely two but several bodies, and that "as the conscious will penetrates into new dimensions it uses a corresponding body." The bodies were of different degrees of density, and Yram sometimes experienced difficulty in passing through walls when he was "using a double of too material a quality." At other times he could pass through them as if they were not there at all because, he said, he had "exteriorized a less material double." His travels were as dramatic as Fox's, and they took him to several parts of the material world as well as through the several planes of the astral. On the lower planes he sometimes was attacked by "rather unpleasant entities," and once he was hardly out of his body when he "received a terrific slap in the face without being able to find whence it came."

To compensate for such unpleasant experiences, Yram sometimes projected to higher spiritual planes where the beings he met and the visions he had were of great beauty and religious intensity. On one stratum he would meet and chat with deceased friends. Explaining this he wrote: "In order to appreciate this properly you must remember that I am not telling you a dream, not a vision, I am telling you of a real fact, a conscious act accomplished with an absolutely clear mind, with perfect freedom, and without any trace of sleep. You are there near your friends, talking affectionately, fully conscious of your double state, which you can terminate immediately whenever you wish. As all your psychical elements are active, a thought is all that is needed to bring you straight back to your body with a lucidity equal to that of any moment of the day."

Yram's writing style tends to be as ethereal and lacking sub-

Passing Through the "Pineal Door"

Below: *Separation of the Spirit Body for Independent Existence.* The book further describes the experience as follows: "The heavenly heart rises to the summit of the Creative, where it expands in complete freedom . . . body and heart must be left completely released. All entanglements have disappeared without trace."

Below: the final stage of meditation, *The Center in the Midst of the Conditions*, in which the spirit body has been fully liberated.

Robert Monroe and the Mind Research Institute

Robert Monroe is probably the leading authority and researcher on out-of-the-body experiences in the United States. Born in Indiana in 1915, Monroe was a writer and producer of radio programs from 1937 to 1949, and is now president of several radio and electronics corporations. He had his first out-of-the-body experience (OOBE) when he was a child, and from 1958 on these became increasingly frequent. In 1965-66 Monroe took part in laboratory experiments in which it was found that during his OOBEs his brain wave pattern was like that of dreaming sleep. There was no change in his heart rate, but there was a fall in blood pressure. Monroe opened the Mind Research Institute at his farm in Virginia in 1971. In further tests there it was found that an OOBE most frequently took place when a person was lying warm and relaxed in bed, in a north-south position. In the successful experiments, about 40 percent were willfully induced; 15 percent were spontaneous; 45 percent were indeterminate. In his book *Journeys out of the Body* (1971), Monroe describes these experiments and also gives step-by-step instructions on how to project yourself out of your body.

stance as his double, and of all the virtuosi of astral projection, his approach is the least critical and scientific. His narrative would not convince any skeptic that his experiences were anything more than vivid dreams or nightmares, though anyone familiar with the literature of projection will recognize in it elements that suggest that at least some of his OOBEs were authentic. At the opposite extreme is Robert Monroe who, as a result of having had many OOBEs, established a Mind Research Institute in Virginia. His book is the most level-headed and analytical of all experients' records.

Monroe recalls two out-of-body experiences from his childhood, one of which involved an apparent projection 30 years into the future and a foresight of television before it was invented. But it was not until much later in life that he began to have OOBEs regularly. It started alarmingly. On several occasions when he lay down he suffered a severe and inexplicable abdominal cramp. Then his entire body began vibrating. The condition lasted for some time, then ceased abruptly. Monroe consulted a physician and a psychologist, but neither could offer any explanation of the experience. He got accustomed to simply waiting patiently for the pain and the vibrations to pass. One evening as the pain occurred, he happened to let his arm fall loosely over the side of the bed. His fingers were resting on the bedside rug, but when he moved them slightly they seemed to pass through the rug to the floor beneath, and when he pushed they seemed to penetrate the floor as well. Curious, he pushed deeper until his entire arm was through the floor and his hand through the ceiling of the room below. He was sure that he was fully awake, and made careful mental notes of the familiar features of his room and the moonlit landscape through the window, but the sensation persisted. His fingers splashed about in a pool of water. When the vibrations began to abate he snatched his arm back onto the bed for fear that the floor might close and sever it.

Some four weeks after this incident, Monroe again experienced the vibrations, and while he was waiting for them to pass he "just happened to think how nice it would be to take a glider up and fly the next afternoon." Soon after this he felt something pressing against his shoulder and back, and thought at first that he had fallen out of bed and was leaning against a wall. Then he realized that it was not the wall but the ceiling. He was floating against it like a balloon, and down below he could see his wife in bed with someone. When he looked closer and saw that the other person was himself, his first thought was that he had died, but when in a panic he tried to get back into his physical body, he found that he had no difficulty in doing so.

This experience started Monroe on a long program of research. In his book he reports several experiments undertaken with the cooperation of other people in which he projected his second body to a distant location and returned with correct information about what those people were doing at the time. Once he projected to visit a woman friend who was on vacation somewhere on the New Jersey coast. He didn't know exactly where she was, and she was not aware that he was going to attempt an experiment. About three o'clock on a Saturday afternoon he lay down and employed one of the techniques he had developed to separate his second body, at the same time willing it to visit his friend wherever she was. He saw a scene in what appeared to be a kitchen. His friend and two teenage girls were sitting there chatting. They held glasses in their hands. He remained a while, and then decided to try something he had never attempted before. He went over to the woman and pinched her just below her ribcage. He was somewhat surprised when she let out a loud "Ow!" Well, he thought, he had given her something to remember the occasion by, and he waited impatiently for Monday,

Monroe's Long Program of Research

Below: this photomontage was taken for Robert Monroe's book *Journeys Out of the Body*, in which he describes his astral travels.

Dream Images and Astral Visions

Below: these dream images were drawn by the Marquis d'Hervey de Saint-Denis for his book on how to direct dreams (*Les Reves et les moyens de les diriger*). Writing in the 1860s, he described these visions, experienced in the state between waking and sleeping, as "wheels of light, tiny revolving suns, colored bubbles rising and falling . . . bright lines that cross and interlace, that roll up and make circles, lozenges and other geometric shapes."

when they would meet again at work. Asked what she had been doing between three and four on Saturday, the woman answered after some thought that she had been sitting in the kitchen of a beach cottage with her niece and her niece's friend. They had been doing nothing in particular, she said, mostly talking and drinking cola. Monroe had to prompt her to remember the pinch, but when he mentioned it she asked in amazement, "Was that you?" She showed him two bruise marks on her side at exactly the spot where he had pinched her.

Monroe does not use the term "astral" when he writes about his OOBEs, but he firmly believes he has visited different planes of reality that he calls "Locales I, II, and III." Locale I is the here-and-now physical world. Locale II is a "thought world" and is "the *natural* environment of the Second Body." Locale III, Monroe writes, "seems to interpenetrate our physical world, yet spans limitless reaches beyond comprehension." In it "reality is composed of deepest desires and most frantic fears. Thought is action . . . it is the well-spring of existence . . . the vital creative force that produces energy, assembles 'matter' into form, and provides channels of perception and communication." What we call heaven and hell are located in Locale II, which is inhabited by various entities and creatures that are really "thought forms." Monroe states that on visits to Locale II he has met the dead,

and he believes that "human personality survives the transition of death and continues in Locale II." Locale III is a physical and material world weirdly like, but at the same time in many details unlike, the world we know. There is a natural environment similar to the Earth's. There are people, cities, roads, businesses, all the signs of a civilization. But it is a civilization based on different technologies and with different customs. There are no electrical devices, no signs of the use of oil or the principle of internal combustion as power sources. Scientific development is apparently less advanced than on Earth, but Locale III cannot be a period of our past history because our science was never at the Locale III stage. On visits there, Monroe has inhabited a different body and lived a different life from his earthly one.

When Monroe writes about his experiences in Locale III he strains his readers' credulity to the utmost. It is interesting, though, and perhaps relevant to note that since 1971 when his book was first published, theoretical physicists working in the field of advanced quantum mechanics have come up with the hypothesis that there exist multiple Universes, all basically similar but with slight differences, and that "transition events" — which could take the form of OOBEs — between these Universes can and do occur. In fact, in the light of these recent developments in theoretical physics, even the convinced skeptic should hesitate before dismissing accounts of astral projection as nothing more than mere fantasy.

Above: these illustrations from *The Art and Practice of Astral Projection* by Ophiel, an occultist, show two stages in the development of clairvoyant vision as one breaks through into the astral plane. "The first thing to appear," writes Ophiel, "is the solid black. Then next the colors begin to appear through the black . . . The black then thins out and away, the colors become more brilliant, and finally burst out into the blinding pure white Astral light."

Chapter 5
Beyond the Veil

We all know we all die. But what about the tantalizing accounts of those who have very nearly died, those who have hesitated on the threshold and then stepped back into life again? What do they have to tell us about the experience of dying, and about the world—if one exists—that lies beyond death? What were they able to observe about the mortal world they so nearly left behind? Some patients clearly recall conversations held over their unconscious bodies on the operating table; others are able to observe the actions of their families far from where their physical bodies drift toward death. What *is* the experience we call death?

There are a number of reported instances of false deaths which seem to suggest that the second body may survive the death of the physical body, at least for a time. One of the most famous and bizarre is the case of the Reverend Bertrand, a Huguenot clergyman. Both Richard Hodgson and William James, two of the most serious 19th-century psychical researchers, heard his narrative at first hand, checked it, and were convinced of its authenticity. The case was reported in the *Proceedings for the Society for Psychical Research* in 1892. While climbing in the Alps with a party of students and an old guide, the Reverend Bertrand felt weary. He decided to rest while the others went up to the summit, which he had in any case visited several times before. He instructed the guide to take the party up by a path to the left and to come down by the right. When they had gone he sat down to rest with his legs dangling over a precipice. After a time he put a cigar in his mouth and struck a match to light it, but suddenly a curious feeling came over him. He watched the match burn his fingers, but he couldn't throw it down, nor could he move his limbs. Realizing that he was freezing to death, he began to pray; then, giving up hope of survival, he decided to study the process of dying.

He remained conscious while the icy paralysis progressively gripped all his bodily functions, then he felt his head become unbearably cold and suddenly had the sensation of separating from his physical body. He could see it below him, "deadly pale,

Opposite: this painting, *Is this not Great Babylon that I have built?*, is by the Irish poet and painter G. W. Russell, better known as A.E. The soul was a recurring theme in A.E.'s work. In this painting it is shown ascending from the physical body. Inclined to mysticism, A.E. was attracted to the teachings of Theosophy and to those of the great Indian mystics.

The Phenomenon of "False Death"

Below: the psychologist, philosopher, and psychical researcher William James. He investigated an out-of-the-body experience undergone by a clergyman, the Rev. J. L. Bertrand, while mountain climbing.

with a yellowish-blue color, holding a cigar in its mouth and a match in its two burned fingers," and he felt that he was "a captive balloon still attached to Earth by a kind of elastic string and going up, always up." He felt exultant and alive and only wished that he could cut the thread that still connected him with the physical. He could see the party continuing their climb, and noted that the guide had disregarded his instructions and gone up by the right instead of the left. He also watched the guide steal a leg of chicken and some drinks from his bottle of Madeira, and he thought, "Go on, old fellow, eat the whole chicken if you choose, for I hope my miserable corpse will never eat or drink again."

Traveling further in his astral body, he saw his wife, who was due to join him in Lucerne the following day, descend from a carriage with four other people and go into a hotel at Lungren. But his only emotion was regret that "the thread, though thinner than ever, was not cut."

Suddenly he had a sensation of being irresistibly pulled downward. The party had returned to where they had left him, and the guide was rubbing his body to restore circulation. He felt that he was a balloon being hauled down to earth. His description of his reentry into the physical body emphasizes the violence of the experience, which numerous other projectors have noted: "When I reached my body again I had a last hope—the balloon seemed much too big for the mouth. Suddenly I uttered an awful roar, like a wild beast; the corpse swallowed the balloon, and Bertrand was Bertrand again."

The old guide might reasonably have expected the revived clergyman to be grateful to him for saving his life, so he was astounded when Bertrand admonished him for disobeying his instructions as to the route and for stealing some of his Madeira and the chicken leg. When the party returned to Lucerne, Bertrand astonished his wife by asking whether there had been five people in the carriage and if they had stopped *en route* at the hotel in Lungren.

"Yes," she said, "But who told you?"

A more modern case of false death is that of Private George Ritchie, who on December 20, 1943, was brought back to life with an injection of adrenalin directly into the heart after being officially dead for nine minutes. The army doctor who had signed the death certificate pronounced the case "the most baffling circumstance of his career," and both he and a nurse signed affidavits attesting that Private Ritchie had died. But during those nine minutes of not being alive the young soldier had a sequence of experiences that he remained grateful for ever afterward. Now a psychiatrist in Charlottesville, Virginia, Dr. Ritchie believes that he was allowed to return to this life "so that I could learn about man and then serve God." He described his strange experience in *Guideposts* magazine in 1963.

Having just completed basic training, Ritchie was given the "unheard-of break for a private" of being assigned to the Army medical school at Richmond, Virginia, but on the day he was due to go there he developed what at first was a chest cold. He tried to combat it with aspirin, but his condition rapidly got worse, he developed a high fever, and finally he lost consciousness. He surfaced slightly with blurred impressions of traveling in an ambulance and of struggling to get to his feet to have an X-ray taken. Then everything went blank until he suddenly woke up to find himself lying in a dimly lit, unfamiliar room. His first thought was that he would miss the train to Richmond, and he sprang out of bed to look for his uniform. It was nowhere to be seen, but when he turned back to the bed he had just left he saw that someone was lying on it. The man was obviously dead. "The slack jaw, the gray skin, were awful," he said. When he looked closer he saw on the left hand of the corpse his own fraternity ring from his college days, which he had worn for two years.

He fled from the room, his only thought being that he must get to Richmond. In the hall an orderly seemed to walk right through him without seeing him. What if the people at the medical school couldn't see him either? he thought as he sped through the dark night toward Richmond. He didn't know whether he was running or flying but he was aware of the landscape slipping by. Then he stopped his headlong flight to take stock of his situation. He was standing by a telephone pole in a town by a large river. He tried to touch the guy wire, but his hand passed right through it. "In some unimaginable way," he later wrote, "I had lost my firmness of flesh, the hand that could grip that wire, the body that other people saw." Realizing that he wasn't going to be able to pursue his medical career in his present nonphysical form, he decided that he must get back and rejoin his physical body as fast as he could.

He had no trouble returning to the hospital. He was there as soon as he thought of it. But the problem was to find his body. He rushed from ward to ward and room to room, scrutinizing the faces of sleeping soldiers, and several times he thought he recognized himself but found that the fraternity ring was lacking. Then he found the ring on the left hand of a figure covered with a sheet. For the first time, the thought occurred to him that, "This is death. *This* is what we human beings call 'death,' this splitting up of one's self."

Then he had a religious illumination. The room filled with light and he felt the presence of God, and simultaneously his whole life, "every event and thought and conversation, as palpable as a series of pictures," passed before him in review. Suddenly he was in another world, or a world coextensive with and "strangely superimposed on our familiar world." It was a world thronged with unhappy and desperate looking people, all trying vainly to make contact with others. He surmised that they were the dead, still preoccupied with earthly cares, as he had been in trying to get to Richmond. He wondered if this was hell. "To care most when you are most powerless; this would be hell indeed," he said.

He went on to visit two other worlds—not, he said, so-called spirit worlds, "for they were too real, too solid." He realized they were also worlds that had been there all along, but could only be seen with "a new openness of wisdom." The first of these was a world of philosophers and artists of all kinds, men concerned not "with earthly things, but . . . with truth," and in it there were universities and great libraries and scientific labora-

Above: this wooden sculpture depicts Belam, a spirit of the Melanau tribe of Sarawak, in Malaysia. Belam is believed to catch the souls of sick people and restore them to their bodies. This is a variation on the widespread belief among primitive peoples that illness is caused by a separation of the astral and physical bodies.

Above: Auckland Campbell Geddes, a British physician and professor of anatomy who described, in a paper read to the Royal Medical Society, an out-of-the-body experience undergone by a person who was critically ill.

tories. He only had a glimpse of the final world, one far away from earth and out of all relation to it, where the buildings and the people were all blindingly bright. "At that time," he wrote, "I had not read the *Book of Revelation*, nor, incidentally, anything on the subject of life after death."

Then he woke up in his physical body. To the astonishment of the onlookers—the doctor, the nurse, and the orderly who had been assigned to prepare him for the morgue and who had noticed feeble signs of life in the corpse—he showed no symptoms of brain damage although he had not drawn breath for the full nine minutes of his excursion into the beyond.

In modern Western societies the accredited method of seeking truth has tended to be the scientific method, and it is an axiom of science that no statement can qualify as truth unless there are tests it can be subjected to. The trouble with the survival-of-death and the second-body hypotheses is that the evidence supporting them is based on subjective reports such as those of Bertrand and Ritchie. Because there are no tests that scientists can set up to prove or disprove the theories, they have tended to ignore the problems. But in recent years there has been a growing dissatisfaction among young scientists with the demarcations of the traditional scientific approach. Charles T. Tart, Professor of Psychology at the University of California, has pinpointed its limitations for the scientifically curious.

Tart argues that Western science has been a science dealing with one state of consciousness only. Because of this it only has access to a limited area of reality and a limited range of truths. He wants to extend the range of scientific inquiry to deal with other levels of consciousness. One way to do this would be to encourage groups of highly skilled practitioners to attain certain states of consciousness and to discuss and compare their findings. Till that time, however, we will have to depend for our knowledge on those recorded accounts which seem to be genuine. Two such accounts are vouched for by doctors, and both appear to be reliable.

Addressing the Royal Medical Society of Edinburgh in 1937, Sir Auckland (later Lord) Geddes, a distinguished professor of anatomy, read his colleagues a description of an OOBE that he said had been given to him by another physician who wished to remain anonymous. The experience, in fact, was probably his own, but he no doubt felt that to present it as such at that time would be to jeopardize his professional reputation.

On November 9, a few minutes after midnight, the physician in question began to feel very ill. His condition worsened in the night, and by morning he realized that his state was critical. He was unable even to ring for assistance, however, and he "quite placidly gave up the attempt." Suddenly he realized that he was separating into two distinct types of consciousness, an "A consciousness" connected with his ego, and a "B consciousness" connected with his body. As his physical condition grew worse, "the B consciousness began to disintegrate, while the A consciousness which was now me, seemed to be altogether *outside of my body, which I could see.*"

At this stage the physician, like the Reverend Bertrand, became clairvoyant in his second body. "Gradually I realized that I could see not only my body and the bed in which it was, but everything in the whole house and garden," he said, "and then I realized that I was seeing not only things at home, but in London and in Scotland, in fact wherever my attention was directed. . . . And the explanation which I received (from what source I do not know, but which I found myself calling to myself *me mentor*) was that I was free in a time dimension of space, wherein *now* was equivalent to *here* in the ordinary three-dimensional space of everyday life." His mentor further explained that there was a "psychic stream" flowing through the three-, four- and five-dimensional Universes, and that individual brains were "just end-organs projecting as it were from the three-dimensional Universe into the psychic stream." The different dimensions interpenetrated each other, and "the fourth dimension was in everything existing in the three-dimensional space, and at the same time everything in the three-dimensional space existed in the fourth dimension, and also in the fifth dimension.

With his clairvoyant vision, the physician began to recognize people in the three-dimensional world, and he noticed that they all had around them "psychic condensation" or auras of different colors and of varying bulk, sharpness of outline, and apparent solidity. Then he saw a friend enter his bedroom, register shock, and hurry to the telephone. He also saw his doctor receive the news, hurriedly leave his patients, and rush to his bedside and examine him. He heard his doctor say, "He is nearly gone," and watched him take a syringe and inject his body with something that he later learned was camphor. Like the Reverend Bertrand he didn't want to return to the physical. "As my heart began to beat more strongly, I was drawn back, and I was intensely annoyed because I was so interested and was just beginning to understand where I was and what I was seeing. I came back into my body, really angry at being pulled back, and once back, all the clarity of vision of anything and everything disappeared, and I was just possessed of a glimmer of consciousness which was suffused with pain."

Geddes invited his colleagues to consider the implications of this experience, and assured them: "Of one thing only can we be quite sure—it was not fake." He said that it had helped him "to define the idea of a psychic continuum, spread out in time like a plasmic net." Furthermore, he believed that it brought "telepathy, clairvoyance, Spiritualism, and indeed all the para-psychic manifestations into the domain of the picturable." These were bold words for an eminent professor to utter in the presence of professional colleagues in 1937. That Geddes ventured so to commit himself and to face possible derision surely indicates that the experience and the understanding he gained through it made a profound impression on him.

Our final false death case was reported as "The Case of Dr. X" in the *Journal of the Society for Psychical Research* in 1957. Dr. X was able to describe in detail what other people were doing at a time when his physical body was so located that he would not have been able to obtain the information by means of his normal sensory faculties, even if he had been in possession of them. He wrote his account 40 years after the event had occurred in 1916, and his memory remained clear as to exactly what had happened.

"Other Levels of Consciousness"

Below: the writer Ernest Hemingway, who had an out-of-the-body experience in 1918 while fighting in World War I in Italy. He had been hit in the leg by shrapnel. As he lay in the trench he suddenly felt as if "my soul or something was coming right out of my body, like you'd pull a silk handkerchief out of a pocket by one corner . . . It flew around and then came back and went in again . . ." Hemingway used this experience in *A Farewell to Arms*, a novel based on his war experiences.

Flying Doctor

Dr. X was a medical officer in World War I, and was stationed on a small country airfield in England. One day word came through that a pilot had been shot down at another airfield. Could Dr. X help to release him from the wreckage?

It was to be an event unique in the history of aviation—the first time that medical help had been taken by air to a casualty. All the top personnel turned up at the runway. Seconds after takeoff, the plane crashed. Dr. X was thrown out into a dip where the airfield was obscured from view. Suddenly he found himself hovering about 200 feet above his unconscious body in a state of pleasant awareness. He could see the frenzied activity at the airfield. The ambulance started up and then stalled. The medical orderly jumped in. Others were running to the crash.

Then Dr. X began to move in what seemed like a delightful journey over the countryside and sea till he felt a kind of retraction and was back again hovering over his body. Then, with a pop, he was aware of an orderly pouring sal volatile down his throat. Later, all the incidents he had seen at the airfield while in his astral body were confirmed by others. Dr. X found the experience so pleasant that it completely removed his fear of death.

Anesthetics and Astral Projection

Opposite: this drawing by Sylvia Leone Mahler (real name Edith Haubold) is entitled *Alpha* and shows man linked to a higher plane of existence via a looped and spiraling cord. While hospitalized after a major operation Sylvia Mahler had her first out-of-the-body experience. She was in pain and about to ring for a painkiller when she began to feel as though the room had faded away. She seemed to be standing at the bottom of a deep well, constructed of transparent leaves, rocks, shells, and flowers, all in beautiful colors. She began to rise upward through the well, observing fascinating and beautiful shapes and colors, until she reached the interior of a vast cathedral, decorated on the walls with intricate designs. Faced by unknown beings who gazed at her, she felt an immediate urge "to declare . . . my dedication forevermore to that indescribable glory for which there is no single name." At that moment, the nurse awakened her to give her an injection. But for those moments she had been "in a world beyond the boundaries of pain . . . containing the greatest joy I have ever experienced." After this occasion she turned to art, finding it a way to express her new insights.

Dr. X, a medical officer with the Royal Flying Corps, crashed seconds after taking off in a small plane from a country airport. He was hurled to the ground where he lay inert and apparently dead. He experienced the abrupt separation of his second body, which seemed to rise to a height of about 200 feet above the scene of the crash. He saw the ambulance leave the airport and a crowd of anxious people gather around him. He next had a sensation of traveling at great speed through the air until he was over the Atlantic. Suddenly he was pulled back into his physical body and regained consciousness. Later, every detail of his account of what had happened after the crash while he was unconscious was confirmed by the other people concerned.

The cases of the Reverend Bertrand, Ritchie, Dr. X and Geddes—whether about himself or someone else as he said—constitute a small sample out of hundreds of recorded false deaths which have been investigated by psychical researchers. Even in this small sample, however, a number of common characteristics stand out, which are typical of many of the accounts of astral projection. All four narrators describe the same sensation of seeing their physical body from a distance, though only one, the Reverend Bertrand, mentions the existence of an attenuating cord or cable between the physical and astral bodies. Both Ritchie and Dr. X reported the feeling of rapid travel, and Ritchie and the physician recorded by Geddes described the feeling that it was only necessary to will oneself to a place to be there. Ritchie and Geddes' physician also believed that they had become aware of other worlds, and had gained in knowledge through their astral experience.

From the similarities between these experiences and those of many other astral projectors it would seem reasonable to class the OOBE as a genuine psychic phenomenon. In these examples it has been associated with the process of dying, but there is another class of evidence: that of people who have experienced separation while under the influence of anesthetics or drugs. In their book, *The Phenomena of Astral Projection*, Muldoon and Carrington wrote: "Anesthetics, producing deep unconsciousness, are . . . ideal for producing astral projection." They also said that although anesthesia was a state of total blankness for most people, "there are many cases on record in which, seemingly, more or less complete consciousness has been retained by the patient, and he has afterwards been enabled to describe all that went on in the operating room, the conversation of the physicians and nurses, and any unusual details which may have developed."

A British surgeon, George Sava, published a volume of reminiscences and reflections in 1953 entitled *A Surgeon Remembers*. In it he says, "It is indeed a disquieting thought . . . that every time one operates, one's activities are under observation from the patient's astral body hovering overhead . . . a fascinating but frightening possibility." The experience that gave rise to these thoughts was connected with an operation he had once performed on an elderly woman, Mrs. Frances Gail.

Mrs. Gail was in a postoperative coma and seemed to be sinking fast. An urgent call from the hospital brought Dr. Sava from his home, and he worked hard to bring his patient back to

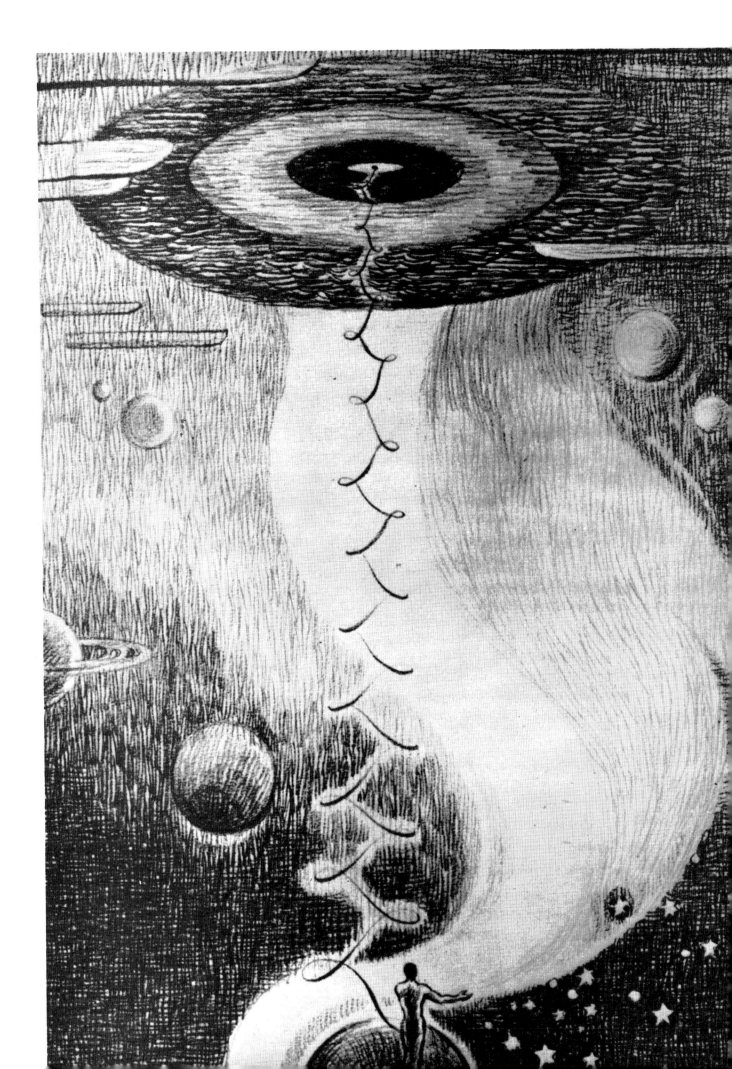

OOBEs in the Operating Theater

consciousness. He was successful, and when she was able to speak Mrs. Gail told him that she had been out of her body and would have preferred to have remained out of it, but she had come back because her friends had called her. Sava was sympathetic but, of course, not particularly impressed by this information, which could be merely an old person's subjective fantasy, but what she said next astounded him.

"You didn't carry out the operation you first intended, did you, Mr. Sava? . . . You kept my body lying there under the anesthetic while you and the others discussed whether it was strong enough to withstand what you proposed to do. You took away some pieces of bone. You were chiefly troubled about the anesthetic and said to the anesthetist: 'Do you think she can stand three hours of it? Heart all right?' The anesthetist just nodded and said, 'She's okay, especially considering she's no chicken.' Is that right?"

It was right. Every detail of Frances Gail's account exactly corresponded with what had happened in the operating theater while she had been under the anesthetic. It was told as an attentive and fully conscious observer might have told it.

A similar experience is recalled by Dr. Russell MacRobert, a staff doctor at the Lennox Hill Hospital in New York City. The patient in this case was a clergyman who was having an ear operation. He was in great pain and was given extra anesthetic for the operation. The surgeon was just about to begin when he discovered that he was lacking a necessary special instrument. He swore, took off his gloves, and went to get his instrument bag from another room down the hall. When he returned he put on fresh gloves and a gown, had a nurse sterilize the instrument,

Below: an Australian aboriginal bark painting depicting a funeral ceremony and the path of the wandering spirit after death. The path is a symbol common to many cultures, both primitive and civilized.

Left: *The Soul of St. Bertin Carried up to God*, a 15th-century painting showing the ascent of a holy man's soul as conceived by medieval Christianity. The artists of the late Middle Ages delighted in painting rich textures, and their portrayals of the afterlife are just as solid and sensuous as their portrayals of the concrete, physical world.

Above: *The Departure of the Astral Body at Death*, an engraving based on a clairvoyant vision of the 19th-century American mystic Andrew Jackson Davis. There are many accounts of people seeing a spirit—or something—leave the body of a dying person.

Images of the Departing Soul

Below: Dr. Karlis Osis, director of research at the American Society for Psychical Research. The apparatus behind him is his own invention, a "soul trap," which is intended to detect out-of-the-body projection. The subject sits in another room, wired to an EEG, and attempts to view, in the astral body, the image inside the hole.

Opposite: three photographs purporting to show the soul leaving the body at death. They were taken early in this century by the French physician Hippolyte Baraduc and show his wife (top), 15 minutes after death, and (middle) one hour after death, and (bottom) his son's body photographed in the coffin nine hours after death.

counterparts" of three patients who had operations under anesthetic. Soon after the first patient, an elderly woman, was brought into the surgery, he saw a form rise and float free in space above the operating table. And "as the anesthetic deepened and the physical body became more relaxed, the freedom of the spirit body became greater. For the spirit form floated more freely away from the physical counterpart during the height of the anesthetic. . . . The spirit was quiet, as though it was also in deep peaceful sleep. I knew that the direct process of surgical activity was not affecting it. . . . At the finish of this operation, while the wound was being closed, the spirit came closer to the body but had not yet reentered its vehicle when the patient was wheeled from the operating theater." In this and in the other two cases, Dr. Hout wrote, he saw the cord connecting the physical and etheric bodies, and it looked like "a silvery shaft of light which wound around through the room in much the same way as a curl of smoke will drift indifferently in still atmosphere."

Crookall has collected many accounts of people seeing the second body leaving the physical body at death. Common features of these accounts are that the vaporous substance emerges from the head, gradually condenses into a form resembling the physical body, remains connected for a time with the physical by means of the silvery cord, and then disappears. A British nurse and psychic, Joy Snell, wrote in 1918 in her book *The Ministry of Angels* that she had often observed this phenomenon. She described the death of a close friend in this way: "Immediately after her heart had ceased to beat, I distinctly saw something in appearance like smoke . . . ascend from her body. . . . This form, shadowy at first, gradually changed and . . . resolved itself into a form like that of my friend but glorified, with no trace on it of the spasm of pain which had seized her just before she died."

Muldoon and Carrington quote the testimony of a missionary who spent many years in Tahiti. He reported that the Tahitians believe that at death the soul is drawn out of the body via the head, and that their clairvoyants described the process of separation in exactly the same terms as their European and American counterparts have described it. Such cross-cultural similarity strongly suggests that the phenomenon is not merely hallucinatory.

In his monograph *Deathbed Observations by Physicians and Nurses*, Dr. K. Osis of the American Society for Psychical Research has assembled a great deal of evidence that supports the view that death is an altered state of consciousness, and that for many people it is attended by experiences of exaltation and ecstasy. The testimonies of people who have experienced false deaths confirm this. The accounts given by Geddes and Ritchie as to the existence of other worlds or dimensions of reality cannot just be lightly shrugged off. Both Osis and Crookall have records of deathbed visions in which the dying person has met and sometimes been "helped over" by a friend or relative who neither he nor anybody present knew at the time was dead. The evidence for some kind of existence "beyond the veil" is strong, and the day will come for each of us when we have the opportunity to conduct our own personal investigation.

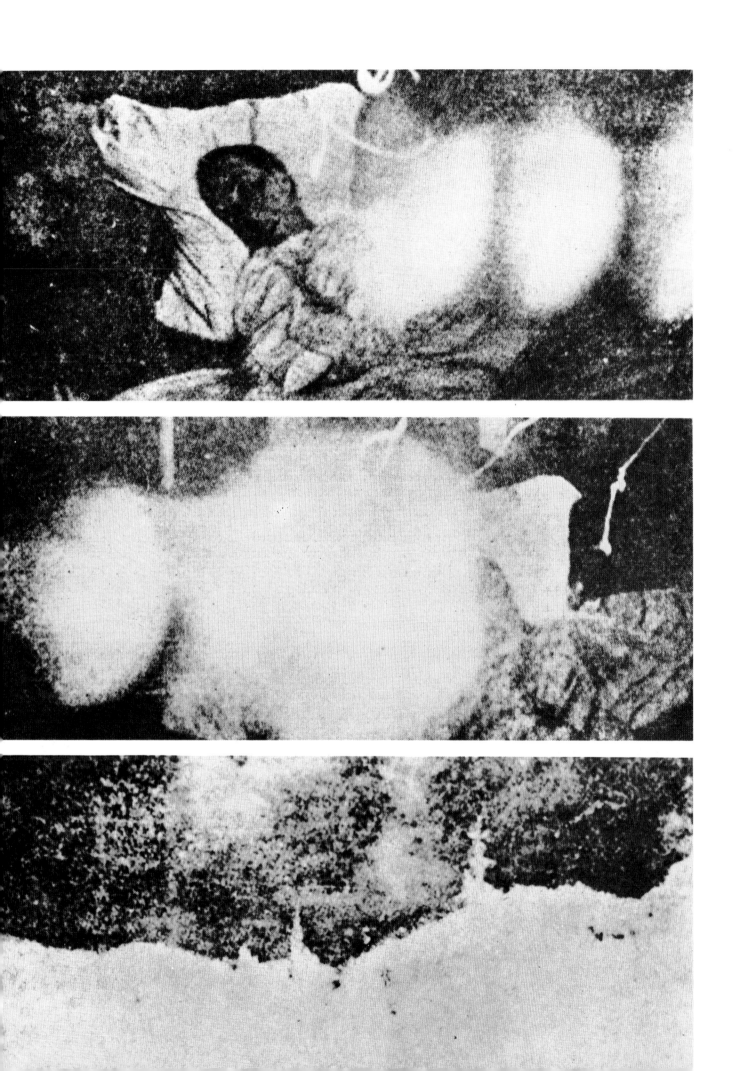

Chapter 6
Possession and Multiple Personality

It is perhaps alarming enough to suggest that your personality can under some circumstances leave your body temporarily. But what about the possibility of another personality entering into your body, and speaking its words through your mouth? The evidence for possession has a long history; psychologists today talk of multiple personality. Hypnotists report disturbing evidence of patients with memories of previous incarnations. What do these terms mean and what must it be like for the person who finds other personalities inhabiting what was once a familiar body? Where do these personalities come from, and—if they are finally dispelled or exorcised—where do they go?

In 1944 the widow of a famous Brazilian author, Humberto de Campos, sued in court for a share in the royalties of five books that her husband had written after his death. The books had issued from the pen of Chico Xavier, a prolific trance-writer, who did not contest the fact that they were the dead man's creation. He even offered to go into trance and produce more specimens of de Campos' work right in the courtroom. Distinguished critics vouched for the fact that the books were typical of the alleged author in style and subject matter. The judge, however, ruled that the dead had no rights in courts of law, and dismissed the widow's suit. The case of Chico Xavier is one of many which suggest that the dead sometimes take possession of the living, and use them as instruments for communication or action in the present world. Although psychological explanations of the phenomena of possession, multiple personality, and the command of unknown languages can often be advanced, there are many cases that do not easily yield to such explanations. That of Chico Xavier is one of them.

Before he died, de Campos himself vouched for the apparent authenticity of one of Xavier's published works, a 421-page volume purporting to be a collection of poems by Brazil's greatest dead poets. De Campos wrote that the alleged authors of these poems showed in them "the same characteristics of inspiration and expression that identified them on this planet." He also said: "The themes they tackle are those that preoccupied

Opposite: this "automatic" painting is by a British housewife named Madge Gill who, before her death in 1961, produced hundreds of drawings and paintings while she was in a state of semitrance. Mrs. Gill believed herself "undoubtedly guided by an unseen force" and attributed many of her works to a spirit she called Myrninerest.

The Mystery of Automatic Writing

Below: the Brazilian medium and automatic writer "Chico" Xavier, born in 1910. By the age of 64, he had written 126 books that he claims are actually written by a number of "spiritual entities." His works include novels, essays, history, and works on the teachings of Spiritism (Spiritualism).

them when alive. The taste is the same, and the verse generally obeys the same musical flow." For Xavier to have produced the work out of his own head would have been a prodigious feat of literary parody, and one for which he was hardly educationally equipped. He had left school at 13 and had worked in a textile factory, as a kitchen hand, and as a salesman before settling in a modest clerical post in the civil service, which he retained until he retired in 1961.

Xavier is still busy trance writing today, and up to 1974 he had produced 126 books in many categories including poetry, fiction, children's books, history, popular science, and doctrine of Spiritualism, or Spiritism as it is known in Brazil. Immense industry and erudition, apart from literary genius, would have been required for any one man to have created this great variety of work. Xavier has suffered from defective eyesight all his life, and can read only slowly and with difficulty. He could hardly have acquired by normal means the vast knowledge that has gone into his books. He has stated that he scarcely understands a word of some of the scientific writings that have flowed from his pen. Since he doesn't claim authorship of any of the work, he has donated the substantial income from the books to the Spiritist cause.

In 1958 Xavier and another Brazilian Spiritist trance-author jointly produced over a period of 40 days a book entitled *Evolution in Two Worlds*. The discarnate, or nonphysical, author of this work seems to have wanted to prove his authorship because he divided the chapters of his book between Xavier and the second writer, Dr. Waldo Vieira, alternating between them. The two trance-writers lived 250 miles apart and were not in communication during the book's composition. Guy Playfair, who has a chapter on Xavier in his book *The Flying Cow*, says that *Evolution in Two Worlds* "reveals an immense knowledge of several sciences that no ordinary writer, even a qualified scientist, could have assembled without copious research and note-taking, and despite the wide education gap between the two writers, the unity of style is total. One chapter frequently begins where the previous one leaves off."

The phenomena of automatic writing and trance mediumship are generally fairly benevolent forms of spirit possession. Both are to some extent controlled by the mediums, at least in so far as they deliberately go into trance and temporarily allow themselves to be taken over for use as an instrument or channel. But the term "possession" is normally used to stand for something more sinister: a total and uncontrollable usurpation of a personality by an invading entity. Of course, to speak of an invading entity is to put a Spiritualist interpretation on the facts, whereas many psychologists would maintain that possession is really acute schizophrenia, and that the forces that usurp the victim's personality originate within his or her own unconscious. There are some cases of alleged possession, however, which contain elements that are difficult to explain in terms of abnormal psychology.

In May 1922 an American minister and psychologist, Walter Franklin Prince, was approached by a certain Mrs. Latimer, a woman later described as "highly cultivated." She was convinced that for two years she had been possessed and tormented by the spirit of a cousin by the name of Marvin. It had begun a few days after Marvin's death when she had distinctly heard his voice saying, "You made me suffer and I will make you suffer." This sentence was to be repeated often over subsequent months. She didn't understand how she had made Marvin suffer until he reminded her of a letter she had written shortly before his death in which she had made a disparaging remark about him. It was true, although she was certain that Marvin couldn't have seen the letter. She was also accused by the spirit of having failed to send flowers for his coffin. She had in fact sent roses, but when she checked she found that they had been placed inconspicuously away from the coffin itself.

Over the two years before she consulted Prince, Mrs. Latimer had hardly had a single night when she didn't wake up screaming loudly and uncontrollably. Her days were also tormented. Marvin often correctly predicted how she would be hurt by the attitudes or actions of other people. He threatened that the torments would continue until she made a sincere mental apology, which she felt unable to do.

Prince had some experience of treating people with troubles of a psychic nature, in the course of which he had found that conventional psychiatric methods of depth analysis combined with persuasion and suggestion were of no avail. He decided to try the experiment of acting on the assumption that Mrs. Latimer really was possessed by the spirit of Marvin, and of giving

Below: Dr. Walter Franklin Prince (right), the American psychical researcher, talking with a farmer, Alexander McDonald, whose family was driven from their farmhouse by ghosts. Dr. Prince once succeeded in freeing a woman from what seemed to be a spirit that possessed and tormented her.

Above: the American psychical investigator
Richard Hodgson, who studied the case of
Lurancy Vennums, a teenage girl who was
apparently possessed by the spirit of a
neighbor who had died at the age of 18,
when Lurancy herself was only 15 months
old. Hodgson finally came to the conclusion
that the case belonged "to the spiritist
category" and was not a case of multiple
personality.

treatment by lecturing the vindictive spirit.

"I wish to talk with you as one gentleman talks to another," Prince began solemnly, and in Mrs. Latimer's presence he proceeded to give Marvin a 15-minute lecture. He reasoned with him and exhorted him to change his ways. "I shall not deny that you may have had provocation," he said, ". . . but feel sure that you are . . . preventing your own development and progress . . . Your habit of ill will against this woman results in what is called her possession. In fact, you yourself are obsessed by the habit . . ." He suggested that Marvin had probably brooded over his cousin's offense during his last hours, giving it an importance far greater than it deserved, and that he should now review the whole matter intelligently and forgive her. If he did so, Prince said, "the time will come when your life will become so transformed that you will be very thankful for the suggestion I make today."

Prince's unconventional strategy worked quickly. Mrs. Latimer's torments ceased. Her first night's sleep after the session with Prince was disturbed only by a dream in which her dead mother appeared and said, "We heard what the man said. I will take care of Marvin. Go to sleep." On two successive nights Marvin appeared to her in her sleep and, she said, "just stood silently and sorrowfully." When she returned for another consultation with Prince and told him what had happened, he addressed the spirit again and solemnly congratulated him. Mrs. Latimer only heard the voice on one or two more occasions, and on one of these Marvin explained that he had been unable to free himself of the embittered thoughts toward her that had preoccupied him at the time of his death, and that in tormenting her he had been urged on by other vindictive spirits. He promised that he would soon be gone. Mrs. Latimer suffered from vague feelings of unease and tiredness for some months. One day something told her, "You are now free," and thereafter she showed no further symptoms of possession or psychic illness.

Did Prince cure his patient by playing along with her delusion and giving her suggestions that enabled her to free herself of it? Or did he really exorcise a possessing spirit? He did not profess to know the answer himself, though he was impressed by the fact that so quick and complete a cure was effected without anything being done or said directly to the patient. Some time later he repeated the experiment with Leonard Tyrrell, who was being tormented by a deceased acquaintance named Murray. Again Prince gave his no-nonsense, man-to-man speech, to which Murray responded through Tyrrell's automatic writing: "Well, there may be something in what you say; I had never thought of it in that light before. I'll think about it. You may tell him I won't trouble him this week." In a later consultation Murray wrote that he was grateful to Prince for his suggestions because he was now making progress on his side, and he wouldn't disturb Tyrrell again. Sure enough, the symptoms instantly ceased. If it was psychotherapy, it was unlike any other psychotherapy in its simplicity and instant effectiveness.

It is difficult to find any psychological theories that would explain the facts of the classic case of possession, the "Watseka Wonder" case. It is an old case, but it was investigated and authenticated at the time by Richard Hodgson, a psychical researcher who was as thorough, knowledgeable, and skeptical about the supernatural as any modern psychologist.

Mary Roff had died at the age of 18, 12 years before the events occurred that seemed to give evidence of her reappearance in her home town of Watseka, Illinois. The bereaved Roffs were neighbors of the Vennums, and for four months in 1878 14-year-old Lurancy Vennums was apparently possessed by the spirit of Mary, who had died when Lurancy was 15 months old. When the possession started Lurancy was so unhappy with her own family that her parents sent her to the Roffs. She greeted everyone with delight using the familiar names, and sometimes nicknames, by which Mary had known them in her childhood. When she was asked how long she would stay, she answered, "The angels will let me stay till some time in May."

During those months hundreds of little incidents occurred which convinced the Roffs beyond doubt that their daughter had returned in the borrowed body of Lurancy Vennums. The child had total recall of virtually everything that had happened to Mary in her lifetime years before. She remembered minor accidents, journeys, family events and habits in minute detail. On one occasion while the child was out, Mr. Roff asked his wife to find a certain velvet headdress that Mary had habitually worn in the last year of her life, and put it on a stand. Mrs. Roff did so, and when the girl returned she immediately noticed it and said, "Oh, there is my headdress I wore when my hair was short." Then she asked if her mother had kept a certain box with letters in it, and when Mrs. Roff produced the box the girl found among its contents a piece of material and said delightedly, "Oh, ma, here is a collar I tatted! Ma, why did you not show to me my letters and things before?"

On May 21 Mary said fond farewells to her family and Lurancy Vennums returned to her own family. Her own personality and memories were restored, and she settled down happily in her former surroundings.

Richard Hodgson, who visited the Roffs' home several times while Lurancy was there, wrote that there were two possible explanations. Either Lurancy had a secondary personality endowed with supernormal powers of telepathy, clairvoyance, and retrocognition, or she really was possessed for those four months by the spirit of Mary Roff. Hodgson, one of the least credulous of men involved in psychical research, admitted that he had formed the personal opinion that the case belonged "to the spiritistic category."

Over the past 80 years some 150 cases of multiple personality have been reported, and invariably they have given rise to debate between the psychologists and the Spiritualists. The psychologists' case was perhaps best put by Theodor Flournoy. Born in 1854, he became Professor of Psychology at the University of Geneva. In a book entitled *Spiritualism and Psychology* he wrote: "As a crystal splits under the blow of a hammer when struck according to certain definite lines of cleavage, in the same way the human personality, under the shock of excessive emotions, is sometimes broken along the lines of least resistance or the great structural lines of his temperament. A cleavage is pro-

The Case of the "Watseka Wonder"

Below: James Hyslop, Professor of Logic and Ethics at Columbia University in the late 1800s. His studies of mediums and of people said to be suffering from hysteria or multiple personality led him finally to believe that there was such a thing as possession of a person by an alien spirit.

Right: a sample of automatic writing by Hélène Smith, the Swiss medium investigated by Théodore Flournoy. She believed that the writing was really produced by one of her spirit controls, called Leopold. One of her other controls was Queen Marie Antoinette.

Opposite top: a sample of Hélène Smith's normal handwriting.

Above: a self-portrait by Hélène Smith showing her with her guardian angel. She claimed to have experienced astral travel and to have visited Mars. Flournoy attributed her experiences to the workings of her subconscious mind.

duced between opposite selves—whose harmonious equilibrium would constitute the normal condition—seriousness and gaiety; optimistic tendencies and pessimistic; goodness and egoism; instinct of prudery and lasciviousness; the taste for solitude and the love of Nature, and the attraction of civilization etc. The differences, in which the Spiritists see a striking proof of an absolute distinction between the spirits and their so-called instruments, awaken, on the contrary, in the mind of the psychologist the irresistible suspicion that these pretended spirits can be nothing but the products of the subconsciousness of the medium himself."

This is plausible, but it is an argument that rests on faith just as much as the Spiritualist case does. One man who was not satisfied with the psychological explanations of the phenomenon of multiple personality was James Hyslop, Professor of Logic and Ethics at Columbia University in New York City. Also born in 1854, he became an active psychical researcher. He devised a method of separating material of subconscious origin from material of external origin in multiple personality. He would take the subject to a medium who had no prior knowledge of the case. If the medium channeled information or manifested characteristics corresponding to those of the alien personality that was intermittently taking possession of the subject, Hyslop considered that there was a strong probability that the other personality really was alien and of external origin. He tried this experiment with several patients and eventually reached the conclusion—which he said he "fought against for 10 years"—that in certain cases traditionally ascribed to hysteria, multiple personality, paranoia, or some other form of mental disturbance, there were strong indications that the person had, in fact, been invaded by foreign or nonphysical agencies.

One of the most famous cases of multiple personality was that of Miss Beauchamp, investigated by the psychologist Dr. Morton Prince. After a series of emotional shocks, Miss Beauchamp developed four distinct personalities each of which differed in health, in knowledge, and in memories. The third personality, Sally, claimed to be a spirit, and she dominated and could hypnotize the others, sometimes tormenting them mischievously. She put toads and spiders into a box so that the first self would get a shock when she opened it. She took the last

Aime

Je veux tenir ma promesse mais tu comprendras sans nul te, qu'aujourd'hui à cet instant je suis force d'être d'une grande et dois m'abstenir de beaucoup

Automatic Painting

Below: an automatic painting made around 1870 by Mrs. Alaric Watts, a medium. She tried at first to repress her automatic painting as she had done with automatic writing: later, she decided that the visions that inspired her work conveyed religious truths. Unlike many automatic artists, Mrs. Watts was a capable artist while normally conscious.

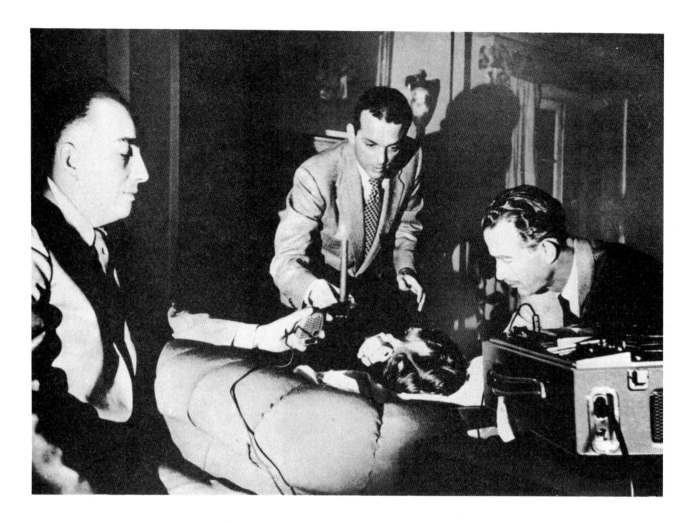

Above: Morey Bernstein, an amateur hypnotist and writer, hypnotizing Virginia Tighe, a Colorado housewife who—while in hypnotic trance—apparently relived an earlier life as an Irishwoman named Bridey Murphy. Bernstein's book *The Search for Bridey Murphy* contained a wealth of details of life in Ireland recalled by Mrs. Tighe (called Ruth Simmons in the book); but later investigation suggested that childhood memories may have produced the material.

public transportation of the day to its terminus in the country and left the first self to walk back to town. She took a particular dislike to the fourth personality and maliciously persecuted her. When Prince tried to integrate the four personalities into one with hypnotic suggestion, Sally remained resistant and independent, always insisting that she was a spirit. Prince then tried the technique that Walter Franklin Prince had used in the Latimer and Tyrrell cases. He reasoned and exhorted. Finally Sally agreed to be squeezed out of existence, and the remaining three personalities were successfully welded into one.

Walter Franklin Prince treated a similar case, that of Doris Fischer, in which one of the personalities was mischievously dominant and seemed more like an invading entity than a projection from the unconscious. In this case there were five personalities involved. They were called Real Doris, Margaret, Sleeping Margaret, Sick Doris, and Sleeping Doris. Margaret was the independent spirit. She stole so that Real Doris would be blamed, hid her school books, jumped into a filthy river with her clothes on, and scratched her body until it bled, leaving Real Doris to suffer the pain. The torments went on for years. James Hyslop cooperated with Prince to treat Doris Fischer, and it was one of the cases in which the assistance of a medium was sought. Corroborative evidence came through suggesting invasion by foreign or nonphysical agencies.

Two modern cases of multiple personality that became well known outside medical literature are the cases of Eve and of Bridey Murphy. The case history of Eve was described in *The Three Faces of Eve*, a book by the two psychiatrists C. H. Tigpen and H. M. Cleckley. Later it became a successful film. Eve White, a married woman with one child, was sent for psychiatric treatment because of persistent headaches and occasional blackouts. She was described as "a neat colorless woman." Orthodox treatment relieved her symptoms, but not long after it was discontinued Eve returned to her psychiatrists. She was sent by her enraged husband because she had been on an expensive shopping spree and had bought a wardrobe of sexy clothes, though she had no recollection of the event. During an interview with the doctors, Eve suddenly changed personality. A "bright unfamiliar voice that sparkled" said "Hi, there, doc!" and Eve Black appeared. Eve Black was contemptuous of Eve White and knew everything about her. She said she had often used her blackouts in order to get out and enjoy herself, go to bars, flirt with men, and buy expensive clothes. Eve White knew nothing of this other self.

This seemed a simple enough case of a split personality, but during the next stage of therapy a third personality emerged. This one, who called herself Jane, professed to know nothing at all about Eve White or Eve Black. Jane was a more aware, intelligent, and integrated personality than either of the two Eves. Although they never became aware of her existence she got to know them both well. She accompanied them wherever they went, observed them closely, and showed sympathy with them over their problems. This weird situation in which Eve White knew nothing about her other two personalities, Eve Black knew all

Who Was Eva White?

Below left: the actress Teresa Wright portraying Virginia Tighe under hypnosis in the film based on the story of Bridey Murphy. While hypnotized, "Bridey" remembered not only details of her life but also her own funeral in Belfast. Investigation in Ireland confirmed the accuracy of many of the terms and figures of speech she used, but failed to discover any conclusive evidence of her existence.

Below: Virginia Tighe as a young woman in the 1950s. As "Bridey Murphy," she had supposedly lived in Ireland between 1798 and 1864. One thing that made her case convincing—apart from the many accurate details it included—was the prosaic nature of Bridey's life. Many—if not most—people who claim to be reincarnated insist that in their previous lives they were royalty or great artists, giving their accounts an element of wishful thinking.

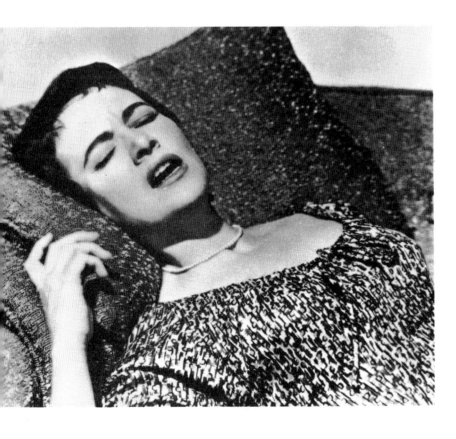

Fraud, ESP, or Reincarnation?

Below: English hypnotist Arnall Bloxham, putting a subject into a trance. He has taken many people back in time to relive previous lives. He and his wife are convinced that all of us pass through several reincarnations until—as in Hindu and Buddhist teaching—we attain a state of perfection.

about Eve White but didn't suspect the existence of Jane, and Jane knew about both of the others, continued for about a year. Then the three became integrated around the predominant personality of Jane, which was a happy outcome for all concerned.

The case of Eve does not challenge the psychologists' contention that the phenomenon of multiple personality is a psychological and not a spiritual one, because the two new personalities that emerged during therapy could plausibly have been respectively repressed and undeveloped aspects of Eve's own personality. In fact, the thought might occur to some people that the case is as well known as it is precisely because it so neatly illustrates the psychologists' case.

In 1956 a book entitled *The Search for Bridey Murphy* became a best-seller. It was written by an amateur hypnotist, Morey Bernstein, of Pueblo, Colorado. Berstein had read about other hypnotists employing age-regression techniques to get information about previous incarnations, and one evening in 1952 he tried the experiment on a friend, Virginia Tighe. Under deep hypnosis, she suddenly became a completely different personality. She spoke with a distinct Irish brogue and claimed to be Bridey

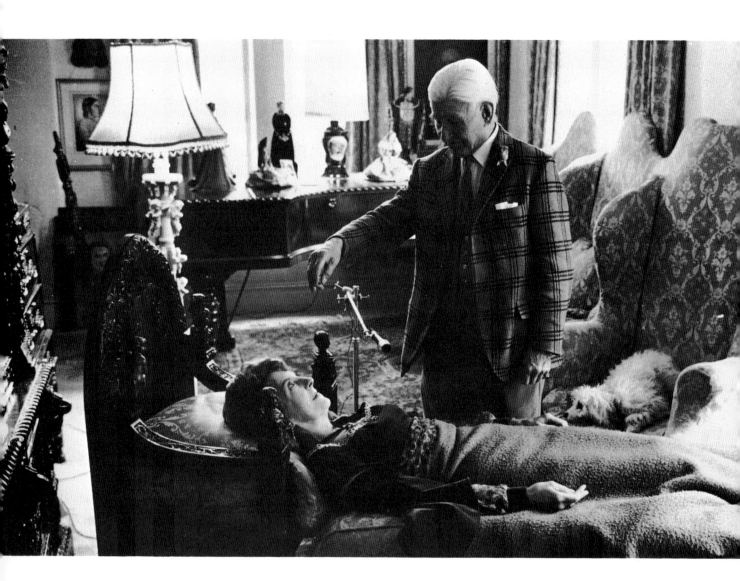

Murphy, who had lived in Cork, Ireland between 1798 and 1864. Over six separate sessions, Bernstein elicited a great deal of information from Bridey, including descriptions of Irish scenes and customs and a number of colloquial expressions. Virginia had never been to Ireland, and it seemed extremely unlikely that she could have obtained the information in any normal way. However, when psychologists studied the material after the publication of Bernstein's book, they discovered that there were experiences in Virginia Tighe's past that resembled material in Bridey's communications. For instance, her childhood home was found to have had many features in common with the house in Cork as described by Bridey. The discovery of such similarities quickly led to the case being discredited, and Bernstein paid the price often exacted of those who enjoy overnight fame. However, Professor C. J. Ducasse of Brown University in Rhode Island, who studied the material carefully, defended Bernstein and Virginia Tighe, and publicly declared his conviction that there was no fraud involved in the Bridey Murphy case.

The emergence of other personalities, allegedly from past lives, when a person is under deep hypnosis is not a phenomenon confined to the Bridey Murphy case. An English hypnotist, Arnall Bloxham, has conducted age-regression experiments with several subjects. His book, *Who Was Ann Ockenden?*, published in 1958 contains impressive circumstantial detail, obtained from a young girl under hypnosis, of a previous existence in prehistoric times. Another of his subjects regressed to the 17th century and claimed to be Henriette, sister of Charles II of England and wife of Philippe, Duke of Orleans. She was able to describe details of daily life at the court of Louis XIV of France. A third subject, a man, remembered his previous life as a naval gunner during the Napoleonic wars, and experts on naval history who have listened to Bloxham's tapes of his sessions with this subject have been profoundly impressed by their authenticity of detail.

Several other hypnotists have come up with material similar to Bernstein's and Bloxham's, which on the face of it looks like evidence for reincarnation. Some psychologists have not taken the easy way of glibly dismissing the phenomenon as fraud, but have been disinclined to accept the reincarnation explanation of it. These have suggested two alternative hypotheses: the workings of unconscious memory or of extrasensory perception. According to the unconscious memory theory, people may, at some time in the past, have registered information that comes through under hypnosis without being aware of it. They may, for instance, have flicked through a book and subliminally photographed and stored away pages of its contents. The ESP hypothesis holds that the information may have been culled from the minds of others telepathically and without awareness that it was happening. Up to the present, no systematic research has been devised in age-regression experiments that excludes these possibilities.

A project completed in 1971 by Alan Gauld, Professor of Psychology at the University of Nottingham in Nottingham, England, suggests a method that might be applied to checking the results of age-regression experiments, and possibly the kind of result that might be expected. Gauld worked with information supplied by "drop-in" communicators who produced informa-

History Relived

Arthur Guirdham is an English psychiatrist. For over 40 years he was afflicted by a recurring nightmare in which a tall man approached him.

Then one day in 1962 a woman patient came to see him and described a nightmare similar to his own. Dr. Guirdham did not tell her of his own dream; but oddly, it never recurred after that. As the woman, whom he calls Mrs. Smith, continued treatment she revealed strange facts about her life: her ability to predict the future and her detailed dreams of life in the southern part of France during the Middle Ages as a member of an heretical sect called the Cathars. She did not at first tell the doctor that she immediately recognized him as her lover, Roger de Grisolles, in those dreams.

It is not unusual for a psychiatric patient to have sexual fantasies about the doctor. But Mrs. Smith's recollections of medieval France, of the persecutions suffered by her coreligionists, and of being herself burned at the stake were extraordinarily detailed. Guirdham had details from them checked by medieval historians, and the most obscure of them were corroborated. Her memories struck a chord in the doctor's own psyche, and he is now convinced that he too lived as a Cathar in France.

Below: a Bible-reading on board ship in the early 19th century. One of Arnall Bloxham's subjects remembered a previous life as a gunner's mate on a British ship during the Napoleonic wars. He described, under hypnosis, a battle in which he had lost a leg. At the point when he was wounded, the subject screamed as if in pain. Earl Mountbatten was so impressed by the authentic details of the sailor's account that he borrowed the tape recording and played it at a dinner to a number of experts on naval history.

tion by automatic writing or at a ouija board session. Drop-in is the name given to spirit communicators who are unidentifiable, and who give information that has nothing to do with anyone present at the session. Such information is later often found to refer to real events and real people. Gauld found after very careful checking that in 10 cases out of 37, information the drop-in spirits had given about their identity and former lives was correct, even including their exact names, addresses, and previous occupations.

Unconscious memory is the explanation usually brought forward to account for the phenomenon of *xenoglossy*, or the speaking of unknown languages. It is a plausible explanation when, as

Arnall Bloxham's Amazing Tapes

Left: Arnall and Dulcie Bloxham with some of the tapes they have collected over a period of more than 14 years of research into reincarnation. They allow interested groups of people to hear the tapes, which they feel add up to a strong case in favor of the theory of reincarnation.

in some recorded cases, a person speaks just a few phrases or verses in a foreign or ancient language, but it seems a very unlikely explanation when the language is used actively and responsively. Nobody can acquire the skill of speaking a foreign language just by mentally photographing a few pages of a book.

The classic case of xenoglossy is the Rosemary case. In 1928 a young Englishwoman suddenly started producing automatic writing. The experience rather alarmed her, so she consulted a doctor who was known to take a particular interest in psychical research. Dr. Wood reassured her, and she came to share his interest and acted as a medium in seances with him. In one seance a communicator appeared who identified herself as Nona, an

Far left: a portrait of Henriette, sister of Charles II of England and the wife of Philippe, Duke of Orleans. One of Arnall Bloxham's subjects revealed, under hypnosis, that she had been Princess Henriette in a previous existence. She disclosed many details of the court of Louis XIV, where she had lived after her marriage.

Left: an English medium called Rosemary who, while in a trance, spoke in a strange language later identified by an Egyptologist as ancient Egyptian. Translated, her speech revealed details of a life lived some 3300 years ago.

Speaking in Tongues -or Evidence of Reincarnation?

Egyptian woman who had lived about 3300 years ago. The Nona seances were held over several years, and in them Rosemary responded in a strange foreign language to questions Wood put to her in English. Nona said the language was her "mother tongue." Wood transcribed the words and phrases phonetically, and when he had obtained a substantial amount of material he showed it to an Egyptologist. That expert was not only able to translate the material, but also to confirm that it consisted of intelligible responses to Wood's questions. Part of the information communicated consisted of details of the life of Vola, a friend and contemporary of Nona's who the latter said was a previous incarnation of Rosemary's. As in Bloxham's Ann Ockenden case, it was impossible to check the circumstantial details of the alleged past incarnation. But over the years some 5000 intelligible words and phrases in ancient Egyptian came through in the communications, and were consistently pronounced in the same way: a phenomenon that defies rational psychological explanation.

In his 1966 article "Twenty Cases Suggestive of Reincarnation," Ian Stevenson, Professor of Psychiatry at the University of Virginia, writes about his own long and careful investigation of a modern case. The subject was the wife of a Philadelphia doctor who occasionally used hypnosis on his patients. One day he tried an age-regression experiment with his wife. In her first trance she had the alarming sensation of being struck on the head and drowned. Then she said, "I am a man," and gave the name "Jensen Jacoby." The communicator spoke broken English and a language that was unfamiliar to the hypnotist, but which he later learned was Swedish. In all, eight seances were held in which Jensen communicated. In the later ones Swedish-speaking people were present, and were able to ask Jensen questions in his own language. Stevenson carefully studied the tapes of the communications and discovered that although Jensen's vocabulary was very limited and he usually replied very briefly to questions, some 60 words were first introduced into the conversations by Jensen and had not been previously used by any of the interviewers. Moreover, though he lacked words for many familiar 20th-century objects, he was able to give the correct old Swedish names for museum objects from the 17th century.

Stevenson's evidence strongly suggests that the Philadelphia doctor's wife became a medium for a 17th-century Swede's communications, and more circumstantial evidence might have been obtained had not the doctor insisted on discontinuing the experiment for fear of "a permanent 'possession' or other transformation of personality." However, xenoglossy, multiple personality, and possession are at best only evidence for fragmented, partial, and temporary reincarnations. Evidence for more complete and permanent reincarnations has also been provided by Professor Stevenson, who has made it his specialty as a parapsychologist to follow up and scrupulously check and test the authenticity of reports of alleged reincarnation phenomena all over the world in our own day.

Opposite: a painting of the Pentecost by a 16th-century Portuguese artist. This was the event, shortly after Christ's Ascension, when the Holy Spirit descended upon the Apostles, and they began to speak in other tongues. Speaking in tongues, or "glossolalia," is believed by Christians to be —if genuine— a gift of God. Advocates of the reincarnation theory tend to regard it as a sign of some previous existence.

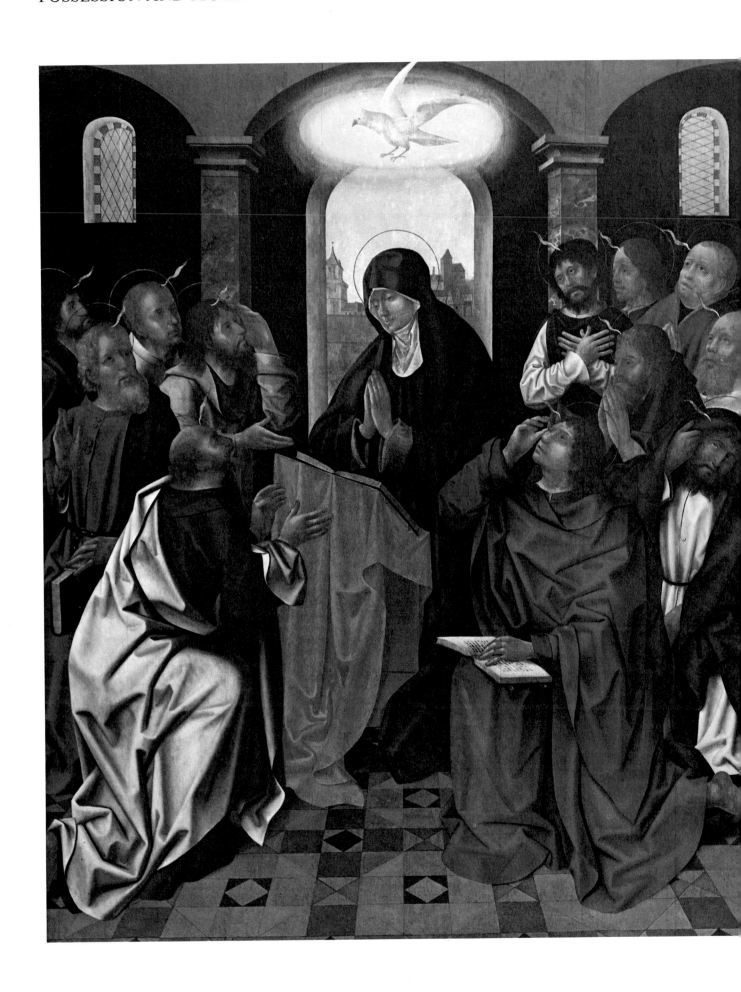

Chapter 7
The Evidence for Reincarnation

Do we have a single opportunity for life upon this earth, or have we several chances? Among the most persuasive arguments for the idea of reincarnation are the apparently spontaneous memories of children of previous existences, sometimes with details which can be checked, and which turn out to be absolutely accurate. How can these children be accounted for by strictly rational means? What is the concept of reincarnation, and what has it meant for the societies which accept it? What might it mean for us as a way of explaining the puzzling and ambiguous stories which suggest that one person lives again and again?

In 1962 Professor Ian Stevenson met a young Lebanese who told him that in his home village of Kornayel there were several children who remembered previous incarnations. He gave Stevenson a letter of introduction to his brother. Two years later Stevenson had an opportunity to visit Lebanon and follow up his interest in reincarnation. He was able to investigate personally the curious case of Imad Elawar, and he tells the fascinating story in an article entitled "Twenty Cases Suggestive of Reincarnation," published in 1966. Imad was born in Kornayel in 1958. As soon as he began to talk, he repeatedly mentioned the names "Jamile" and "Mahmoud," although no members of his family had such names. He also talked about Khriby, a village some 30 kilometers from Kornayel across the mountains. One day when he was two years old, he was out for a walk with his grandmother. Suddenly he rushed up to a stranger in the street and hugged him. The bewildered man asked, "Do you know me?" and little Imad answered, "Yes, you were my neighbor." It turned out that the stranger was from Khriby.

Though the Elawar family belonged to an Islamic sect that believes in reincarnation, Imad's father did not like the suggestion that his son was a reincarnate. He became angry when Imad talked about his previous life in Khriby and said he belonged to the Bouhamzy family. So the boy suppressed such talk in his father's presence, but continued to tell his mother and grand-

Opposite: in this 19th-century French painting, ghosts of warriors who died for their countries are depicted entering Heaven, where they are welcomed not by St. Peter but by the legendary Gaelic warrior Ossian. Many cases of apparent reincarnation involve people who died violently, often in battle. Assuming reincarnation to be possible, perhaps the shock of sudden death leaves a vivid memory that is likely to remain with the reincarnated spirit, and so make recall of a previous existence relatively probable.

A Convincing Case History

parents about his memories. He talked a great deal about the beauty of Jamile. He mentioned an accident in which a man had had both his legs crushed beneath the wheels of a truck, and had died soon afterward. He remembered the accident very vividly, he said, but he had not been the man who was killed. This statement was puzzling, because as Imad grew older he repeatedly expressed delight in the fact that he was able to walk. He also repeatedly begged his parents to take him to Khriby, but his father refused.

When Professor Stevenson arrived in Kornayel, Imad was just over five years old, and had been describing memories of his former life for the past three years. He had never left the village. Stevenson collected all the facts he could. He talked to members of Imad's family and to Imad himself. Among other information, the boy gave him a detailed description of the house he had lived in in Khriby. Stevenson then traveled the rough mountain road to Khriby to check the information he had received.

He soon learned that Bouhamzy was the name of a local family, and that in 1943 Said Bouhamzy had been run over by a truck, had both his legs crushed, and had died after an unsuccessful operation. He was shown the house where Said had lived, but it did not correspond with Imad's description of his former home, nor did the facts he managed to learn about Said's life match Imad's memories of his previous existence.

Stevenson continued his investigations, however, and discovered that Said had had a cousin and close friend named Ibrahim Bouhamzy. Ibrahim had scandalized the village by openly living with his mistress, the beautiful young Jamile. His happiness had been short, though. In 1949 at the age of 25, he had died of tuberculosis. He had spent the last six months of his life bedridden and unable to walk, which had distressed him greatly. Like his cousin Said, Ibrahim had been a truck driver. He had himself been involved in a couple of accidents, and he had never gotten over Said's death. Mahmoud was the name of an uncle of Ibrahim.

Right: Professor Ian Stevenson, an American physician and professor of psychiatry who has contributed to several branches of parapsychology and written an article, "Twenty Cases Suggestive of Reincarnation," based on his own research into the subject.

On his first visit to Khriby, Stevenson was also able to confirm that the house Ibrahim had lived in matched Imad's description, and that the man who lived in the neighboring house was the person Imad had embraced on the street in Kornayel three years before. In all, Stevenson on this visit confirmed that out of 47 facts Imad had given him about his previous life, a total of 44 matched exactly with facts about the life of Ibrahim Bouhamzy.

He returned to Kornayel and persuaded Imad's father to let him take the boy to Khriby. The three of them went, and during the drive Imad produced seven correct statements about the route, which he had never traveled before. In Khriby, Imad produced a further 16 facts about Ibrahim's life and his home, and Stevenson was able to confirm 14 of these as completely correct. Ibrahim's house had been locked up for several years and was opened especially for their visit, so Stevenson was able to check

Below: this ancient Indian board game, called The Game of Heaven and Hell, is based on the Hindu concept of reincarnation.

The Golden One

In 1865 in India, Jayaram Banerji and his wife Sundari had a son whom they named Haranath. His birth had been preceded by a strange clairvoyant dream of his father's, involving a *sadhu*, or holy man; and early in his life the young Haranath showed signs of possessing strange powers. He frequently went into trances. Later, he experienced astral travel and claimed to communicate with divine beings. He was widely venerated for his healing and for his obviously sincere love of God.

One day in 1896 Haranath was about to begin a journey when he suddenly lost consciousness. Ten hours later he still lay inert; his heart had stopped beating and all other signs of life had disappeared. His traveling companions made plans for his cremation.

Then he suddenly returned to consciousness. During his coma he had in fact been experiencing intense mental activity. He had been in communion with a "Great Being," whom he had seen once before as a child. This being was a 16th-century saint called Gouranga. While Haranath lay unconscious, the spirit of the saint was absorbed into his body.

After this experience, Haranath's complexion took on a golden hue (Gouranga means "the golden one").

Opposite: this 18th-century Tibetan painting is based on a text called the *Ch'os-nyid Bar-do*, which describes the third of several transitional stages undergone by the soul after death and before rebirth. The painting shows the advent of the peaceful deities that appear at this stage, which is called "Experiencing Reality."

immediately statements that Imad made about its furnishings. In his former life as Ibrahim, the boy said, he had owned two rifles, one of them double-barreled. This proved to be correct, and when they entered the house he was able to go directly to a place where Ibrahim had hidden one of the rifles.

Stevenson has collected reports of over 1000 cases that are, as he cautiously puts it, "suggestive of reincarnation." The Imad Elawar case is one of the strongest, not just because of the quantity of corroborative evidence, but also because of the circumstances in which the evidence was obtained. Stevenson stumbled upon the case by a lucky chance. He arrived in Kornayel unannounced and began his investigation immediately, so there could be no question of fraud or deception because such an elaborate hoax would have taken some time to set up. Nor could there be any question of misconstruing and subsequently distorting the child's information to match the verification, consciously or unconsciously. In this case Stevenson collected the facts at first hand and not by hearsay, and wrote them down before attempting verification.

There seems to be no doubt that, for whatever reason, the mind of the child Imad Elawar contained memories and impressions that corresponded with experiences in the life of the dead Ibrahim Bouhamzy. Whether this suggests that Imad was a reincarnation of Bouhamzy is, of course, another question.

Belief in reincarnation is fundamental in the Hindu and Buddhist religions, so it is not surprising that some of the classic cases on record come from India. In 1961 and again in 1964 Stevenson visited the village of Rasulpur in Uttar Pradesh, India, to interview people and collect facts that might corroborate an apparent reincarnation case that had been brought to his attention. In 1954 a child of the village, Jasbir Jat, had fallen ill with smallpox at the age of three and a half, and had apparently died. Preparations for burial were made, but the child began to show faint signs of life. Some weeks passed before he was fully recovered, and when he was able to express himself clearly again, Jasbir spoke and behaved in a manner that distressed his family. He insisted that his name was Sobha Ram and that he was the son of a Brahmin, Shankar Lil Tyagi, of the village of Vehedi, which is about 20 miles from Rasulpur. He introduced into his speech sophisticated words characteristic of the Brahmin caste, and he refused to eat his family's food. Fortunately, a Brahmin woman heard about him and volunteered to cook Brahmin food for him.

This situation continued for several years. Communication between the villages of Rasulpur and Vehedi were virtually nonexistent. In 1957, however, a Vehedi woman who had been born in Rasulpur paid a visit to her home village. She had not been back since 1952, when Jasbir was only 18 months old, but he recognized her. From others she learned the story of his strange claim and behavior, which she repeated to her own family when she returned to Vehedi. When the family of the late Sobha Ram Tyagi heard about it, they paid a visit to Rasulpur to meet Jasbir. The child greeted them all by name, showing that he knew the relationship of each to Sobha Ram and many facts about their life in Vehedi. He also gave an exact account of how Sobha Ram had died, which was as a result of a fall from a carriage during a

Above: a wooden figure of the chief lama of
Bhutan. According to some sects of
Buddhism, the chief lamas of the
monasteries are Bodhisattvas, or seekers of
enlightenment on their way to becoming
Buddhas, and are reincarnated in the same
status—that is, as potential chief lamas—
that they occupied in the former life.

marriage procession. After the visit, Jasbir was allowed to go to
Vehedi several times and stay with the Tyagi family. He was much
happier than in Rasulpur, and showed intimate familiarity with
the family life and past history.

When Stevenson investigated this case he did not have the
good fortune he had had in the Imad Elawar case of being present
when the verifications took place. But by visiting the two
villages and talking to the people involved he compiled a list
of 39 facts about Sobha Ram's life that Jasbir had mentioned
before he paid his first visit to Vehedi. Of these, 38 could be
corroborated. The one that could not be verified was the most
intriguing of all. Jasbir stated that Sobha Ram's fatal fall had
been caused because he had been poisoned, and he even named
the murderer. There was no way of proving this, but Stevenson
discovered that the Tyagi family had suspected that Sobha Ram
had been murdered. Furthermore, he found that the time of
Sobha Ram's death had coincided with the time of Jasbir's
smallpox illness, during which he too had almost died.

In a significant number of apparent reincarnation cases the
previous life ended violently or prematurely. Believers maintain
that this does not mean that only those that meet violent deaths
are reincarnated, but simply that those who die a natural death,
particularly in old age, do not carry over distinct memories from
one life to another. Violent death, it seems, can leave strong
impressions not only on the soul, but also in some cases on the
physical body. Several researchers have noted birthmarks in
alleged reincarnates situated where fatal wounds were apparently
sustained in the previous life.

Guy Playfair quotes such a case in his book *The Flying Cow*.
It is from the records of the Brazilian Institute for Psycho-
Biophysical Research and concerns a woman named Tina. She
was born in the town of Araraquara, 175 miles from São Paulo,
and still works there as a lawyer with a public utility company.
Tina is an unusual reincarnate in that as an adult today she clearly
remembers incidents from her previous life. Normally such
memories fade in childhood.

Tina remembers that she lived in France and that her name
was Alex Amadado Barralouf. Her father's name was Jean
Paris and her mother's Angala. She believes that she came from
the town of Vichy, and remembers shopping with her mother, a
tall, blonde, well-dressed woman. When she was two and a half
years old she recalls being taken to Le Havre and seeing the ships
tied up on the quay. She learned French easily and has a strong
sense of identification with France. She detests everything
German because she believes she had been shot and killed by a
German soldier during World War II. On the front and back of
her left side are two marks that she has had from birth. They
correspond with the positions that would have been marked if
a bullet aimed at her heart had gone in and out.

Family anecdotes such as this one cannot be regarded as
providing the same kind of evidence as Professor Stevenson's
scrupulously objective investigations. But they are common in
parts of the world where reincarnation is widely believed in, and
they give an interesting insight into the belief.

Although belief in reincarnation is far less frequently found in the contemporary Western world, most people at some time have had a strange type of experience that is sometimes explained by the idea of reincarnation. This experience is generally known by the French term *déjà vu* which means "already seen." It refers to those instances in which a person has a strong feeling of having been in a place or a situation before. Various psychological explanations have been put forward to account for this. It has been suggested that the experience is a hallucination, or that it is an evocation of a memory that seemed to have been completely forgotten. Physiological explanations have also been advocated. One is that the brain receives two visual signals from the retina within a split second of each other, and that the so-called memory is implanted by the first of these two signals.

Although such explanations may be relevant to many ephemeral and rather vague sensations of *déjà vu*, they do not explain cases in which detailed knowledge, which could not have been acquired by normal means, is possessed. An example is if a person visiting a place for the first time can correctly describe present or former features of the town or landscape before

The Buddhist Belief in Rebirth

Below: a Buddhist New Year dance in Sikkim celebrating rebirth.

"Life Without Death"

Right: the Greek philosopher and mathematician Pythagoras lived from 580 to 500 B.C. He claimed, however, that he had lived other lives: once as a Trojan warrior named Euphorbus who was slain during the Trojan War, once as a prophet named Hermotimus who was burned to death by his rivals, once as a Thracian peasant, once as the wife of a shopkeeper in Lydia, and once as a Phoenician prostitute. His doctrine of the transmigration of souls was only one of his mystical teachings.

Above right: Edward Ryall, who remembers being slain in the battle of Sedgemoor in 1685 during the Duke of Monmouth's attempt to gain the English throne. In this previous life he was a Somerset farmer. His book *Second Time Round* depicts 17th-century living in minute detail and contains obscure facts that have since been verified—such as his recollection of brilliant northern lights before the battle.

Opposite: *The Morning of Sedgemoor*, a painting of the battle in which Ryall believes he lost his life as John Fletcher nearly 300 years ago.

actually seeing them.

Nils Jacobson, a Swedish psychiatrist, cites the following case in his book *Life Without Death?*, published in English in 1974. A patient had from time to time experienced throughout his adult life a kind of trance vision in which he was a World War I soldier who met his death in Flanders. The experience was always preceded by a sensation of profound depression and dullness, and began with an OOBE. He felt himself leave his body and glide out "into a milky-white, dense mist where everything was deathly silent." Then he was on a crowded railroad station with a lot of soldiers amid great scenes of emotion and distress as relatives said goodbye to the men embarking for the front. When he was aboard the train he hung out of the window, clasping the hands of a pretty young woman who gazed desperately into his eyes and whispered repeatedly, "Marcel, o mon Marcel," to which he replied, "Catherine, ma Cathy. . . ." Then the train pulled away and he experienced a long clattering journey through the dark. Finally the train arrived at a destination that he learned was near Arras. With hordes of other soldiers he disembarked and trudged through rain and mud to an encampment near the front line.

Time passed—he couldn't tell how long—and a day came when it was the turn of his company to attempt to take a village by storm on a height in front of them. He wormed his way with other soldiers along the trough of a deep ravine at the bottom of which a stream flowed. This afforded the only protected approach to the village. They finally arrived at the point from which the attack was to be launched, and at a given signal he went over the top and ran toward the village, which he saw clearly in front of him. He was suddenly stopped by a powerful blow and burning pain in his chest, and everything went blank.

Jacobson's patient had experienced this harrowing vision several times before 1966 when, during a journey, he found himself near Arras. He decided to take the opportunity to discover

Left: Christian Henry Heinecken, the "Infant of Lubeck," who shortly after his birth in 1721 began to speak fluently. By the age of one year he knew all of the Bible; by the age of four he had learned Latin and French. He died before reaching the age of five. Proponents of the reincarnation theory cite cases of child prodigies in support of the theory, suggesting that the astonishing faculties are an inheritance from a former life.

Below: Mozart as a child performing with his father and his sister Nannerl. The greatest musical prodigy in history, Mozart was already composing music at the age of five.

whether the vision had any foundation in reality. He drove into and around the town, but everything was unfamiliar. Then he came to a crossroads and saw a signpost with the name "Bapaume," and his heart rose in his throat. About three miles down that road he began to recognize features, and when they arrived at the village his recall became crystal clear. He was able to take his family through the maze of narrow streets to a field. There he pointed out the winding ravine from which rose steep slopes toward another village beyond, the place where in his vision he had died. When they went to this village he was disappointed to find it unfamiliar. Neither the church nor the buildings were as in his vision. But his son, by chatting to an elderly inhabitant, learned that the village had been completely destroyed during violent fighting between French and German forces in November 1914, and that the church and the buildings around it had been rebuilt in the 1930s.

This case is interesting not only because the subject had told others about his vision before some of its details were confirmed, but also because others were present at the time of verification. *Déjà vu* is not normally preceded by a visionary experience that the person consciously remembers, and cases in which paranormally obtained knowledge is communicated to another before the event are rare. This may partly be, however, because people are reluctant to communicate such apparently baseless information for fear of being proved wrong and thought foolish.

A 26-year-old German woman recorded a strange *déjà vu* experience in 1967. Her husband became impatient with her when, during a journey by car through a part of Germany which neither had previously visited, she suddenly exclaimed that she knew the area because she had lived there before. Although he knew that it was the first time she had been in that part of the country, she insisted that it was familiar to her. She pointed out a house where, she said, she had lived with her parents and two brothers in a previous life when her name had been Maria D. They stopped at a village tavern and she immediately recognized the proprietor as someone who, when much younger, had served her family. This finally made her husband wonder whether her talk had been more than mere fantasy, and he casually inquired of the old man about the "D. family." The parents, the older son, and the daughter were all dead, he told them sadly, and the death of "poor little Maria" had been most tragic. She had been savagely kicked to death by a horse in a stable. This information awakened what seemed like vivid and terrifying memories in the wife, who broke down and cried as she recalled the details of her previous death.

All the cases we have looked at are, in Stevenson's phrase, "suggestive of reincarnation." But there may be other explanations. The first that springs to mind is that they are all due to fraud or some sort of delusion. However, there are too many anecdotes and too many carefully investigated cases on record for this easy solution to be acceptable. The only other explanation that seems at all tenable is that the alleged memories of former lives are acquired by extrasensory perception.

Modern parapsychological research has established fairly conclusively that telepathy, clairvoyance, and precognition do

Child Prodigies – or Second Lives?

Above: the French mathematician, scientist, and philosopher Blaise Pascal (1623-62). His brilliant mind was evident in childhood, but his early education consisted almost entirely of literature. The boy taught himself geometry, and at the age of 11 discovered a new geometrical system. The following year he wrote a treatise on the subject of acoustics.

Memories of Other Lives

Below: the English novelist Joan Grant, who has recalled memories of several previous lives and has put them into her books. Although classified as novels, they are regarded by her as autobiographies.

take place, particularly in heightened states of consciousness. It is theoretically possible that information in the mind of any living person may be paranormally acquired by another, or that past, present, or future events or scenes can be clairvoyantly experienced. But the conditions that normally facilitate ESP, such as the existence of a bond between sender and receiver, or circumstances of crisis, or the development of a general psychic faculty, are not to be found in the experiences described in this chapter. None of the subjects had any connection with or prior knowledge of the deceased, and none of them showed any ability to acquire information paranormally about any other facts except those about their former life experience. Imad and Jasbir had no knowledge of events in Khriby and Vehedi after the deaths of Ibrahim and Sobha Ram, and the knowledge that they possessed had a continuity and coherence that suggests the functioning of memory rather than ESP. ESP tends to supply

Left: an ancient Egyptian wall-painting showing a group of maidens. When she visited Egypt, Joan Grant was overcome by a flood of memories, which she used as a basis for her book *Winged Pharaoh*. In the book she describes her life as Sekeeta, an Egyptian princess.

Left: a wall-painting in a house in Pompeii showing part of an initiation ceremony of the cult of Dionysus. It was in Pompeii a few years ago that a Brazilian woman discovered the familiar features of a previous life that had haunted her for years. Born into an upperclass family, Celia (whose story is told in Guy Playfair's book *The Indefinite Boundary*) showed signs of sexual precociousness even in childhood, and throughout her life suffered from vividly violent, recurring dreams. In middle age she visited Pompeii, and recognized it at once. She led her companions to "her" house, which turned out to have been the house with the wall-painting shown in the photograph—and formerly the city's brothel.

Western Scientists and the Buddist Reincarnation

fragmentary and discontinuous information, and to mix information received from the external source with contents of the consciousness of the receiver. The ESP hypothesis is also inadequate to explain the existence of, for example, birthmarks on the skin of an alleged reincarnate that correspond exactly with wounds received in an alleged previous life. Nor can it account for sustained creative work such as, for example, the extraordinary novels of Joan Grant.

Joan Grant was born in England in 1907, and as a child became aware that she possessed memories of previous lives in other centuries and other lands. Her claims were an embarassment to her family, and she did not fully develop her psychic gifts until adulthood, when a visit to Egypt brought a flood of intense and detailed memories of that land in ancient times. She wrote down the memories as they came to her, which made a great deal of fragmentary material. With the cooperation of her husband, a psychiatrist, she put the fragments into a novel that was published in 1937 under the title *Winged Pharaoh*. She had done no research before or while writing the book, which was presented as the story of the life of Sekeeta, the daughter of an Egyptian pharaoh who had lived 3000 years ago. When scholars, critics, and Egyptologists evaluated the novel, they unanimously praised the accuracy of its historical detail, though they were understandably dubious about Joan Grant's claim that her accuracy was due to the fact that she *was* Sekeeta. Other books followed, and in her autobiography, *Far Memory*, she wrote: "During the last 20 years, seven books of mine have been published as historical novels which to me are biographies of previous lives I have known." It is a seemingly outlandish claim, but to attempt to apply the ESP hypothesis to the Joan Grant case only produces the scarcely less fantastic explanation that she acquired her information by telepathically picking the minds of Egyptian scholars unknown to her, and focusing and sustaining her telepathic powers in a manner without precedent in ESP research.

When all the evidence has been examined, it seems that the ancient and widespread belief in reincarnation offers an explanation for many otherwise incomprehensible occurrences. Hindus and Buddhists, among others, believe that a single human lifetime is only one stage in the development of a soul, which has to return to Earth many times in many different bodies before it can attain perfection. They believe that a person's actions generate a force known as *karma*, which determines his destiny in the next existence. If the soul brings with it into life an accumulation of bad karma acquired through wrong action in a previous life, it will have to spend a lifetime expiating it in order to advance its process of growth. Such a belief accounts for the apparent injustices and inequalities of earthly life. It explains differences of personality and endowment, precocity in some children and special gifts in people of genius. And it serves, as no other philosophical or religious concept does, to reconcile man to his fate while at the same time encouraging him to change himself. It also may account for many of the strange memories described in this chapter. It is a belief that is surely worthy of more serious consideration than it has been given.

Opposite: a Tibetan painting showing the Wheel of Life, which represents in pictorial form the basic principles of Tibetan Buddhism. The sages of the East have long believed in the idea of survival after death, and Western scientists are at last beginning to investigate the concept seriously.

126

Chapter 8
Pictures in the Mind

Few of us have the waking experience of moving outside our bodies, but nightly each of us makes a strange voyage into the unknown, in the realm of dreams. What are the dreams that absorb us so completely in our sleep—and then most often disappear into such total oblivion that only a few scattered remnants remain with us in the morning? Some dreams seem to look into the future, like Rudyard Kipling's dream which he described as an "unreleased roll of my life film." Some dreams seem to suggest that mind can reach directly into mind. And some dreams seem to be purest nonsense. What, then, is a dream? And why do we dream?

The girl woke suddenly from a terrifying dream in which she had seen a fierce wolf in the cellar, restlessly prowling and snarling. But waking did not relieve her terror, for she instantly became aware that someone was lying beside her in the bed. She put out her hand and felt the soft naked shoulder of a woman, who turned to her and said, "I have not been in bed for a hundred years." In a very quiet gentle voice the creature beside her told her that it was a hundred years since she had been a woman. At that time she used to slip away from her husband's side at night and run about the woods in the form of a wolf, killing lambs and hens. She made the girl feel the dry scars on her back where the wolves had bitten her in play. Her husband, she said, had tried everything to keep her in at night. After failing repeatedly, he had finally murdered her. Since then she had never known human comforts or been able to take possession of a human soul. "But now," she said in her soft voice, "You . . ." She took the girl's hand and drew it slowly toward her breast, and the girl knew that if the creature laid it on her heart "her wolf soul would take possession of my body." The pull was irresistible and the girl felt paralyzed with panic, but suddenly she was able to use her free hand to make the sign of the cross. At this she woke up trembling and in a sweat, but immensely relieved to find that her earlier awakening had been part of her nightmare.

This adolescent dream, recalled by the English painter Gwen Raverat in her book *Period Piece*, has characteristics that any-

Opposite: World War I propaganda, showing Emperor Franz Josef of Austria tormented by nightmares of the war dead and bereaved. Many believe to this day that evildoers will be punished by nightmares of their victims.

Above: *The Nightmare*, in which the sleeping girl is haunted by an incubus sitting on her stomach. The "night mare," illustrated literally as a demonic horse, pokes its head in through the bed curtains. In medieval times, an incubus (from the Latin word for nightmare) came to mean a devil, often in the semblance of a human being, who seduced or raped women.

one who has known the terrors of the nightmare will recognize. It is dramatic, and has an internal logic, structure, and development that might have been created by a storyteller. It is, for the dreamer, as vivid an experience as any a person might undergo in the waking world, with emotions of an intensity rarely experienced in daily life.

Even much milder, pleasant dreams may engage the senses of touch, hearing, sight, and smell, as well as vision, and combine to create an impression of reality much more vivid than is obtained, for instance, by watching an engrossing film. The dreaming mind accepts the dream world as completely as the

Why do We Dream?

Left: this 19th-century engraving, *Preparing for a Nightmare*, supports the "heavy supper" theory of nightmares. The pork pie and pickles, plus the lurid tale, are bound to cause bad dreams.

awake mind accepts the real physical world. Only rarely does it realize that what it is experiencing is only a dream. Moreover, the dreaming mind is extremely inventive, subtle, and complex. So weird and yet so common is the dream experience that since the beginning of recorded time people have been fascinated by dreams, and have speculated about how and why they occur, where they come from, and what they signify.

Every age and every culture has proposed answers to these questions. The favored theory in the West in the 20th century has been that dreams are the language of the unconscious mind, that everything a person fears, inhibits, or secretly desires emerges in the dream experience. The dreaming mind disguises the repressed ideas by putting them into symbolic form, but the meaning of the symbolic language can be discerned with the help of psychoanalysis. Gwen Raverat's dream would be a joy to a psychoanalyst—particularly one who subscribes to the teachings of Sigmund Freud. To a Freudian analyst, hers is a clear case of fear and repression of sexuality. The cellar symbolically represents the girl's unconscious mind; the prowling, snarling wolf her repressed animal nature; and her struggle with the female werewolf a dramatic enactment of an internal struggle to subdue and control her sexual feelings. But if the artist, who was born in the Victorian period, had told her parents about her dream, they would probably have told her that it was nonsense. They might also have explained it away as a result of eating a heavy supper and reading too many horror stories. There are still people who hold the "heavy supper" theory today, but their numbers are getting fewer. Laymen as well as psychologists and psychiatrists take for granted many modern discoveries about dreams that would have astounded our ancestors. These discoveries would not, however, have astounded many of the great writers of the past. Coleridge, Baudelaire, Goethe,

Above: *The Call of the Night* by the 20th-century Belgian painter Paul Delvaux. Delvaux was a leading member of the Surrealist art movement, and like all Surrealists deliberately created a disturbing dreamlike world. His abstracted figures wander sleepily in odd situations or dead landscapes. The Surrealists drew upon the dream symbolism of post-Freudian psychology for their imagery, and their paintings are often as difficult to interpret as dreams are.

Stevenson, Poe, and Mary Shelley, among others, not only made literature of their own dreams but also recognized, long before the age of psychoanalysis, that dreams are the language of the unconscious. "The language of the unconscious" is, however, inadequate as a definition of the dream. Both modern research and ancient traditions suggest that the dream phenomenon may be stranger than psychoanalysts imagine. There are dreams that call in question some of our fundamental notions of reality. The poet Coleridge posed this intriguing question: "What if you slept, and what if in your sleep you dreamed, and what if in your dream you went to heaven and there plucked a strange and beautiful flower, and what if when you awoke you had the flower in your hand? Ah, what then?" To dismiss this as an idle question, a poet's fancy, would be to miss Coleridge's point that reality is ambiguous, and that there are some human experiences—including certain dreams—that challenge our basic concepts of space, time, and causality.

Take for instance the story of John Chapman, a poor tinker and peddler who lived in Swaffham, England in the 15th century. A legend like this is not evidence that a skeptic would accept, but is worth retelling both as an illustration of a paranormal dream and as a charming story.

To this day John Chapman's generosity is commemorated in the village church in Swaffham, where wood carvings and stained-glass representations of him and his family can be seen. As the story goes, Chapman one night had a dream in which he was told to go to London and wait on London Bridge. There he would meet a man who would give him news of great good fortune. The dream was so convincing that he obeyed its instructions. It took him three days to walk the 100 miles to London. For a further three days he waited on London Bridge, which in those days had shops and houses on it, but not one of the many people who passed to and fro stopped to speak to him. He was about to give up and trudge back to Swaffham to face the reproaches and mockery of his family and neighbors when a shopkeeper, who had observed him curiously for the three days, came out and asked him what he was waiting for. Without revealing his name or where he came from, Chapman told the shopkeeper about his dream. The man laughed and said, "Now if I heeded dreams I might have proved myself as very a fool as thou hast; for it is not long since that I dreamt that at a place called Swaffham Market, in Norfolk, dwells one John Chapman, a peddler. He hath a tree in his back garden, so I dreamed, under which is buried a pot of money. Now suppose I journeyed all the way thither because of that dream in order to dig for that money, what a fool I should be!" The legend does not record what John Chapman replied to his unwitting benefactor, but he made good time back to Swaffham, and found a vast fortune in gold and silver coins buried under the pear tree in his back garden.

The story has no doubt been embellished with frequent re-telling over the centuries, and it is easy to dismiss it as mere folklore too far-fetched to be true. Yet similar experiences are not uncommon today, and have been well authenticated by scientific investigators. The parapsychologist Louisa Rhine gives many examples in her book, *Hidden Channels of the Mind*. Here is one about the dream of an amateur geologist:

He says that he dreamed "of a large, beautiful, agate-encrusted, crystal geode [hollow stone] lying in shallow water quite near the shoreline in the W————— river which flows something like 15 miles southeast of the city. The exact location, shoreline, a long gravel bar, everything just as plain as though I were seeing it as it is, was clearly shown. When we arose on the following Sunday morning I told my wife of my dream experience and suggested we take our lunch and drive to the scene of my dream. We had only lived in this city approximately six months

"Language of the Unconscious"?

Above: an engraving of 1827 of *The Lady's Dream*, a charmingly obvious wish fulfillment, in which the sleeping girl sees herself besieged by adoring suitors.

Dreaming of Future Events

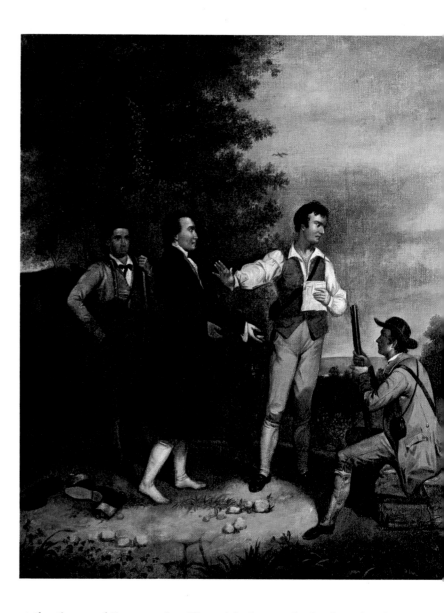

Right: *The Capture of Major André* depicts how John André was searched for incriminating papers during the American Revolution. He was later executed as a spy. Six years before, an Englishman had dreamed this very scene the night before meeting André at the home of a friend. The dreamer had had a second dream the same night in which he saw the young officer hanged.

at the time and I was unfamiliar with the particular location but inquired along the way a couple of times describing landmarks, etc., in detail; and within a half-hour after we parked our car, we walked up to the big, beautiful geode lying exactly where I'd seen it in my dream. Later I was offered $300 cash for it but did not care to sell."

The geologist's story is almost as strange as that of the Swaffham tinker. Both are tales of perceiving in a dream a piece of reality that one had no prior knowledge of. The Chapman story seems to imply the possibility of dreaming the future—which is even more startling than seeing an object clairvoyantly, as the geologist apparently did. According to modern scientific and philosophical principles both of these feats are impossible. As the Cambridge philosopher C. D. Broad has pointed out, there are certain "basic limiting principles" which "form the framework within which the practical life, the scientific theories, and even most of the fiction of contemporary industrial civilizations are confined." We take it for granted, for instance, that a person cannot obtain information about what is in another

Far left: a contemporary engraving shows the death of Major André. One of the most interesting aspects of the precognitive dream about André's capture and execution is that it occurred in two parts, almost like a serial.

Left: John Chapman, the 15th-century peddler who, according to legend, was led by a dream to a vast fortune buried in his own backyard. This wood carving of Chapman is on a pew in the Suffolk church that he helped build with the money he was said to have found under his pear tree. Stained glass windows in the church retell the story of the peddler's dream.

person's mind, or perceive a physical event or material object unless the information or perception is obtained through one of his five senses. This basic limiting principle rules out the possibility of telepathy or clairvoyance. We also take it for granted that an event cannot begin to have any effects before it has happened, which rules out the possibility of precognition. These basic limiting principles are what most people would call common sense. If asked to justify these principles, people would be at a loss and might resort to the argument that "it stands to reason." Telepathy, clairvoyance, and precognition do not stand to reason—in fact they stand directly opposite. Common sense endorses the claim for established science and philosophy that such phenomena cannot happen. But evidence steadily accumulates that paranormal events do happen, and a lot of the evidence comes from the study of dreams. When Lewis Carroll's Alice protested in Wonderland that "one can't believe impossible things," the Queen replied: "I daresay you haven't had much practice. When I was your age I always did it for half-an-hour a day. Why, sometimes I've believed as many as six impossible things before breakfast." Anyone who goes deeply into the subject of dreams and dreaming will continually find himself challenged to develop the facility that the Queen boasted.

Take an example of an apparently precognitive dream also reported in Louisa Rhine's book. A college girl had a date to go on a picnic one Sunday with a young man she knew only slightly. In the morning her mother phoned her. The mother sounded agitated and upset and begged the girl to stay in her room that day, saying she would explain later. To comfort her the girl said she would stay in, but she went on the picnic as arranged. The two young people drove 50 miles and spent the day by a lake, where they swam and had their picnic. But on the return journey the young man stopped the car in a remote forest area and raped the girl. She was so shocked and ashamed that she didn't men-

The Beckoning Grave

In her dream the little girl was walking up the path of an old church graveyard. Her hair was long and seemed to be clinging to her. Around her she saw several horses just moving aimlessly about. All at once she felt herself drawn irresistibly toward one particular grave. She couldn't help but go to it, and when she reached it, she had a horrifying sensation of falling. At that point she woke up in a depressed state.

The girl had the same dream over and over from the earliest time she could remember, and it never varied in any way. At the age of 12, however, she had an experience that chased away the haunting dream. She wrote about it to British author J. B. Priestley in response to his appeal for experiences in which the conventional idea of Time was upset. Here is her story:

While on vacation, she got caught in a thunderstorm alone on her way to her relatives' home. Suddenly she came upon the church of her dream, exact in every detail. In fact, she was living the dream. Her long wet hair clung to her, some ponies were wandering about the area, and a certain grave drew her toward it. When she got to the grave she saw on the headstone: "Died April 29th 1934." That was her birthday!

After this shock, she never had the old dream again.

"Unreleased Roll of My Life Film"

Above: Rudyard Kipling. Anything but psychic, he had a prophetic dream that puzzled and intrigued him. He dreamed he was attending some ceremony which he couldn't see properly, and at the end a stranger spoke with him saying, "I want a word with you." Six weeks later his dream came true. But "the word" turned out to be an anticlimax. Kipling said it "was about some utterly trivial matter that I have forgotten."

tion the event to anyone. When she went home the following weekend her mother asked her if she had stayed in her room on the Sunday, and she assured her that she had. Then her mother explained her request by telling the dream she had had on the previous Saturday night. She described in detail the scene by the lake, the appearance of the young man—whom she had never met—and the traumatic event that her daughter still kept a secret.

Such tales confound logic and reason, by which they could only be explained as coincidences or lies. But there are too many well-authenticated cases of dream precognition for the coincidence theory to hold water, even allowing for the fact that in the millions of dreams that occur every night, at least some of the contents are likely to coincide with future events.

Rudyard Kipling is a good example. This eminent writer was frankly scornful of people who professed to have psychical experiences. However, in his autobiography he recorded a curious dream. In it he had seen himself standing in a line of men, formally dressed, in a large hall floored with rough slabs of stone. He was aware that he was attending some kind of ceremony, but from where he was he couldn't see what was happening. When the ceremony was over and the spectators dispersed, a stranger approached him from behind, took his arm, and said, "I want a word with you." That was all there was to the dream. It was an apparently insignificant and meaningless sequence of events, remarkable only for being extraordinarily clear. Kipling forgot about it entirely until some six weeks later he was attending a war memorial service in Westminster Abbey. A large man standing on his left prevented him from seeing the ceremony, and when he looked down at the stone-flagged floor he suddenly realized that he had been in this situation before, in his dream. When the ceremony was over a man came up to him from behind, put a hand on his arm, and said, "I want a word with you, please." Writing about the incident Kipling asked, "How, or why, had I been shown an unreleased roll of my life film?" But he didn't attempt to answer the question.

Curiosity, speculation, and an interest in subjective experiences are a writer's stock in trade, and it is not surprising that much of the evidence for the strangeness and variety of the dream experiance has come from poets and novelists. Kipling's dream, though perplexing, was simple, but the English poet Robert Graves has recorded one that is extraordinarily complex and appears to contain elements of both telepathy and precognition.

Graves had been discussing with friends a famous book on dream precognition, J. W. Dunne's *Experiment with Time*. In it the author recommended that readers examine their dreams to see how much of their contents referred to events that occurred within two days of dreaming them. For example, to dream of a rag doll lying in a mud puddle and then to see this scene the following day might be evidence of precognition; to see a doll in a mud puddle three weeks later would seem only a mild coincidence. The longer the time lapse between a dream and the occurrence of an event in it, the greater the probability of such an event happening by chance, and the less likely that the dream is precognitive. On the night following this discussion, Graves had a dream which he describes as follows:

"The chief scene was where I was being introduced to a man who came up to me at a cocktail bar and shook my hand saying: 'Perhaps you prefer not to meet me; my name is Oscar Wilde.' With him were two others whom I knew to be writers of the same literary period, and I liked neither of them.

"The scene faded. There came a queer word, flashed on the screen of my mind. It was in capitals, and it was either TELPOE or TELTOE, PELTOE, or TELSOE, or something like that. In my dream it baffled me, and when I awoke it baffled me."

The poet remained baffled until, two days later, he received a letter from a complete stranger. The letter had been forwarded to him from his old home in Islip, near Oxford. The letter contained some unintelligible lines of verse:

"'Attercop, the all wise spider.'
The poet at Islip scrawled;—Re
Oscar Wilde at the tipplers;

Above: *Titania's Awakening*, based on the play *A Midsummer Night's Dream*, in which the dream experience of confused awakenings and insistent illogic is woven into a complex pattern of dreams of love and magical charms. It ends—all the lovers reunited—with a question of what is real and what has been the dream.

Above: *Dicken's Dream*, a painting showing
the author in a doze, surrounded by the
vivid creations of his imagination. Like
many writers, Dickens used material that
came to him in dreams to construct his
thickly textured novels, full of characters as
memorable now as when he wrote.

'Whistler, do let's appreciate
Walter Pater's polish, deceit.' "
Graves' correspondent commented: "Something is wrong with
these anagrams, I fancy. I lack the monkey-wit to worry them
out. What did you intend?"

From this Graves understood that his correspondent had been
puzzling over the meaning of the line "Attercop, the all wise
spider," which Graves had written some years ago when he was
living in Islip. His correspondent had suspected that the word
'Attercop'—which in fact is just an old Scottish word for a
spider—must be an anagram. So he had made four anagrams
from the whole line, and put them one under the other to form a
single nonsensical sentence. (Each line of the verse is made up
of exactly the same letters.) Nonsensical though the sentence
was, it contained elements that strangely corresponded with
Graves' dream: Oscar Wilde, the cocktail bar ("the tipplers"),
and the names of two literary acquaintances of Wilde's—the
poet Walter Pater and the artist and writer James McNeil
Whistler—whom Graves disliked. This verse also made him

understand the baffling capitalized words of the dream. They must have been leftover letters that his correspondent had been toying with in his attempt to make his anagrams.

In some way Graves' dream thoughts had linked up with the thoughts of a complete stranger who, living hundreds of miles away, was puzzling over the meaning of one of Graves' early poems. The letter had been written two days before Graves had his dream, and reached him two days after he had recorded it. Had he while dreaming telepathically read the contents of his correspondent's mind? Or clairvoyantly seen the contents of the letter on its way to him? Or foreseen his actual reading of the letter two days later?

This story suggests another explanation for a commonplace dream experience: the occurrence of images or incidents that bear no relation to the dreamer's own waking experience, and that seem unintelligible to him. While psychoanalysts would maintain that such images and events can ultimately be interpreted symbolically in terms of the dreamer's own wishes, fears, and attitudes, some recent research suggests that such dreams may have external causes. They may be the contents of other people's minds which the dreamer somehow tunes into while asleep.

In discussing direct mind-to-mind communication Professor Broad has proposed that the term "telepathic interaction" should be used instead of "telepathy." He believes that interaction between minds independently of the channels of sense happens much more frequently than we suppose. He also thinks that it is rare for the entire contents of one person's consciousness to be conveyed telepathically to another person's, but that it is common for bits of information or imagery to be conveyed.

Perhaps this is what happens in many of our nonsense dreams. We pick up bits of information from other minds and incorporate them in our ongoing dream process. This may account for the nonsense dream that the novelist Charles Dickens wrote down:

"I dreamed that somebody was dead. I don't know who, but it's not to the purpose. It was a private gentleman, and a particular friend; and I was greatly overcome when the news was broken to me (very delicately) by a gentleman in a cocked hat, top boots, and a sheet. Nothing else. 'Good God!' I said, 'is he dead?' 'He is dead, sir,' rejoined the gentleman, 'as a doornail. But we must all die, Mr. Dickens, sooner or later, my dear sir.' 'Ah!' I said, 'Yes, to be sure. Very true. But what did he die of?' The gentleman burst into a flood of tears, and said, in a voice broken by emotion, 'He christened his youngest child, sir, with a toasting fork.' I never in my life was so affected as at his having fallen victim to this complaint. It carried a conviction to my mind that he never could have recovered. I knew that it was the most interesting and fatal malady in the world; and I wrung the gentleman's hand in a convulsion of respect and admiration, for I felt that this explanation did equal honour to his head and heart."

Dreams can be nonsensical, fantastic, dramatic, harrowing, symbolic, diagnostic of emotional problems, creative, telepathic, clairvoyant, and precognitive—to mention but a few of their possible characteristics. No single theory can comprehend the

Creative Dreamers

Below: Mephistopheles appearing to Faust. Goethe once explained that much of *Faust* was worked out during an unconscious process lasting several decades. *Faust* itself has many dream images. For many people, caught in what feels like a creative dead end, the best solution is the traditional one of "going to sleep on it" in the hope that the problem may be unraveled in dreams or, at the least, appear more manageable in the fresh light of morning.

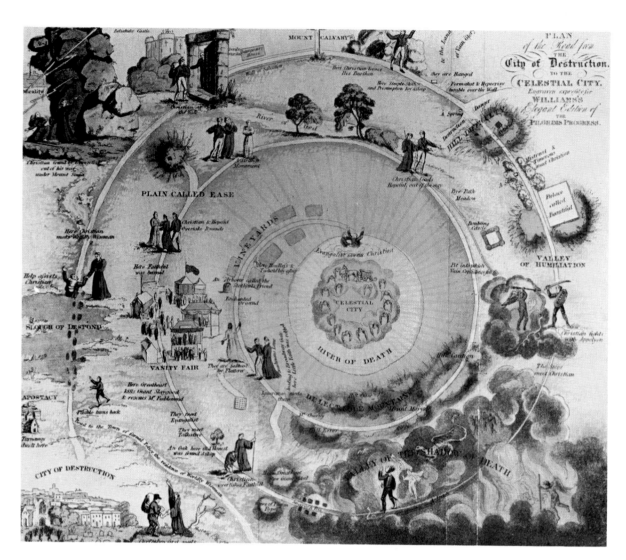

Above: a map in the form of a spiral of Christian's journey in *Pilgrim's Progress* by John Bunyan, one of the great English books. The story is cast in the form of Christian's dream, during which he travels over a path strewn with obstacles—and some rewards—from the worldly City of Destruction to the Celestial City.

Right: an early title page of *Pilgrim's Progress* only 10 years after the original publication, when it was already in its 11th edition. Here the frontispiece shows the pilgrim dreaming.

full range of dream experiences, but certainly the least comprehensive of all is the "heavy supper" theory, which attempts to reduce dreams to irrelevant phenomena produced by indigestion. Freud's revolutionary book *The Interpretation of Dreams*, published in 1900, made people take their dreams seriously and helped them understand some of their symbolic significance. However, the theory on which his book was based has since been found inadequate. Rigid Freudian interpretations have distorted and devalued many dreams in order to make them fit the theory. Poets, even in the West, have always been respecters of dreams. It is no accident that the last three dreams described were experienced by writers, for creative people are naturally interested in subconscious inventive powers as well as conscious ones. But the scientific culture of the West—of which Freud was a product—emphasized the values of the waking consciousness and the active life. Freud was in many ways a man of his time, with little comprehension of the kinds of experience that poets might praise and explore. For him, and for most of his followers, the unconscious mind was a kind of storage area for unacceptable or painful thoughts. More recently however, a respect for the positive potential of the unconscious mind has arisen among many psychologists.

Other cultures, which the West has often regarded as primitive, have had much different attitudes toward dreams. In dreams they have sought knowledge of unseen worlds, communed with their ancestors, and received counsel about future events and

The Dream as Artistic Device

Left: *The Dream of Ossian* by Ingres. Ossian, a legendary Gaelic warrior and bard, came to the attention of the literary world in the late 18th century through the supposed translations of James Macpherson. They seem now to be mainly traditional Gaelic poems edited and interlaced with Macpherson's own writings. In the Ossianic poems, dreams play an important part, often providing the motivation for action. In this dream, Ossian is warned of trouble to come, and promptly sets sail.

Above: *Dream of a Turtle Hunt*, an Australian aboriginal painting. Dreams have an important place in primitive cultures worldwide. The traditional aboriginal myths tell of the spirit ancestors of the Dreamtime, who moved across the bare silent land and created all the animals, plants, waterholes, and rivers needed for human life. Their last act of creation was to form the Dark People, aborigines themselves. Then they vanished into the land, leaving behind only their forms in shapes of curious rocks, or painted figures deep in caves, or engraved outlines on flat rock surfaces. The meaning of these obscure messages was explained to the young men of each generation by the initiated men of the previous generation in solemn coming-of-age rituals.

conduct. For example, the warlike Masai tribe of Africa had a witch doctor chief who, shortly before he died in the mid-18th century, called his people together and told them about a dream he had had. In it, he said, he saw "a great snake stretching right across the country of the Masai. Huge birds will fly over, and the shadow of their wings will be on the veld. These things the white man will bring." He warned his people that if they shed the blood of the whites there would be a great pestilence and half the tribe and nearly all the cattle would die. Some time later, when the British started to build the Uganda Railway, they were unmolested by the Masai because the tribesmen regarded the railway as the "great snake" that their late chief had seen in his dream. In 1896, however, the Masai went against their chief's last warning and killed an Englishman who had raided their cattle. This event was followed by an epidemic of smallpox that killed half the Masai, and an epidemic of rinderpest that exterminated nearly all their cattle—the chief's vision come true. The "huge birds" casting their shadows over the veld suggests that the chief foresaw the great airliners of modern times.

One of the most peaceable and democratic groups known to anthropologists is the Senoi tribe of the Malay Peninsula. Among these people the use and interpretation of dreams is an important part of everyday life. Children are taught to recall their dreams every morning, and to try to bring back from the dream world a poem, a dance, or an idea that they can contribute to the cultural life of the community. They learn how to combat hostile "spirits" met in bad dreams by calling on the help of friendly "spirits," and to turn frightening dreams of falling into pleasant dreams of flying. The standard of mental health and sense of community among the Senoi suggests that these so-called primitive people possess some kinds of knowledge and expertise that Westerners in their restless pursuit of power and material progress have bypassed. Today we are paying much more serious attention to the beliefs and customs of other cultures, and some of our own schools of thought about dreams reflect attitudes similar to those of non-Western peoples.

One of the strangest uses of dreams in a non-Western culture is recorded by Arthur Grimble in his book *Pattern of Islands*. When Grimble was land commissioner in the Gilbert Islands in the Pacific, he was taken one day to a remote village to witness a ceremony known as the calling of the porpoises. Porpoise meat was prized as a delicacy by the islanders. Grimble learned that it was obtained through the offices of a hereditary porpoise-caller who, in a dream, would project his spirit out of his body and seek out the porpoise-folk in their home under the western horizon. He would invite them to follow him back to the village for dancing and feasting, and if he put the invitation in the right way the porpoises would follow him with cries of joy.

When Grimble reached the village everything for the great feast had been prepared and laid out. All that was lacking was the porpoise meat. He met the porpoise-caller, a fat, friendly man, who then went into his hut and remained there for several hours. The islanders waited patiently and in silence until suddenly the porpoise-caller rushed out of his hut and fell on his face, then rose and clawed at the air and whined like a puppy. "Teirake! Teirake!" he cried. "They come, they come." The villagers all rushed into the water and stood breast-deep in it waiting for the porpoises. Here is Grimble's description of the arrival of the porpoises:

"They were moving towards us in extended order with spaces of two or three yards between them, as far as my eye could reach. So slowly they came, they seemed to be hung in a trance. Their leader drifted in hard by the dreamer's legs. He turned without a word to walk beside it as it idled towards the shallows... The villagers were welcoming their guests ashore with crooning words ... As we approached the emerald shallows, the keels of the creatures began to take the sand; they flapped gently, as if asking for help. The men leaned down to throw their arms around the great barrels and ease them over the ridges. It was as if their single wish was to get to the beach." When the porpoises were finally beached, they were slaughtered and eaten.

Arthur Grimble's odd tale casts new light on the old question: what precisely is a dream? We tend to think of the dream as involuntary mental imagery experienced during sleep, and such a definition adequately covers the majority of common dream experiences—even those that have paranormal elements. But the tale of the porpoise-caller suggests that the mental imagery of the dream is not necessarily involuntary. Grimble's account suggests that the man was not so much asleep as in a state of trance. Was his dream a channel for exerting psychic control over another species? Few of the recorded dreams in history can match this one in its mysterious power. Many dreams, however, have had powerful effects upon the dreamers, and some have literally changed the world. The more we study dreams, the more we are dazzled by the complexity, subtlety, and mystery of the human mind.

Dreams Among Primitive Tribes

Below: a woven picture by shaman Ramon Medina of the Huichol Indians of Mexico. His woven pictures, called nearikas, are created to represent the dreams he experiences after eating peyote, a hallucinogenic cactus. In this painting, a boy goes in search of corn, but meets the Ant People who nibble away his clothes, hair, and even eyebrows while he is asleep, leaving him only his bow and arrows. A bird lands on the tree above him. He aims at it, but she reveals herself as the Mother of Corn and leads him to the rich source of corn.

Chapter 9
The Royal Road

What do the strange pictures we see in our dreams mean? For the founder of psychoanalysis, Sigmund Freud, they represented a royal road to the unconscious. His disciple (and later his rival) Carl Gustav Jung accepted the importance of the dream but differed with Freud on how a dream should be interpreted. What did Freud and Jung claim was the symbolic meaning of some of the dream images that their patients most frequently reported? Where do these two great psychoanalysts differ, and what are the elements they have in common? What can we learn about ourselves from the images in our dreams?

The man dreamed that he was in the upper story of a two-story house which was unfamiliar to him but which he knew was his own. Looking at the fine old pieces of furniture and the valuable paintings on the wall, he thought, "Not bad!" He decided to explore further and went downstairs. On the ground floor the furnishings were medieval, the rooms were dark, and the floors were of red brick. He opened a heavy door and found a stone stairway leading to a cellar, an ancient, beautifully vaulted room which he decided, after a close look at the walls and floor, must date from Roman times. The floor was of stone slabs, and in the middle of one of these was an iron ring. He lifted the slab and discovered another stone stairway which led him down into a low cave cut into the rock. The floor of the cave was covered with thick dust in which old bones and bits of broken pottery were scattered. Among these relics from prehistory he found two human skulls. Then he woke up.

The man related his dream to a colleague who had something of a reputation as a dream interpreter. This person was particularly interested in the skulls, wanting to know whose they were and trying to connect them with a wish. The dreamer realized that the dream interpreter was suggesting that he had a secret death-wish toward certain people. Though he felt sure he had no such wish, he also felt he had to name someone whose death was worth the wishing, and he said the skulls were those of his wife and his sister-in-law. His colleague, he noticed, was greatly

Opposite: Sigmund Freud in a portrait by American artist Ben Shahn. For the giants of 20th-century psychoanalytic theory, Freud and Jung, dreams assumed an immense importance as a diagnostic tool. Freud wrote, "The interpretation of dreams is the Via Regia [the Royal Road] to the knowledge of the unconscious in mental life." From that starting point, the Royal Road broadened with the increasing variety and complexity of the methods of interpretation.

Freud and Jung:the Parting of the Ways

Right: Carl Gustav Jung. Born in 1875, Jung was a devoted disciple of Freud from 1907 until 1913. Their parting of the ways then was traumatic for both men. Freud distrusted Jung's interest in the paranormal, and Jung felt that Freud's theories were being based too much on sexuality.

relieved by his reply.

Although neither the dream nor the interpretation of it was particularly remarkable, the event was a significant moment in the history of dream theory. The dreamer was Carl Gustav Jung, the interpreter was Sigmund Freud, and the incident was one of several that led to the parting of the ways of the two great psychoanalysts.

Jung had studied the writings of Freud, whom he held in high regard and whose friendship he valued. But as his own views developed and matured, he discovered more and more areas of sharp disagreement with Freud, including the interpretation of dreams. Jung was not mocking Freud when he gave him the kind of answer he knew Freud wanted to hear about the skulls. At the time he not only wanted to learn from the older man, but also did not feel equal to quarreling with him. Moreover, he did not entirely trust his own judgment. But he suspected that Freud simply could not deal with certain kinds of dreams, and he had his own ideas about what the dream of the house meant.

The house, Jung believed, was an image of his state of consciousness at the time. The upper story, with its cozy inhabited atmosphere, represented his consciousness; the ground floor was the first level of the unconscious; and the deeper and darker recesses represented levels of his own personality which had affinities with primitive ancestors and culture that could never be illuminated by consciousness. The dream was one of particular importance to him because it led him for the first time to the concept of the "collective unconscious." This is the concept that

humans inherit not only physical characteristics but also unconscious memory traces that may have their origins in mankind's
earliest experiences.

At about the same time Jung had another dream which foreshadowed his future break with Freud. In this dream he was at a
customs post in a mountainous region on the Swiss–Austrian
border, and he saw an elderly man dressed in the uniform of an
Imperial Austrian customs official walk past him. The man was
stooped and his expression was "peevish, rather melancholic, and
vexed." Someone explained to him that the old man was not
really there but was the ghost of a customs official who had died
years ago. "He is one of those who still couldn't die properly,"
his informant said.

When he analyzed this dream, Jung was obliged to recognize in
the peevish customs official a hitherto unconscious image of
Freud. The official in the dream was a man of a bygone age whose
life's work had obviously brought him little pleasure or satisfaction. Freud in life had occasionally shown evidence of inner
dissatisfaction regarding his work. The dream, Jung thought,
compensated for or corrected the extremely high opinion he still
consciously held of Freud. He did not believe that seeing Freud
as a ghost expressed a secret death-wish toward him—which
would have been Freud's own interpretation. On the contrary, he
thought that the final sentence of the dream was an allusion to
Freud's potential immortality. Applying the Freudian method
of association, Jung thought that the word "border" suggested

Left: Freud and Jung together in 1909
during the period in which they were
working closely together. They are shown
in the United States, at a conference in
which Freud gave an account of the subject
matter and development of psychoanalysis.
Freud is seated at the left, and Jung is
shown sitting at the far right.

the border between consciousness and the unconscious, and also between Freud's views and his own. The fact that the dream incident took place at a customs post was significant because he immediately associated customs with "censorship," a key word in the Freudian theory of the unconscious. He thought of the process of a customs examination, the opening of private suitcases, and the search for hidden contraband as corresponding to the process of psychoanalysis. His dissatisfaction and disillusionment, both with Freud the man and with Freudian theory and method, were in this way symbolically expressed.

There is a certain irony in the fact that in analyzing the dream which presaged his break with Freud, Jung had to apply the Freudian interpretive method, or at least a part of it. Anyone who practices or writes about dream interpretation today is in the same position. He may deplore Freud's theories as rigid, and

Below: common dream images came to have widely differing meanings in Freudian and Jungian analysis. For instance, the image of a house—most particularly the rooms within it—in Freudian theory is interpreted as representing woman.

Theories and Interpretations

Left: in Jungian theory a house represented the Self—an idea that had a long and well-documented history as shown in this 18th-century Hebrew encyclopedia in which the body and a house are compared in detail. The turrets are ears, the windows eyes, the furnace a stomach, and so forth.

regard his insistence on the hidden sexual content of dreams as distortion. He may feel that Freud understood human dream experience too narrowly and left too much out of account. But in spite of all this the dream interpreter of today must acknowledge his debt to Freud for his insights, the seriousness of his approach to the subject, and the workability of some of his methods.

For example, here is a dream that lends itself easily to Freudian interpretation. It was sent by a young man to a psychiatrist who ran a syndicated newspaper feature on the interpretation of dreams.

"I dreamed that I was reshingling our roof. Suddenly I heard my father's voice on the ground below, calling to me. I turned suddenly to hear him better, and, as I did so, the hammer slipped out of my hands and slid down the sloping roof and disappeared over the edge. I heard a heavy thud, as of a body falling. Terriby frightened, I climbed down the ladder to the ground. There was my father lying dead on the ground, with blood all over his head. I was brokenhearted, and began calling my mother, in the midst of my sobs. She came out of the house, and put her arms around me. 'Never mind, son, it was all an accident,' she said. 'I know you will take care of me, even if he is gone.' As she was kissing me, I woke up."

The young man who had this dream volunteered the information that he was 23 years old and a married man separated

Above: the House as Woman was not exclusive to Freud. Cartoonist James Thurber drew an overwhelming picture of the henpecked husband confronted with his appalling House-Wife.

Sexual Dreams

Below: a patient's dream interpreted by Freud. She dreamed she dived into the water "just where the pale moon is mirrored." Freud, knowing that the French word "lune" (moon) is slang for "bottom," and that children think babies come from there, interpreted the dream as a birth dream. Such dreams must be interpreted by reversing the order of events. The young woman was thus coming out of the water, expressing a wish to be reborn—or, according to Freud, to continue treatment.

from his wife for a year. His father had insisted that he go back to her, which he refused to do. Apart from this disagreement, he had always had good relations with both his parents.

Freud's theory maintains that the dream is always the fulfillment of a wish which the dreamer keeps suppressed or "censored" in his unconscious, and which breaks through in a disguised form in his dream. The commonest such wish is to escape from the responsibilities and emotional demands of mature adulthood, and to seek refuge in the infantile security of the parent-child relationship. The failed husband's dream would have been a gift to any psychiatrist, being as it is the clear expression of a thinly disguised wish to escape from the problems of marriage and mature love, eliminate the father, and return to the inviolable

security of the mother's arms.

Wish fulfillments in dreams are rarely as obvious as this. Normally the censor functions much more efficiently in disguising the latent or hidden content of the dream, as in the following example quoted by Freud's biographer, Ernest Jones:

"A patient, a woman of 39, dreamed that she was sitting in a grandstand as though to watch some spectacle. A military band approached, playing a gay martial air. It was the head of a funeral, which seemed to be of a Mr. X; the casket rested on a draped gun-carriage. She had a lively feeling of astonishment at the absurdity of making such an ado about the death of so insignificant a person. Behind followed the dead man's brother and one of his sisters, and behind them his two other sisters; they were all incongruously dressed in a bright gray check. The brother advanced 'like a savage,' dancing and waving his arms; on his back was a yucca-tree with a number of young blossoms."

In the course of analyzing the dream, several facts emerged. The Mr. X of the dream was the brother of a man the patient had once been deeply in love with and engaged to. Like her husband, this man had a brother and three sisters. He had ruined his health and a promising career through addiction to drugs. Her husband was an alcoholic. She had married him on the rebound after her parents had engineered the breaking off of her engagement to Mr. X, and she felt nothing but contempt for him. Possessed of these facts, her analyst was able to interpret her dream. Mr. X was a disguise for her husband, whom she wished was dead. The fact that her husband was an officer in the volunteers accounted for the military funeral, and her feeling of contempt for him was reflected both in the gaiety of the occasion, which made it clear that nobody mourned his passing, and in her own thought that he was not worthy of a ceremonial funeral. The brother who danced like a savage was her former fiancé, and his wild exuberance was an expression of joy that their long frustrated passion could now be consummated. The yucca-tree he carried on his back was a symbol of the phallus, and the young blossoms represented children. The dream, therefore, revealed that she had a deep unconscious wish for her husband to die and leave her free to marry the man she loved and have children by him.

"The interpretation of dreams," Freud wrote, "is the Via Regia [the Royal Road] to the knowledge of the unconscious in mental life." The function of dream analysis is to penetrate the manifest, or apparent, content of the dream and lay bare its latent content. To be able to do this, the analyst or dream interpreter needs to understand the mechanisms by which the unconscious converts the latent content, which is unacceptable to the conscious self, into an acceptable form. Freud called this process of conversion the "dream work." The purpose of the dream work is to relieve psychic tensions by enabling suppressed wishes to be gratified in the dream, and so enable a person to sleep. Freud distinguished four mechanisms by which dream work is accomplished: displacement, condensation, symbolization, and secondary revision.

A good example of *displacement* appeared in the woman's funeral dream in which her feelings about her husband were

Above: what is surely a "typical" dream—the appearance of the dreamer nude in the middle of a fully dressed group. For Freud the interpretation of this very common dream was a clear wish by the dreamer for uninhibited sexuality, often representing a wish to return to childhood when it was acceptable to be unclothed.

Below: a patient's drawing of a dream with a lighthouse and a serpent twisted around it —both phallic symbols in Freudian theory. For Jung both were healing symbols, the serpent symbolizing medicine, and the lighthouse casting light over the dangerous and dark sea. The cross in this particular picture was taken by Jung as a sign that the patient recognized he was then at a crucial point in his personal development.

Above: a cartoon of Freud peering anxiously down his trousers. Because in his theories everything directly or indirectly has a sexual basis, his obsession on the subject was not only largely responsible for the split with Jung but also caused considerable hostility and derision from those who did not understand his work.

Right: Freud's theory of the sexual nature of dreams appears to have some physical evidence supporting it, shown by this graph charting a man's sleep. Research has shown that penile erections, indicated by red line peaks, coincide with Rapid Eye Movement (REM) or dreaming sleep, indicated by black bars.

transferred, or displaced, to Mr. X. Another way displacement works is by pushing the main emotional content away from the central theme of the dream. What may seem to be the emotional focus of the dream is really the least significant part of it, while the key to its real significance, the true focus of its psychic intensity, may lie in some fleeting or apparently trifling feature.

A dream that can be written down in a few lines may require several pages for its analysis. This is because dream thoughts undergo a process of *condensation*. Every feature of the dream, every person, incident, or symbol that occurs in it, may represent several or many ideas and emotions. For instance, a person in a dream may resemble the dreamer's father in his looks, an ex-schoolteacher in his dress, and his boss in speech or mannerisms. This composite figure symbolizes the dreamer's conceptions of male authority. The process of disclosing the latent content of the dream would involve drawing out the dreamer's associations to each of the people whom his dream image brought together. The same applies to places, events, buildings, objects, and animals. Every word in the report of the manifest dream may have gathered into it any number of memories or associations which collectively constitute its latent content.

Freud's ideas on the disguise mechanism of *symbolization* in dreams form the most controversial part of his theory. The basic idea that the unconscious "thinks" in images and translates ideas into dramatic and easily visualized forms is as old as the art of dream interpretation itself, and no psychologist would quarrel with it. But Freud maintained that objects and events in most adults' dreams are symbolic representations of sexual organs or sexual activities. On this basis any object that is long or pointed, or that is used for penetration, or from which water flows—sticks, umbrellas, steeples, trees, guns, swords, fountains, taps, for example—symbolically represents the penis. Circular objects and containers—pits, cavities, boxes, pockets, cupboards, and also doors and gates—represent the female genitals. Dreams of pleasurable movement—riding, rocking, climbing, flying, floating—symbolize masturbation or sexual intercourse.

In analyzing a particular dream that had no overt sexual content, Freud started out with the remark that "dreams which are conspicuously innocent invariably embody coarse erotic wishes." The dream under discussion, as related by his patient, was as follows: "Between two stately palaces stands a little house, receding somewhat, whose doors are closed. My wife leads me a little way along the street up to the little house, and pushes in the door, and then I slip quickly and easily into the interior of a

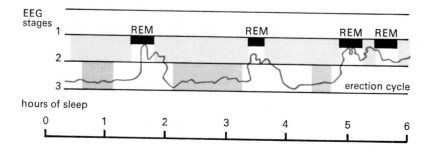

EEG stages

REM   REM   REM   REM

erection cycle

hours of sleep

0   1   2   3   4   5   6

courtyard that slants obliquely upward." Freud interpreted this dream as a wish by the man to have sexual intercourse from behind ("between the two stately buttocks of the female body," as Freud says) with a young girl from Prague (the little house between the palaces reminded the man of a place in Prague) who had entered his household the day before. Although in waking life he was deterred from attempting to seduce the girl out of consideration for his wife, his unconscious wished that his wife would condone the act (push open the door). Freud does not report how his patient reacted to this interpretation.

The fourth mechanism of the dream work Freud called *secondary revision*. This is really more an activity of the conscious than of the unconscious mind. Through secondary revision the dreamer on waking gives the dream coherence and pattern. The conscious mind gathers up the fragments of dream experience, puts them in order, fills in gaps, and reconciles inconsistencies to construct out of a profusion of images and experiences an intelligible whole which it can then call "a dream." This secondary revision completes the process.

Jung did not dispute Freud's contention that dream interpretation is the "royal road to knowledge of the unconscious," but

Freudian Dream Analysis and Modern Research

Below: *The Caterpillar*, a sardonic painting of a Freudian nightmare. In it a girl lazes in a hammock, and is apparently unaware of the enormous black hairy caterpillar creeping steadily toward her.

Jung and the Unconscious Mind at Work

Right: Freud's insistence that any object in an adult's dream is a symbolic representation of sexual organs might have been an extreme statement, but the idea of sexual symbolism certainly did not begin with Freud. In this early 19th-century Indian miniature, a woman embraces a tree (long and pointed, trees obviously symbolize the penis in Freudian thought), which was originally painted to illustrate true love "longing for union."

he vehemently disagreed with Freud's view that the unconscious is obsessively preoccupied with sexual wishes and frustrations. "It is true," he wrote, "that there are dreams which embody suppressed wishes and fears, but what is there which the dream cannot on occasion embody? Dreams may give expression to ineluctable truths, to philosophical pronouncements, illusions, wild fantasies . . . anticipations, irrational experiences, even telepathic visions, and heaven knows what besides."

The difference between Freudian and Jungian dream interpretation may best be illustrated by considering how the two theories would be used on the same dream. J. A. Hadfield, in his book *Dreams and Nightmares*, gives the following example:

"I dreamt that I was staying in a country house, and after everyone had gone to bed I went downstairs to the sitting-room to get the coal that was left on the sitting-room fire to take to my own bedroom. When I had taken the fire and reached the passage outside, I was met by a Negro . . . who threatened me. I tackled him and got him down, but then did not know what to do next. Then came a female form and said, 'Don't kill him, and don't hurt him, but send him to a reformatory.'"

The Freudian would interpret this as a sexual dream. The fire that the dreamer steals would symbolize sexual wishes that are forbidden and suppressed. The black man and the female form would represent father and mother figures respectively, and the overcoming of the black man in the fight would express a wish-fulfillment to get rid of the father and possess the mother. The female's recommendation to "send him to a reformatory" might be interpreted as the mother's suggestion for getting rid of the father without incurring the guilt of murdering him.

A Jungian interpretation of the dream would pick out features in it that resemble perennial myths. The theft of fire from heaven was the offense through which Prometheus incurred the wrath of the gods and endless trouble for himself. The figure of the black man would represent forces of the collective unconscious—that is, primitive drives which can lead to trouble when they enter consciousness. The female figure would be the anima, the feminine principle in a man's personality which balances and compensates for these forces. The final recommendation of the anima, to put the attacker in a reformatory, would signify an attempt to reconcile and integrate the conflicting forces within the unconscious.

The important differences between Freudian and Jungian theories of dreams are highlighted in this comparison. The chief difference is in their ideas of the contents of the unconscious. In Freud's view the unconscious contains only repressed material—thoughts, wishes, and experiences that the individual does not want to admit to the conscious level of awareness and therefore represses and disguises. Jung called this collection of repressed material the "Personal Unconscious" and distinguished it from the "Collective Unconscious." The collective unconscious contains elements that do not derive from personal experiences but from racial memories and experiences. Just as humans have anatomical and physiological characteristics that relate them to prehistoric time and to rudimentary forms of life, so Jung believed, they have mental characteristics that are a throwback to their primitive origins—and that they are unconscious of. These characteristics take the form of passions, impulses, and often irrational acts that can disrupt and completely unbalance an individual, a community, or even an entire nation. These powerful forces of the impersonal, or collective, unconscious have found expression in the myths of mankind. Jung noted that widely separated ages and cultures have produced myths containing similar situations, actions, problems, and personalities. He used the term "archetypal" to describe these universal images thrown up by the collective unconscious. These archetypal images, themes, and personalizations, he noted, often occur in the dreams of people who have no knowledge of mythology.

A remarkable document that illustrated and substantiated Jung's theory was brought to his attention by a fellow psychiatrist. It was a record of a series of dreams that the psychiatrist's daughter had had at the age of eight, and had written out and presented to her father in a booklet for Christmas. "They made up the weirdest series of dreams that I have ever seen," Jung wrote. "Though childlike, they were uncanny, and they contained images whose origin was wholly incomprehensible to the father." Here are four of the themes from this series of 12

Below: Jung's theory of the dream image of a tree being the Self growing is prefigured in this diagram by an 18th-century mystic, William Law, in which a beam of light pierces the dark world of the unconscious roots, and passes through the "fireworld" of real suffering and experience to open out toward the light of God.

Carl Jung saw his theories of the collective unconscious exemplified in the dream paintings of his patients, who used symbols that had no particular significance as far as they consciously recognized but which were in fact well-known nearly universal symbolic ideas.

Right: one woman patient painted this picture of a dream in which she saw the dark wing of Satan descending over Jerusalem to darken the city. In Jungian theory this dream would have a collective meaning that reaches beyond the personal, prophesying the descent of a divine darkness upon the Christian hemisphere—but perhaps pointing to a further evolution.

dreams as summarized by Jung:

Dream 1. "'The evil animal,' a snakelike monster with many horns, kills and devours all other animals. But God comes from the four corners, being in fact four separate gods, and gives rebirth to all the dead animals.

Dream 2. "An ascent into heaven, where pagan dances are being celebrated; and a descent into hell, where angels are doing good deeds.

Dream 4. "A small mouse is penetrated by worms, snakes, fishes and human beings. Thus the mouse becomes human. This portrays the four stages of the origin of mankind.

Dream 5. "A drop of water is seen, as it appears when looked at through a microscope. The girl sees that the drop is full of tree branches. This portrays the origin of the world."

Nine of the 12 dreams concerned the theme of destruction and restoration. All of them contained archetypal material, events, and imagery that are found in ancient myths which the eight-year-old girl could have had no direct access to. In the first dream, for instance, the idea of the God who consists of four gods coming from the four corners to give rebirth harks back to pre-Christian concepts of the divine quaternity—a connection between the quality of "fourness" and the divine. The horned serpent was a symbol known in alchemy to represent either Mercury or an antagonist of the Christian Trinity. The second dream depicting the performance of pagan dances in heaven and good deeds in hell, astonished Jung for its statement of the relativity of moral values. How had an eight-year-old child acquired such a revolutionary notion? The fourth and fifth dreams have affinities with ancient myths of the Creation, and they also contain sophisticated philosophical concepts—for example, the evolutionary chain of being from primitive forms of life up through more complex organisms, and the identity of the microcosm—the world in miniature—and macrocosm, or universe. All the other dreams in the series contained similar material. Where did it come from? Jung had his own answer ready: it came from the collective unconscious. But why?

Jung had considered the question of the function of dreams long before the little girl's uncanny examples were brought to his attention, and he had come to the conclusion that they are compensatory and purposive. They are *compensatory* in that they make up for deficiencies consciously or unconsciously felt by the dreamer. Obvious examples include a coward dreaming of acts of heroism and an ascetic dreaming of sensuous pleasures.

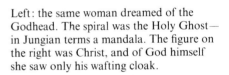

Jung's Patient Paints Her Dreams

Left: the same woman dreamed of the Godhead. The spiral was the Holy Ghost—in Jungian terms a mandala. The figure on the right was Christ, and of God himself she saw only his wafting cloak.

Below: a mandala painted by Jung—an expression of Self—after his highly significant dream of a magnolia tree growing in the city of Liverpool, in which all paths led to the center of enlightenment.

The Magnolia Tree

The Swiss man dreamed he was in Liverpool,
England, with a group of his countrymen.
He thought they were near the harbor and
that they had to go up on some cliffs to get
to the heart of the city. It reminded him of
the Swiss city of Basel, where the market is
below the rest of the city and the way up is
a street called Totengasschen (the alley of
the dead).

When the men reached the plateau above
the harbor, they found a broad square. It
had many street lights, but still looked dim
in the smoky atmosphere of Liverpool. In
the center of the square was a large round
pool, and in the center of the pool a small
island. Through the fog, brilliant sunshine
lit up the island. On it stood a single tree: a
magnolia in full blossom.

Only the dreamer saw the tree and the
island. His companions complained about
the frightful weather and wondered why
another Swiss friend had settled in this
dirty city. The dreamer, enthralled by the
island scene, thought to himself, "I know
very well why he has settled here." Then he
woke up.

The man who had this dream was
internationally known for dream interpretation. It was the psychologist Carl
Jung—and the dream about the magnolia
tree was a turning point in his approach to
the subject.

Right: snakes have haunted the dreams of men and women from time immemorial. Freud saw dreams of snakes as phallic; Jung suggested that for women dreams of snakes often suggested assault. This picture by Franz Stuck of a woman and snake has the simple suggestive title of *Sin*.

Above: *Oh, How I Dreamt of Things Impossible*, an engraving by William Blake in which humans fly. To Freud such an image was sexual. In Jungian theory it can also mean liberty and escape from the rules and requirements of the ordinary world.

Dreams also express unfulfilled potentialities of the personality. "The general function of dreams," Jung wrote, "is to try to restore our psychological balance by producing dream-material that reestablishes, in a subtle way, the total psychic equilibrium." In other words, the dream fulfills not merely a wish, as Freud maintained, but also a profound need for the integration and wholeness of the personality. The dream in this way is also *purposive*. The unconscious, according to Jung, "is no mere depository of the past, but is also full of germs of future psychic situations and ideas," and it is often wiser and possessed of more foresight than the conscious mind. Dreams, he believed, are not backward-looking and concerned with the fulfillment of infantile wishes, but are more often forward-looking, a message from the unconscious which seeks to order the dreamer's life and psychic functioning and to indicate the direction he must follow.

Dream theory occupies a central position in both Jungian and Freudian psychology, and both men wrote hundreds of pages on the subject. To present their ideas fully would require a large volume. A few of the essential differences between the two theories may, however, be indicated by examining the meanings of some common dream images and themes according to Freud and to Jung.

Houses. Freud interpreted dreams of pursuit through the rooms of a house as expressing a wish to visit a brothel. For him, houses had a predominantly female symbolism, though their façades could represent the bodies of erect men. The Jungian view would be that the house represents the self, that its different rooms represent different aspects of the personality—as they did in Jung's own dream—and that everything that happens in the dream house should be examined by the dream interpreter for its symbolic relevance to events in the life of the dreamer.

Staircases. For a man to dream of climbing a staircase is, according to Freud, to dream of having an erection. To descend stairs symbolizes detumescence after orgasm. For a woman, a dream of descending stairs symbolizes normal sexual activity. Jungians

Some Dream Images Explained by Jung and Freud

Below: *The Rape*, an etching of 1878 in which a birdlike monster appears in a nightmarish scene. Freud saw birds as an indication that the dreamer longed to be adept at the sexual act. Jung considered that the dream bird is primarily an image of the Self.

From Flying to Losing Teeth

would take the view that stairs more frequently symbolize passage from one stage of life to another. Artemidorus, a Roman dream interpreter of the 2nd century A.D., expressed a similar view. He thought that dreams of staircases signify an advancement in rank.

Birds. There is some support in the German language for the Freudian claim that the bird is a phallic symbol, for in everyday speed *vogeln* (from *Vogel*, bird) means sexual activity. But for Jung the bird was primarily an image of the soul, the part of human beings that is free and can soar. For him, as for Artemidorus, dreams of birds were good omens except when the birds were caged or injured. In such cases the dream might signify that the soul, or imagination, of the dreamer was trapped, held down by the circumstances of life.

Flying. One of the commonest dream disguises for sexual activity according to Freud is the dream of flying. To slip through the air with ease, to glide or to hover, are activities that might afford ecstatic or pleasurable sensations like those enjoyed in sex. The Freudian interpretation of flying dreams is probably often apt. But flying in dreams according to Jung is an activity that signifies liberty and transcendence, escape from the level of the mundane and ordinary. Flying dreams can therefore signify, as they did for the ancients, achievement, confidence, or ambition.

Snakes. Snakes are another of Freud's phallic symbols. Their shape and movements, and the ability of certain kinds of snakes to rear, thrust and spit, suggest obvious comparisons to the phallus. The symbolism of the snake in myth, as Jung would look at it, has varied and contradictory meanings. It may represent Woman, the Devil, resurrection, and healing. Snakes in dreams, according to Jung, are a sign of a conflict between conscious attitudes and instincts and a warning of such a conflict.

Spiders. Like snakes, spiders are cold-blooded and represent a form of life totally alien to humans. Freud regarded the spider as a symbol of the overpowering mother who comes between the son and the young woman, and will devour one or the other rather than permit them to relate sexually. Jung considered the strangeness of the spider to be its main symbolic significance, and thought that it represented a psychic world whose contents would long remain inaccessible to consciousness.

Losing teeth. The sexual theory regards dreams of teeth falling out as representing a loss of semen for the male and childbirth for the female. But such dreams may also represent a process of growing up, of passing from infancy to childhood, and may be interpreted as indicating that the dreamer recognizes either that he is growing up or that he needs to do so.

Exhibitionism. One writer on dreams quotes this dream of a woman patient who suffered chronically from blushing: "I am walking down Regent Street with no clothes on, but I am surprised to find that I am not embarrassed and nobody else seems to notice." The Freudian interpretation of such a dream would be that it clearly indicates a wish for uninhibited sexuality. Regarded from the Jungian point of view, however, it expresses a need and a striving for psychic equilibrium. It is also a message from her unconscious that draws attention to her neurotic self-consciousness, and tells her that it is a totally subjective and groundless feeling. She is in the most embarrassing situation she

Above: in Jungian theory, the horse symbolizes powerful and instinctual feelings, and the sea within a dream is often a symbol of the unconscious from which such feelings emerge. This painting by one of Jung's patients shows her reluctantly beginning to turn to face her unrecognized emotions.

can possibly imagine, and yet "nobody else seems to notice."
Death of the father-figure. Dreams in which a figure representing
the father either dies or is killed by the person dreaming are
regarded by Freud as expressing the "Oedipus complex," the
desire to get rid of the obstacle to incestuous possession of the
mother. But what about the fact that such dreams occur even
when there is a strong bond of affection between father and child?
The Jungian view of dreams as compensatory and purposive
would regard the dream of the death of the father as indicating a
need for independence of action and decision, and need to
develop full individuality.

This brief survey of some of the imagery and themes that
commonly occur in dreams illustrates the necessity, stressed long
ago by Artemidorus, of relating the dream material to all the
circumstances of a person's life, and the general characteristics
of his or her personality. Dream symbols may signify different
and even contrary things for different people. The dream theories
of Freud and Jung stand as helpful signposts on "the Roya
to the unconscious." But they are far from infallible, and if
followed too slavishly can lead the dream interpreter far astray.

Left: *The Key of Dreams* by René
Magritte. In a deceptively simple
commentary on the ambiguity of symbols
and their interpretation, the Surrealist
painter includes one symbol that has no
double meaning: a valise is a valise. We are
left with the teasing question—is he
mocking Freud and Jung and all the dream
analysts, or illustrating their theories?

Chapter 10
Ancient Theories of Dreams

Men have always dreamed, and for the men in ancient times their dreams were often considered vitally important as signposts for the future. What meanings did they give their dreams? How were dreams used in classical times? In the dream temples of Aesculapius, sufferers would sleep in hopes of dreaming of the god himself, who would perhaps offer some advice or even cure them in the course of their dream. Interpretation of dream symbols did not begin with Freud: what were the early suggestions of their significance? Why have all civilizations puzzled over the dream experience and sought to find meaning in it?

The people of the ancient world tended to believe that some dreams were sent by the gods to convey information to mortals. From this belief the Greeks personified the dream. They regarded a dream as a kind of phantom, able to assume various forms, and dispatched by a god to a sleeping person with a specific message to implant in the dreamer's mind.

The Greek gods—prone as they were to meddling in the affairs of mortals—were not above using dreams to convey misinformation. In *The Iliad*, the story of the last days of the Trojan War, the poet Homer tells how the god Zeus, in order to punish King Agamemnon for some transgression, sends him a false dream.

Under Zeus' instructions, the dream goes to the sleeping Agamemnon and insinuates itself into the king's mind. It assumes the form of the king's most trusted adviser, Nestor, who tells him that Zeus is concerned for him. Now is the time for Agamemnon to assemble his army and attack Troy, says the dream, for the gods are united on his side. and he will be sure of victory.

Agamemnon wakes, confident that he can easily capture Troy, and calls a meeting of his council. On hearing the king's dream, Nestor, pleased no doubt at being the "star" of the dream, observes that if anyone else had had such a dream, one would be reluctant to believe it. But since it was sent to their Commander-in-Chief, he says, it is undoubtedly true. This settles the matter, and the Greeks prepare for battle. But the

Opposite: *Jacob's Ladder* by William Blake, with the angels ascending and descending the heavenly stairs as the sleeping prophet dreams.

The Significance of Ancient Dreams

Above: Achilles grasps the shade of Patroclus, his dear friend. As told in the *Iliad*, Achilles was stubbornly remaining in his tent, seething with anger about a grievance, when Patroclus, clad in Achilles' armor, was slain on the field of battle. In a dream Patroclus appeared to Achilles, begging him to bury his body so that he could pass through the Gates of Hades. Achilles, grief-stricken, agreed, and returned to battle to avenge his death.

epic poem reveals that it was not the easy victory they expected. It was a prolonged and bitter struggle in which the gods frequently intervened on both sides, aggravating the hostilities.

Since the beginnings of civilization dreams have been considered important. One of the oldest texts in existence, the *Epic of Gilgamesh*, written 4000 years ago in Babylonia, is full of dreams and dream imagery. For example, Gilgamesh dreams that he is pinned to the ground by the weight of a god who has fallen on him. At another point in the story he and his companion Enkidu climb to the top of a mountain that immediately collapses. In a nightmare vision of the afterlife, a creature with feathered arms and nails like an eagle's talons leads Enkidu to the "kingdom of dust" where the dead, part-human and part-bird, dwell in darkness. Even the daylight events of the story are full of dreamlike images: a plunge into the sea to obtain a plant that will bestow eternal life; a serpent that sheds its skin and so renews its youth; the wild man Enkidu himself. Such images and situations recur in dreams today.

We have now rediscovered the fact that a dream is not just nonsense but information in disguise—a truth known to ancient peoples. Unlike them, however, we generally believe that the dream is a product of the dreamer's own unconscious mind, not a message from some external mind or deity. And while we accept that a dream may be highly significant for the dreamer personally, we tend to be skeptical of claims that a dream can foretell the future, or that the correct interpretation of a dream can influence the course of history.

Such concepts were taken for granted by the people of ancient times. Perhaps the most familiar example of this belief in the power of dreams is the Old Testament story of Joseph.

Joseph fell out of favor with his family when he reported to them two dreams that symbolically foretold his elevation to such power that his brothers had to pay homage to him. Eventually the dreams came true. Moreover, his own dreams came true as a result of his skill in interpreting other dreams. While in prison in Egypt he accurately interpreted the dreams of his cellmates, and this uncanny skill brought him to the attention of the Pharaoh. Having had a disturbing dream that none of his own wise men or magicians could interpret, Pharaoh sought Joseph's help. In his dream, Pharaoh had stood by a river out of which came seven fat cattle to graze in a meadow. Then seven lean cattle also came out of the river and ate up the seven fat ones. In a second dream immediately following the first, Pharaoh saw seven good ears of wheat appear on a stalk; then seven thin ears blasted by the east wind sprang up after them. Joseph interpreted the dreams as a warning message from God. "Behold," he said, "there come seven years of great plenty throughout the land of Egypt; and there shall arise after them seven years of famine; and all the plenty shall be forgotten in the land of Egypt, and the famine shall consume the land." He followed his interpretation with advice as to how Pharaoh should administer his land in order to provide for the years of famine out of the abundance of the years of plenty. By heeding his advice the Egyptians were able to survive the famine, which occurred as predicted.

Left: *The Palace of Dreams* from a 17th-century engraving. The Greeks believed that the figures in dreams were people from near the underworld, who entered our world by the two gates shown here. True dreams, relevant to the problems of everyday life, entered through the Gate of Horn over which a cow stood guard. False dreams, meant to mislead, entered through the Gate of Ivory, watched over by an elephant.

Below: a 16th-century view of a scene from the ancient Greek epic poem the *Odyssey*, showing Ulysses' wife Penelope at her loom. Like other examples of classical literature, the *Odyssey* has many dreams. Penelope, after having a disturbing dream, remarks, "Dreams, sir, are awkward and confusing things: not all that people see in them comes true."

Above: Joseph, brought out of prison because of his skill in dream interpretation, explains the Pharaoh's dream of the cattle and corn as a warning from God, a prophecy of the seven years of famine to follow seven years of particularly abundant harvests.

Psychologists opposed to any paranormal theory of dreams have argued that Pharaoh could have had intuitive knowledge, accessible to him only under the condition of sleep, of factors that would influence fertility in Egypt over a period of 14 years. This theory is almost as improbable as the idea that God revealed the future to Pharaoh in His usual cryptic way. In dealing with an ancient legend such as this one, we can't draw any firm conclusions. What the story does show unequivocally is the important status enjoyed in those times by a gifted interpreter of dreams.

Other dream stories from ancient times also suggest the possibility that the dreamer possessed subconscious knowledge that surfaced symbolically in the dream. The literature of Islam includes a tale about King Nushirwan, who dreamed that he was drinking out of a golden goblet when a black hog put its head into the cup and drank too. The king told his dream to his vizier, or minister, who interpreted it as meaning that the king's favorite concubine had a black slave as a lover. The vizier suggested that the woman and the entire harem should be made to dance naked before the king. The command was issued. One member of the harem, who showed reluctance to follow the command and whom the others tried to shield, was found to be a Hindu male slave. This apparently clairvoyant dream might be attributed to a subconscious suspicion on the part of the king. The image of the black hog sharing his goblet was perhaps put forward by his unconscious mind as a symbol of knowledge that his conscious mind kept suppressed.

The dream records of the ancient world consist largely of the dreams of kings—probably because it was considered more likely that the gods would communicate with royalty than with ordinary mortals. To judge from accounts of these royal dreams, however, a king's life in those days was far from carefree, for many of them are obvious anxiety dreams. Nebuchadnezzar, King of Babylon in the 6th century B.C., dreamed that he saw an immense and fruitful tree which reached up to heaven and spanned the entire earth. Then, said the king, "an holy one came down from heaven" and commanded that the tree should be hewn down, its branches cut off, and its fruit scattered, but that its stump should be left and should be bound with iron and brass. "Let his heart be changed from man's," decreed the holy one, abandoning the tree symbol and referring to the king himself, "and let a beast's heart be given into him. . . ." This dream foretold not only the collapse of Nebuchadnezzar's rule but also the collapse of his mind into madness.

Another anxious ruler, a contemporary of Nebuchadnezzar, was Astyages, King of Media. Astyages went to great lengths to forestall the prophecies that his wise men told him were contained in his dreams. For example, he dreamed that his daughter Mandane urinated until she flooded first his city and then the whole of Asia. According to ancient traditions of dream interpretation, urine symbolized procreation. The king feared that his dream meant that his daughter would marry someone who would wrest the throne from him and that they would found a new dynasty. So when she became of marriageable age he arranged for her to marry a Persian whom he considered to be an unambitious and inferior young man. During Mandane's pregnancy, however, the king had another dream in which there sprang from her womb a vine that spread over the whole of Asia. This reawakened his anxieties about the security of his regime, so he laid plans to have his grandchild murdered when it was born. But the plans were frustrated, and Mandane gave birth to a child who eventually became the conqueror known as Cyrus the Great.

Herodotus, an historian of early Greece, relates an anxiety dream attributed to Croesus, King of Lydia. The king had two sons, one a dumb and retarded child and the other, Atys, the most brilliant youth of his generation. Croesus dreamed that Atys would be killed with the point of an iron weapon. The dream worried him so much that he removed Atys from his military command, forbade him to engage in military exercises, and had all the weapons in the men's chambers in the palace locked away. Atys was forced to live a sheltered life that must have been particularly frustrating for a youth in an age when prowess in the martial arts was the mark of manhood. Understandably, he grew restive. One day he prevailed upon his

Dreams in the Old Testament

Below: one of Job's dreams as visualized by William Blake. In his version, God-the-tempter who torments Job appears with cloven hooves: the supreme deception of Satan is his claim to be God.

Above: the dream of Nebuchadnezzar,
which Daniel interpreted. The king
dreamed that a tree was felled by "a holy
one" who said: "let his heart be changed
from a man's, and let a beast's heart be
given into him." Daniel predicted the king
would be deposed and would eat grass like
the oxen.
Below: the madness of Nebuchadnezzar in a
watercolor by William Blake. The king went
mad just as his dream had foreshadowed.

father to let him join a hunt for a large boar, and though
Croesus agreed, he took the precaution of putting Atys in the
charge of an experienced and trusted soldier, Adrastus. The
boar was hunted down and surrounded, and when javelins
were hurled at it from all sides, Adrastus missed his target and
fatally wounded Atys.

Was Croesus' dream prophetic or self-fulfilling? Modern
psychological and anthropological studies have demonstrated
the extraordinary power of suggestion. For example, people
have been known to die after a curse was placed on them; they
are literally frightened to death. It may be that Adrastus was
made so nervous by the king's obsessive anxiety and by the
responsibility placed upon him that he did precisely the thing
that he most feared. Anyone who plays a game of skill knows
that anxieties about his performance have a tendency to be
self-fulfilling. Normal explanations can also usually be applied
to most of the other seemingly precognitive dreams from ancient
sources. Nebuchadnezzar's dream, with its symbolism of the
tree (a perennial symbol of the dreamer's self-image), could
clearly be a case of the king's subconscious expressing fears and
knowledge that he would not consciously admit to himself or
to his subjects.

It is easy to submit the ancient dream records to modern
interpretation and demystify them in this way, but it is presumptuous to assume that because we can do this we are wiser
and more knowledgeable than the ancients. It is arguable that
in the importance they attached to dreams the ancients were
wiser than we are. Freud is credited with the discovery of the
relation between dreams and mental and physical health, but
he was not the first to suspect such a connection. In the 2nd
century B.C. there were 320 temples throughout Greece and other
Mediterranean lands devoted to inducing dreams and dedicated

to Aesculapius, the god of healing. These were no new fad, but belonged to a tradition extending back into ancient Egypt and Mesopotamia. At one point in the *Epic of Gilgamesh*, the poet describes a ritual for the deliberate inducing of dreams:

"After twice twenty hours they took some food;
after twice thirty hours they took some rest;
they dug a ditch facing the Sun god;
Gilgamesh stood on the slope of the ditch
and he poured flour into it, saying:
'O mountain, bring us dreams!'"

In this case, dreams were sought as a means of guidance before setting out to kill a monster. Many primitive societies even today induce dreams to help in making decisions or as preparation for hunting. In ancient Egypt there were temples devoted to dream incubation with resident priests who were known as "Masters of the Secret Things." The interpretation of dreams was apparently something of a business in these temples. Archaeologists have unearthed a kind of professional plate which announces: "I interpret dreams, having the gods' mandate to do so; good luck; the interpreter present here is Cretan."

Increasingly dreams were induced with a view to diagnosing and treating illnesses. Near the temple of Hathor in Egypt are the ruins of a sanatorium where the goddess allegedly worked miraculous cures. Running water flowed over her four-faced statue and into the corridor.

The dream incubation rites at the temple of Aesculapius were somewhat complicated. The prospective dreamers were first required to practice various kinds of abstinence—from certain foods such as wine, meat, and broad beans, and from sexual intercourse. They also had to undergo ritual cleansing in cold water. The supplicants then had to make offerings to the god and attend sermons on his miraculous cures. At night there were torchlight services including fervent prayers to Aesculapius. Finally, the patients settled down to sleep in a special dormitory containing large harmless yellow snakes. On awakening the next day many of the patients reported that the god had, in their dreams, prescribed certain medicines or diets to treat their illness. In a few cases patients were apparently cured in the night. A certain Clinates of Thebes, who was afflicted with lice, dreamed that Aesculapius undressed him and swept him clean. The next morning his lice had disappeared.

Equally extraordinary was an experience reported by the Greek physician Claudius Galen, who lived from A.D. 130 to 200. Galen claimed that he received surgical advice from God in a dream. Twice he was directed in a dream to cut the artery lying between the forefinger and the thumb in order to relieve a pain he suffered from in the area of the liver. He followed the advice, and the pain disappeared. Galen did not take the credit for his discovery himself or attribute it to the subtle processes of his subconscious, but adopted what is basically a magical view of the phenomenon and attributed it to God.

Religious, astrological, and other supernatural theories of dreams were refuted by the Greek philosopher Aristotle, who

Dream Theory and Dream Cures

Below: Croesus, the king of Lydia, from the Greek vase painting showing him on his funeral pyre. Croesus dreamed his brilliant son Atys would be killed. In spite of elaborate precautions, his son was killed accidentally by one of the men charged to look after him.

Aristotle's Scorn for Divine Dreams

Right: the healing temples of Aesculapius in Greece. Patients retired after ritual abstinences and cleansing to receive a dream from a god, which would instruct them in the medicine or diet required to cure their disease. Originally these incubated dreams were not necessarily dreams of healing, but could be an answer to any personal problem. But as the large specialized sanctuaries developed, people came to expect to be cured of their illness.

lived in the 4th century B.C. Accepting that dreams might sometimes yield insight into one's state of health, Aristotle put this down to the fact that during sleep, when distracting external stimuli are absent, the mind is able to pay more attention to tiny internal sensations. He held that cases of apparently prophetic dreams could be attributed either to coincidence or to self-fulfilling behavior influenced by suggestions in the dream. He poured scorn on the idea that dreams were of divine origin by pointing out that animals had them as well as human beings—it being assumed that the gods would not communicate with animals. It was Aristotle who laid the intellectual foundations of the scientific-rational culture of the West, and his demystification of dreams has delighted and influenced skeptical minds down the centuries. His teacher Plato, however, differed from him in believing that some dreams might be of divine origin. Plato put forward the theory that repressed aspects of personality emerge in dreams, anticipating Freud by some 2300 years. The famous statement in Plato's *Republic* that "even in good men there is a lawless wild-beast nature, which peers out in sleep," could come from Freud's *Interpretation of Dreams.*

After Aristotle, the most eloquent skeptic to disparage all paranormal theories of dreams was the Roman orator Cicero. In his book *On Divination,* he applied his considerable powers of logic and satire to demolish what he regarded as the crude superstition of people who look to dreams for occult knowledge. But the phenomenon that Cicero so ably derided struck back at him in an extraordinary way. He had a dream in which he saw a noble looking youth come down from the skies on a chain of gold and stand at the door of a temple. The following day, attending an official occasion at the capitol, he saw a young man whom he instantly recognized as the one in his dream. It was Octavius, a great-nephew of Caesar's. Cicero curried favor with Octavius because he thought his dream meant that the young man would rise to supreme power in Rome. In fact Octavius did emerge as the victor from the struggle that followed the assassination of Julius Caesar. But the succession of Octavius was followed by a political purge and Mark Antony, a powerful enemy of Cicero's, got him executed. Commenting on the case, Sir Thomas Browne wrote in his essay *Of Dreams*: "Cicero is much to be pitied, who having excellently discoursed of the vanity of dreams, was yet undone by the flattery of his own."

A Roman who devoted his life to an exhaustive study of dreams was the soothsayer Artemidorus, who lived in the 2nd century A.D. He traveled widely, visited dream incubation centers, consulted dream interpreters, collected old manuscripts, and gathered together all the information about dreams and dreaming that was available in his day. His *Oneirocritica*, meaning "The Interpretation of Dreams," presented a system of classifying and interpreting dreams that is in many ways compatible with modern ideas. He distinguished five types of dream: symbolic (Pharaoh's dream of the cattle and the ears of wheat for example), oracular (divine revelations), fantasies (wish-fulfillments), nightmares, and daytime visions. He further distinguished *insomnium* and *somnium* dreams. The former are dreams influenced by physiological conditions or daytime concerns, and the latter are those with profound allegorical meaning often relevant to future events. Jung was later to make a similar distinction between ordinary and great dreams.

Dream interpretation prior to Artemidorus had tended to run along mechanical lines with certain symbols having fixed meanings regardless of the personality or circumstances of the dreamer. Artemidorus said that such interpretation is virtually worthless. He insisted that not only must individual dream images be analyzed in the context of the dream as a whole, but also the entire dream must be interpreted with reference to the dreamer's total personality and circumstances of life. This

Above: a wooden statue of the Egyptian god Bes, who was the guardian of sleep. He chased away evil spirits and sent the sleeper sweet dreams. Insomniacs made appeals to Bes in rituals and magic spells involving curious potions.

Left: the stone inscription on the giant sphinx in Giza tells how Thutmose IV cleared the sands from the statue in obedience to a dream in which the god Hormakhu—whose likeness is the sphinx—promised him the kingdom.

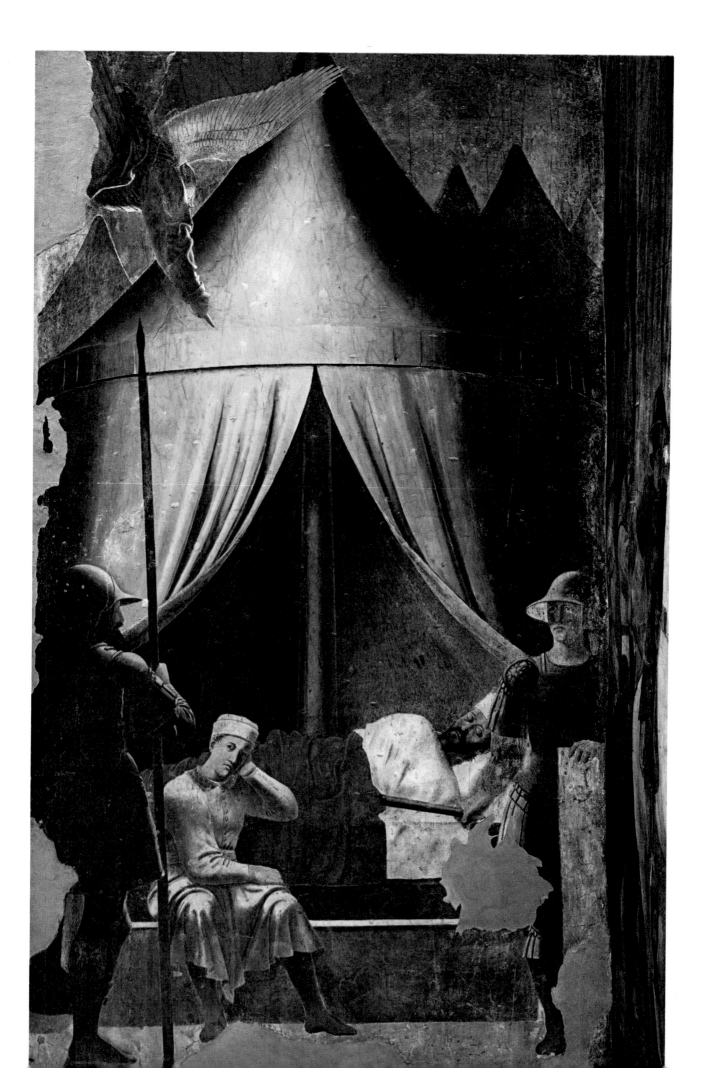

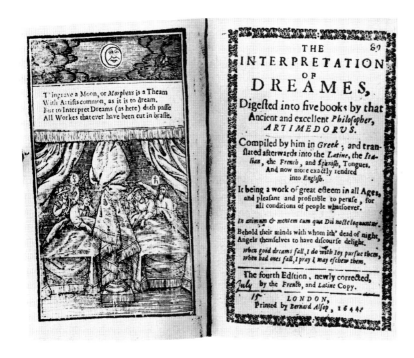

The ingrave a Moon, or *Morpheus* is a Theam
With Artifts common, as it is to dream.
But to Interpret Dreams (as here) doth paffe
All Workes thatever have been cut in braffe.

THE
INTERPRETATION
OF
DREAMES,
Digefted into five books by that
Ancient and excellent *Philofopher*,
ARTIMEDORVS.

Compiled by him in *Greek* ; and tran-
flated afterwards into the *Latine*, the *Italian*, the *French*, and *Spanifh*, Tongues,
And now more exactly rendred
into *Englifh*.

It being a work of great efteem in all Ages,
and pleafant and profitable to perufe , for
all conditions of people whatfoever.

In animum & mentem cum qua Dii noſte loquantur

Behold their minds with whom ith' dead of night,
Angels themfelves to have difcourfe delight.

*when good dreams fall, I do with Ioy purfue them,
when bad ones fall, I pray I may efchew them.*

The fourth Edition, newly corrected,
by the *French*, and *Latine* Copy.

LONDON,
Printed by Bernard Alfop , 1 6 4 4

Interpretation by Contraries

Left: the title page of a 1644 edition of Artemidorus' treatise, *The Interpretation of Dreams*. Artemidorus lived in Greece in the 2nd century A.D., and his book is one of the first serious attempts at dream analysis.

Opposite: *The Dream of Constantine* by Piero della Francesca. In this dream the emperor, who was then grappling with the problem of coping with the conversion of Rome to Christianity, saw a cross which convinced him that that was the direction in which he should look for divine aid in overcoming all his opponents.

approach resembles the modern psychoanalytic method of dream interpretation.

While allowing for factors of the dreamer's personality and circumstance, Artemidorus' system also includes some basic symbols to guide the interpreter of a dream. Some of these, as in Freud's system, have sexual significance. In Artemidorus' book, dreams of sowing, planting, and tilling the soil signify a desire to marry and have children, and the plough itself is a phallic symbol. Ditches dug in the soil and places where grain is stored are symbols for woman, wife, or concubine.

An ancient principle of dream interpretation which Artemidorus incorporated is that dreams often go by contraries. To dream of the death of a brother signifies the disappearance of an enemy or deliverance from adverse circumstances. Dreams of illness portend long life, and natural calamities such as earthquakes promise a change of circumstances for the better. This belief that dreams signify their opposites is found not only in the amost ancient dream books but also in modern anthropological studies. In 1926 the anthropologists A. G. O. Hodgson and H. J. Rose reported a study of dream interpretations by ten headmen of a tribe in Nyasaland. The idea that dreams go by contraries was only one of the correspondences they found between the tribesmen and Artemidorus. There are also striking parallels in the symbolism of the two systems. For Artemidorus, a dream of fire in the sky meant famine or war; for the Africans a bush fire in a dream meant war. To dream of losing a tooth, according to Artemidorus, meant to a lose a member of one's household; to the Africans such a dream showed that the dreamer would lose a wife or child. A flood dream in Artemidorus' book indicated bad luck in a law suit or ill-tempered masters; and it had essentially the same meaning for the Africans. The ancient Greek said the dream of a dragon around the body symbolized bondage, while the headmen saw

Interpretations of Dreams, 1850

Opposite: interpretation of dream images for the general public—a French version printed in 1850. The translations are below.

Picking grapes: means pleasure and happiness, wealth, and good health.
Nightmare: a nightmare means opposition in your undertakings.
The Virgin: to pray to the Virgin means relief from troubles.
Breeze: to dream of a gentle breeze predicts inconstancy in others.
Worship: to dream of praying to God means joy and happiness.
Gardens: working in a garden means one will enjoy good health..
Murder: to dream of murdering signifies safety in the future.
Nose: to dream you possess an enormous nose signifies you will enjoy great wealth and power.
Fire: to see a fire forecasts danger; to put it out forecasts an inheritance for the dreamer.
Grapes: to dream of eating a grape means happiness and prosperity.
Lords and Ladies: to be entertained by grand people means prosperity.
Snake: to see a snake means sorrow; to kill one predicts future success.
Housework: to watch someone who is spinning thread means prosperity.
Music: to dream of music promises a happy outcome from your troubles.
Gallantry: to dream of gallant behavior means happiness and health.
Blindness: to dream of going blind means extremely hard work ahead.
Lending money: to dream of profit from money-lending foretells a difficult time in the future.
Ghosts: to see a ghost forecasts happiness and success to come.
Robber: an attack by thieves suggests the death of a relative.
Burial: dreams of attending a burial mean future happiness.
Bed: to dream of a bed signifies danger in store for the dreamer.
Fruit selling: to sell fruit, or watch others, promises prosperity.
Hunting: a dream of hunting means one will be accused or deceived.
Argument: dreams of women arguing means serious trouble to come; men arguing means jealousy in store.

a snake winding itself around the leg as a symbol of slavery.

Such correspondences strongly suggest that the human mind in different ages and cultures spontaneously generates the same symbolism and ideas to express its most profound experiences, fears, and desires. The ancient dream books of India, China, and Japan support this conclusion. They also show that in all civilizations people have sought and valued the dream experience, have puzzled over it, and have regarded it as a key to profound truths about human life, experience, relationships, and the perennial questions of the nature of time and of reality. There are many points of correspondence between Oriental and Western theories of dreams and between their interpretations of dream symbols. But many Eastern writers on dreams are more preoccupied than their Western counterparts with what might be called the philosophical aspects of dreaming. In their writings we find a recurrent suggestion that the ambiguities of the dream experience may point to ambiguities inherent in reality itself.

The following tale was recounted by Lie-tzu in the 5th century B.C. It concerns a man of Tcheng who, while looking for fuel in the bush, came upon a stag. He killed the stag, hid it in an empty ditch, and covered it with branches. Later, when he came to look for the stag, he found that he had forgotten the place where he had hidden it, and after a long and fruitless search he came to the conclusion that he had dreamed the whole incident. But he told people about his dream, and another man went to look for the stag and found it. When he got home, he said to his wife: "Before me, a man who gathered fuel dreamt that he caught a stag, but he forgot the place where he had left it. I found it. So was his dream real?" His wife replied that it might have been he who dreamed the whole thing, wood gatherer, stag and all. The man shrugged off the perplexities of the question, declaring: "I have found a stag. What do I care whether it was the other man who dreamt or I!"

The matter did not end there. The first man, the fuel gatherer, had another dream in which he clearly saw both the place where he had hidden the stag and the man who had found it. The next day, following the directions of his dream, he sought out the man and disputed his right to the stag. The issue was brought before a judge, who said to the fuel gatherer: "Did you really find a stag and afterward did you not believe wrongly that you had only seen it in a dream? Or did you really dream that you had found a stag and you are wrong now, maintaining that you really found it? Your wife goes so far as to claim that you saw the man and the stag in a dream and that no one found the animal. The fact remains that there really is a stag in front of us. I order it to be cut in two and that the prince of Tcheng be consulted about the problem." But the prince of Tcheng was of no help. He complicated the question further by wondering whether the judge in turn might not be dreaming that he cut the stag in two. So he consulted his minister, who said: "Was it a dream? Was it not a dream? I cannot decide. To distinguish what is dream and what is reality would need the competence of Huang-ti or K'ong-tzu. But they are no longer here. Let the judge's words be obeyed."

Chapter 11
Dreams that Changed the World

Have dreams influenced the course of history? Sacred scriptures of many faiths tell of how the lives of Jesus Christ, of Buddha, and of the Prophet Muhammad were foretold and enlightened by strange and significant dreams which clearly identified them as particularly favored beings. But other men dreamed dreams as well, and used those dreams to influence their actions, which in turn altered the unfolding of events. The questions remain forever unanswerable and tantalizing: what would have happened if Hannibal, if Descartes, if Hitler had not dreamed their dreams? How would history have been different? Can the illogical and perverse world of dreams convey messages to the rational waking mind?

To reconcile a man to the pregnancy of his bride-to-be if he knew that he had not been the cause of it would require a better-than-average explanation. Such an explanation, conveyed in a dream, is related in the Gospel of St. Matthew. When Joseph learned that Mary, his betrothed, was expecting a child, he was at first "minded to put her away privily. But while he thought on these things, behold, the angel of the Lord appeared unto him in a dream, saying, Joseph, thou son of David, fear not to take unto thee Mary thy wife: for that which is conceived in her is of the Holy Ghost. And she shall bring forth a son, and thou shalt call his name Jesus: for he shall save his people from their sins. . . . Then Joseph being raised from sleep did as the angel of the Lord had bidden him, and took unto him his wife."

Dreams play a significant part in the legendary lives of the founders of the world's religions. They announce, confirm, or direct the founder's unique vocation. The faithful will believe them to be true—direct revelations from God to man. The skeptical will consider the possibility that they might be projections of unconscious wishes, ambitions, or fears. The cynical will regard them as the inventions of biographers intent on sanctifying their subjects with tales of mystery and miracle. But however we regard them, the dream anecdotes connected with the founders of religions testify to a widespread belief in the importance of dreams, and such dreams may literally be said to have changed the world.

Opposite: A Tibetan painting of Queen Maya giving immaculate birth to the son who became Buddha. The queen had had a symbolic dream foretelling the birth of a universal monarch.

The life of the infant Jesus was saved from Herod's massacre when the angel of the Lord again appeared to Joseph in a dream and urged him to flee with the child into Egypt. The three Wise Men also had a divine dream in which they were warned not to return to Herod and tell him where the child was but to go back to their country by another route. Later, when Herod was dead, Joseph was informed of the fact in a dream and instructed to return to the land of Israel. When he arrived he received further instructions in another dream that led him to find safety and security in Galilee. Unlike the cryptic dreams through which the Lord made His will known elsewhere in the Bible, these dream messages surrounding the birth of Jesus are clear.

The dreams connected with the birth and vocation of Buddha are, by contrast, exotically symbolic. Maya, his mother, fell asleep in a copse and had this strange dream which she told to her husband, King Cudhodana, and his soothsayers: "White as snow or silver, more brilliant than the moon or the sun, the best of elephants, with fine feet, well-balanced, with strong joints, with six tusks hard as adamant, the magnanimous, the very beautiful has entered my womb. I must understand the meaning of this dream." Demonstrating an extraordinary faculty of foreknowledge or of dream interpretation, the soothsayers promptly told Maya that her dream signified that she would bear a son who would become a universal monarch whose sovereignty would be based on detachment and compassion, and they added that he would become a wandering monk and would abandon all desires. King Cudhodana had a prophetic dream that corroborated this interpretation. In it "he saw the Boddhisattva leave the house in the peaceful night escorted by a troop of gods, and then set forth, a wandering monk, clad in a reddish garment." But it was Gopa, Buddha's wife, who had the most fantastic dream recorded in Buddhist scriptures. Her dream contains an overwhelming succession of universal images of doom and disaster. According to the scriptures:

"Gopa and the prince were both asleep, side by side, in their bed. In the middle of the night Gopa had a series of dreams. She saw the earth quaking, with its rocks and its peaks; she saw trees that had been raised by the wind and uprooted fall back to the ground. She saw the sun and the moon, haloed with their brightness, fall out of the firmament onto the earth. She saw herself cutting off her hair with her right hand and felt her diadem fall to pieces. Then she saw herself, with both hands cut off, both feet cut off, and completely naked; she saw her pearls scattered and the jewels of her girdle broken. She saw the four legs of her bed broken and lying on the floor; she saw the brilliant richly decorated shaft of the prince's parasol broken as well, his garments scattered, thrown down at random and carried away by the waters, all her husband's jewelery, including his diadem, pell-mell on the bed. She saw a meteor leave the town and the city plunged into darkness; then, in her dream, she saw the beauteous necklaces bedecked with pearls hang down and fall apart, the oceans raised and Meru, the king of the mountains, shaken to its foundations."

The cause of these cataclysmic images is Gopa's anguish over her husband's forthcoming departure to become a wandering

Above: medieval sculpture of the dream of the three wise men, who were warned by an angel not to return to Herod to report upon their visit to the child Jesus. Instead, they traveled home secretly. Like the rest of the dreams surrounding the Nativity, theirs was perfectly clear and straightforward: a command given plainly, not in ambiguous and symbolic dream images.

Christ, Buddha, and Muhammad

Left: the dream of Queen Maya in which she saw a beautiful white elephant. When she reported the dream to her husband King Cudhodana and his soothsayers, it was interpreted as meaning she would bear a son. He, "detached by compassion," would "by the sweetness of his ambrosia" be able to satisfy all the worlds.

monk in order to fulfill his vocation. When she tells him about her dream, the prince tells her tenderly: "Be of good cheer, you have not seen anything evil," and he proceeds to interpret each separate image as a favorable portent. These interpretations are not merely a mechanical application of the universal practice of interpretation by contraries, but more an illustration of the fundamental Buddhist philosophy that pain and disaster only occur on the plane of existence ruled by desire and attachment. To experience anguish as poignantly as Gopa does in her dream signals—according to the idea of contraries—her real emancipation from the grief attendant upon desire and attachment, and her entry upon the plane of perfect bliss.

Dreams also play a major part in the story of the beginnings of the youngest of the world's great religions, Islam. The first part of the holy scripture, the *Koran*, was supposed to have been given to the Prophet Muhammad by God in a dream. The possession of the holy city, Mecca, was promised to the faithful in another of the Prophet's dreams. It was as a result of one of his disciples' dreams that the practice of "Adhan"—the calling of the faithful to prayer from the minarets of the mosques—was instituted. Muhammad himself attached great importance to dreams. Every morning he would exchange reports of the night's dreams with his closest disciples, and interpret theirs for them. The most extraordinary document in the early literature of Islam is the *Nocturnal Journey of Mahomet*, an account in 14 chapters of a dream of the Prophet's which could have left him in no doubt as to the importance of his vocation. The flavor of this curious document is apparent in its opening paragraph:

"I was sleeping between the hills Safa and Meeva [near Mecca], when Gabriel approached and woke me. He was leading Elborak, a silvery gray mare, so quickly that the eye could scarcely follow him in his flight. Placing her in my charge, he ordered me to mount; I obeyed. We set off. In a moment we were at the gates of Jerusalem. Elborak stopped. I dismounted and tied her to the rings to which the prophets were accustomed to tie their steeds. On entering the temple I met Abraham, Moses, and Jesus. I prayed with them. When it was over, I remounted Elborak and

Below: a painting of Alexander the Great and a dream he had at the age of 10. In it a dragon gave him an egg to eat. Such dreams of great men were usually said to be a portent of success.

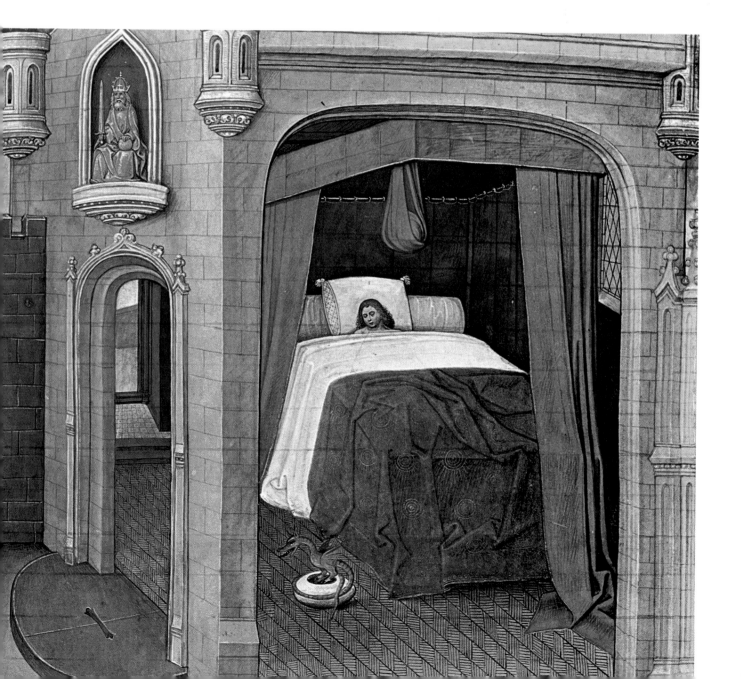

we continued our journey. We traversed the vast expanse of the airs with the speed of lightning. When we reached the first heaven, Gabriel knocked on the door. 'Who is there?' someone asked. 'Gabriel.' 'Who is your companion?' 'Mahomet.' 'Has he been given his mission?' 'He has.' 'Then welcome to him!' With these words, the door opened and we entered. 'There is your father Adam,' Gabriel said to me. 'Go and greet him.' I greeted Adam and he returned my greeting. 'Heaven,' he added, 'is accomplishing your wishes, O my honored son, O greatest of prophets!'"

After traveling through 13 heavens and being greeted and congratulated by all the great prophets of antiquity, Mahomet in his dream passes through the Garden of Delights and visits the House of Adoration, where every day 70,000 angels pay homage to God. In the course of an interview with the Almighty he is instructed to say his prayers 50 times a day. Urged on by Moses, he doggedly bargains with God until he gets the number of daily prayers reduced to five, a practicable demand for homage which the faithful to this day fulfill. Having secured this concession, he mounts Elborak and is returned to the spot from which he had started his journey some hours before.

Just as the followers of Christ and Buddha accept the importance and interpretation of dreams connected with their spiritual leaders, believers in Islam accept the *Nocturnal Journey of Mahomet*. It is a dream containing great archetypal images. And it has profoundly influenced the lives and conduct of a large section of the world's population down to the present day.

Records of dreams that have influenced the course of political history are rarer. Perhaps this is because those who make secular history tend to be less mystically inclined than those who found religions. They are more apt to rely on their own judgments and the counsels of their generals or ministers than on occasional and ambiguous dream messages. But there are a number of dreams that have changed history, most of them associated with men who have won renown as conquerors.

Some of these political and military dreams may be regarded as

"Nocturnal Journey of Mahomet"

Below: Xerxes and his army cross the Hellespont in their invasion of Greece—as advised by the strange apparition in the king's dream, which even appeared to his skeptical minister Artabanus.

Eve of Battle Nightmares

Right: the dream of Richard III the night before Bosworth when he was killed on the field of battle. Richard, traditionally the villain held responsible for the murder of the two young princes in the Tower of London, was said to be so tormented by nightmares of "evil spirits haunting evidently about it, as it were before his eyes" that he went into the battle despondently, and was defeated.

messages from the unconscious that served to strengthen wavering resolve or approve a course of action already considered. On the night before he crossed the Rubicon to march his legions upon Rome, for example, Caesar dreamed that he was sleeping with his mother. Freud would describe this dream as an undisguised Oedipus complex, but Caesar read it to mean that he might dare to violate Rome, the mother-city. He entered that city without encountering the expected resistance, as his dream had foretold.

A later conqueror of Rome was the Carthaginian general Hannibal. He also had a meaningful dream, recorded by the Roman historian Valerius Maximus as follows:

"Hannibal cherished a raging hatred for the Roman Empire and that is why he had reason to rejoice when the horrifying vision he had one day, in a dream, corresponded point by point with his plans and desires.

"While he slept, Hannibal saw a young man, as beautiful as an angel, appear. He assured him that he had been sent from Heaven to urge Hannibal to invade Italy. Turning round, Hannibal also saw an immense serpent which violently and furiously overthrew and destroyed everything that got in its way. The sky behind this reptile was obscured by smoking clouds and pierced by lightning.

"Sorely dismayed by this sight, Hannibal asked the handsome young man what it meant. 'You see,' was his reply, 'the ruin of Italy and the disasters which await it. Go! The fates are going to be accomplished.'

"Is there any need," comments Valerius Maximus, "to recall the evils with which Hannibal ravaged Italy after he had this

dream and obeyed its predictions?"

A more complex dream that had a crucial bearing on the course of political events in antiquity is related by the Greek historian Herodotus. It concerns Xerxes, the young Persian conqueror of Greece. In conference with his advisers the young ruler had urged a policy of invasion, but he had met opposition, particularly from his elderly minister Artabanus. Pondering the question before he slept that night, Xerxes decided to follow the old man's advice and call off the invasion preparations, which he had already ordered. But in a dream he saw a man, "tall and of noble aspect," who stood beside his bed, reproached him for changing his mind, and told him to "continue to tread the path which you chose yesterday." He put the dream out of his mind when he met his ministers the following day, and announced that he had decided that there would be no war against Greece. But the apparition again came to him in a dream, and warned him that if he didn't prosecute the war he would be brought low as quickly as he had been raised to greatness. This troubled him so much that he sent for his minister there and then, told him about his recurrent dream, and suggested that they change places. Artabanus was to sit on Xerxes' throne and sleep in his bed to see if he had the same dream. If he did, they would know that the dream was sent by God. Artabanus gently suggested that the apparition, if it were divine, would hardly be taken in by the proposed disguise. But Xerxes insisted, and the unhappy minister had to obey. He donned the king's clothes and slept in his bed. Once asleep, he had a dream in which the same apparition lambasted him for trying to alter the course of destiny by dissuading the king from

Above: the dream of Napoleon before Waterloo was filled with eerie figures, some holding the symbols of his victories, but one in chains and fetters—clearly a portent of coming defeat after the triumphs of his glorious past.

Corporal Hitler's Dream of Destiny

In the third year of World War I on the Somme front, Bavarian and French troops faced each other in trenches across no-man's land.

One day Corporal Adolf Hitler of the Bavarian Infantry woke suddenly from a fearful dream. In it he had been buried beneath an avalanche of earth and molten iron, and had felt blood coursing down his chest. He found himself lying unharmed in his trench shelter not far from the French front. All was quiet.

Nevertheless his dream worried him. He left the shelter, stepped over the top of the trench, and moved into open country between the armies. A part of his mind told him that he was being stupid because he could be hit by a stray bullet or shrapnel. But he went forward almost against his will.

A sudden burst of gunfire, followed by a loud explosion, made Corporal Hitler fall to the ground. Then he hurried back to the shelter—but it was not there. In its place was an immense crater. Everyone in the shelter and that section of the trench had been buried alive. Only he survived. From that day on, Hitler believed that he had been entrusted with a special mission which promised him a great destiny in world events.

Below: a painting of *The Dream of Tartini.*
Giuseppi Tartini, an 18th-century musician,
dreamed that he made a compact with the
devil, who agreed to be his servant and was
a most satisfactory one. He imagined he
gave his violin to the devil to see what kind
of a musician he was, and the devil played
such a beautiful solo that it surpassed
everything Tartini had ever heard before.
His delight was so great that he awoke, and
instantly seized his violin to try to express
what he had heard. The best he could
manage was a piece he called *The Devil's
Trill,* which has been regarded as the best of
his works. But Tartini himself felt it was so
inferior to the music he had dreamed that
he said he would have broken his violin
and abandoned music if he could have
figured out any other way to earn his living.

making war on Greece. The apparition was about to burn out his
eyes with hot irons when the minister awoke with a shriek, ran to
Xerxes, and admitted that he had been mistaken. The invasion
plans were resumed with Artabanus' support, and Xerxes
achieved his greatest triumph in the sacking of Athens.

This story has a curious sequel. After he had decided to fight,
Xerxes had another dream in which he saw himself crowned with
an olive tree, the branches of which spread all over the earth.
Suddenly this crown vanished from his head. His dream interpreters correctly read this as an omen foretelling success in the
war, but they either failed to see or deliberately suppressed the
significance of the vanishing crown as a possible symbol of
vanishing power. The Persian dominion over Greece was in fact
of brief duration. This detail of the one unfavorable omen may
lend credibility to the story of Xerxes' dreams, but we have to
bear in mind that Herodotus, who told the tale, was a Greek and
would be inclined to play up the defeat of the Persians.

The olive tree dream of Xerxes would have to be classified as
prophetic rather than as one that changed the course of events.
Many other historical figures have reported such prophetic
dreams. In one instance a gigantic woman appeared to Oliver
Cromwell in a dream and told him he would become the greatest
man in England. Before the fateful battle of Bosworth Field in

1485, King Richard III had a dream in which "horrible images as it were of evil spirits" danced before his eyes and would not let him rest. He interpreted this correctly as foretelling his defeat. Napoleon's dream before the Battle of Waterloo, in which he saw a black cat run from one army to the other and his own army cut to pieces, also correctly predicted disaster. President Lincoln foresaw his own assassination in a dream. Marie Antoinette's dream of a red sun rising above a column which then immediately collapsed was regarded as a portent of her execution. Chancellor Otto von Bismarck reported to the Emperor William I a dream in which he had foreseen the successful outcome of a campaign against the Austrians though, at the time of his dream, things looked bad for his Prussian forces. Such dreams, which refer to future events that influenced the course of history, cannot themselves be said to have caused events that changed the world; they did, however, predict the changes—which may be even more remarkable.

A dream that was both prophetic and far-reaching in its effects upon the world was experienced by an Austrian soldier in a battlefield of World War I. One day in 1917, Corporal Adolf Hitler of the Bavarian Infantry awoke suddenly from a dream in which he had been buried beneath an avalanche of earth and molten iron, and had felt blood flowing down his chest. He was actually lying unharmed in his shelter in a trench not far from the French army. All was quiet. Nevertheless, his dream worried him. He left the shelter, stepped over the parapet of the trench, and advanced into the no man's land between the armies. A part of his mind told him that he was being stupid, that he was in danger of being hit by a stray bullet or by shrapnel; but he continued like a sleepwalker. A sudden burst of fire, followed by a loud explosion nearby, made him fall to the ground. Corporal Hitler decided that he would be safer in the shelter than in the open country, so he hurried back. But the shelter was no longer there. In its place was an immense crater. Everyone in the shelter and that section of the trench had been instantly buried. The experience nurtured Hitler's conviction that a great destiny awaited him. And had he not acted on his dream premonition, the history of our time would have been entirely different.

When we turn from religion and politics to consider cultural history, we find one supreme example of a dream experience that changed our world. The dreamer was the 17th-century French philosopher René Descartes. He perhaps more than any other individual was responsible for giving the modern scientific age its methods, its principles, and its underlying philosophy.

In 1619 Descartes was 23 years old and going through a period of great emotional and intellectual stress. He had conceived an ambitious plan for a unified mathematical science, but had not yet put it down on paper. He still had some problems to solve in the plan, and some of them seemed insurmountable. Equally troubling were some of his personal problems relating to his sexual and religious feelings. On the night of November 10 he had three successive dreams, which he later said "could only have come from above." The first two were frightening experiences of menace, violence, and impotence. He interpreted them as representing the consequences of his sins and faults. The

Inspiration From Dreams

Above: woodcut of Jerome Cardan, a 16th-century Italian man of letters. He decided to write his most famous work because it was revealed to him in a recurring dream. He continued to have the same dream while he wrote the book and, in fact, had it more often when he was not working hard enough. The dream stopped entirely when his book had been published.

Scientists Find Solutions in Sleep

Below: Kekulé, the great 19th-century German chemist, saw a snake with its tail in its mouth in a dream and applied its circular structure to the benzene molecule. The dream came to him when he was struggling for a new approach in his research.

third dream was the one that determined the future course of his life and work. He believed on waking from it that he had been visited by "the spirit of Truth which had wanted to open to him the treasures of all the sciences," and that he had received a command from the Almighty to devote his life to the search for truth by the application of mathematical method. Several days later he started writing again. For the rest of his life he developed a philosophy that incorporated both rationalist and religious elements, and that continued to influence Western science for the next 300 years. Whether his philosophy would have developed in the same way without the dreams is an unanswerable question. The fact is that his dreams had a powerful impact on Descartes himself, and so in all probability on the scientific world.

The story of Descartes' dreams raises the question of the relation between dreaming and creativity. Writers, artists, poets, scientists, and inventors have often attributed to their dreams creative ideas, insights, or formulations that they felt they could not have achieved by way of the predominantly rational processes of waking consciousness. Although only a few of these dreams have literally changed people's lives in a significant way, they have all to some extent enriched the world.

Many people have experienced the phenomenon of finding a solution to a problem by "sleeping on it." It is generally supposed that we can do this because the subconscious carries on processes of thought begun at the conscious level. This is probably true when we retrieve a fact that has eluded recollection. The French philosopher the Marquis de Condorcet claimed he often left difficult calculations unfinished after spending several hours on them and went to sleep. Then he would find them automatically completed in his dreams. The novelist Charlotte Brontë told her biographer that she frequently woke up with solutions to writing problems if she deliberately concentrated on a difficulty before going to sleep. In such cases it is reasonable to suppose that normal thought processes have been carried on during sleep. But some creative or inspirational dreams produce results that could not conceivably be arrived at by conscious deliberation. Many of these dreams suggest that the unconscious possesses an ordering faculty and a means of gaining knowledge that does not resemble the step-by-step reasoning of the conscious mind, but goes more directly to its mark.

The German chemist Kekulé revolutionized organic chemistry when he discovered the formula for benzene. It came through a dream at a time when his research had come to a standstill. Later, Kekulé told a conference of scientific colleagues it had happened like this: "I turned the chair to the fireplace and sank into a half sleep. The atoms flitted before my eyes . . . wriggling and turning like snakes. And see, what was that? One of the snakes seized its own tail and the image whirled scornfully before my eyes. As though from a flash of lightning, I awoke. I occupied the rest of the night working out the consequences of the hypothesis." The circular image of the snake suggested the structure of the benzene molecule, a hexagon with a carbon and a hydrogen atom at each point. Kekulé concluded his speech with a recommendation that must have caused many an academic eye brow to be raised: "Let us learn to dream, gentlemen, and then we may perhaps find the

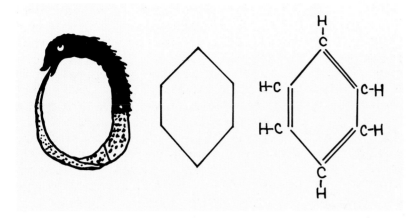

Left: the snake next to the formula for benzene it inspired. It was to revolutionize the development of organic chemistry.

Below: Niels Bohr, the Danish physicist who developed the idea of the atomic "mushroom" 15 years before it was proved by research. In 1913 he had a dream that led not only to this theory, but also to the discovery of a particular type of atom.

truth."

A man who would not have raised an eyebrow if he had been present at Kekulé's lecture was Niels Bohr, the Danish physicist. Bohr was a key figure in the scientific revolution of the 20th century which led to the development of atomic energy and quantum mechanics. He attributed to a dream both his discovery of the type of hydrogen atom that is named after him and of the idea of the atomic "mushroom." This concept was not substantiated by research until 15 years after Bohr's dream experience.

The language of dreams is predominantly visual and symbolic, and the explanation for dreams that solve problems may be that the unconscious throws up a clue to a solution in a symbolic form which suggests a new approach. All the knowledge required for the solution is present in the person's mind. What the dream image supplies is a fresh angle, a new way of seeing the problem which makes all the bits of information necessary for the solution suddenly come together. In other words, conscious and unconscious processes of thought parallel and complement each other. The first lesson in learning to dream, in the sense that Kekulé recommended it, is to pay attention to the visual language of the unconscious, and to remember that it thinks in terms of symbols that condense knowledge rather than in terms of a chain of logically linked concepts.

Another example will illustrate this idea. In 1893 archeologists from the University of Pennsylvania excavated the ancient Babylonian ruins of the temple of Bel at Nippur in what is now Iraq. Dr. H. V. Hilprecht, professor of Assyrian at the University, was later given detailed drawings of two fragments of agate bearing inscriptions which members of the expedition wanted translated. After weeks of effort Dr. Hilprecht still had not succeeded in deciphering the inscriptions. With some hesitiation he conjectured that the fragments had belonged to ancient Babylonian finger rings. Then he had a remarkable dream in which, he said, "a tall, thin priest, of the old pre-Christian Nippur, about 40 years of age and clad in a simple abba," appeared to him and led him into the treasure chamber of the temple. This was a small low-ceilinged room without windows. It contained a large wooden chest and some scraps of agate and lapis lazuli scattered on the floor. The priest told him that the fragments were not finger rings and gave him a detailed account

Right: a drawing of Robert Louis Stevenson writing in bed, where he composed most of his work. He claimed that two crucial scenes of *Dr. Jekyll and Mr. Hyde* came to him in a dream, which enabled him to work out the rest of his popular and haunting tale.

of their history. King Kurigalzu, said the priest, had once presented an inscribed votive cylinder made of agate to the temple. Some time later, the priests had received an order to make a pair of agate earrings for the statue of the god Ninib. Because they had no other raw material for the earrings they cut the cylinder into three parts, two of which they used for the jewelry. The priest concluded by saying: "If you put the two together you will have confirmation of my words. But the third ring you have not found in the course of your excavations, and you will never find it." Then he disappeared. On waking, the professor told his wife about his strange dream. When he examined the drawings, he was amazed to discover "all the details of the dream precisely verified insofar as the means of indentification were in my hands." Later in the year he had an opportunity to visit the museum in Constantinople (now Istanbul) where the actual fragments were kept. Since no one had suspected that the two pieces of agate were related, they were kept in different parts of the museum. When Hilprecht put them together they fitted perfectly and the joined inscriptions made sense. His dream had given him the right information.

The ancients believed that the souls of both the dead and the living can travel in time and space and enter people's dreams, and they would have found nothing improbable in the story of the priest of Nippur's timely visit. The modern view, however, would be that Professor Hilprecht had worked out the problem posed by the puzzling fragments and their inscriptions at the subconscious level, and that the solution was presented to his conscious mind in the form of an intensely visualized experience. Whatever the explanation, one commentator has pointed out that the Professor obtained from his dream no fewer than six specific points of information that he had not previously known, and that these were later found to be correct. Of course the dream also contained information that could never be proved correct or false, namely the elaborate explanation of why and how the votive cylinder had been made into earrings.

The last point illustrates another extraordinary faculty of the dreaming mind: its ability to weave complex narratives. Charlotte Brontë, as we have seen, looked to dreams for help in composing her stories. Ann Radcliffe, the 18th-century author of numerous Gothic romances, is said to have frequently dreamed up novel horrors for her tales by stuffing herself with highly indigestible food before going to sleep. But the supreme example of literary creation through the dream is Robert Louis Stevenson. He deliberately cultivated the ability to dream narratives in such detail and of such complexity that they took the form of serials continued and developed night after night. He gave the credit for many of the plots, scene, and characters of his stories to his "Little People" or "Brownies." Stevenson gave this explanation of how a dream helped him to write the story for which he is probably best known, *Dr. Jekyll and Mr. Hyde*: "I had long been trying . . . to find a body, a vehicle for that strong sense of man's double being which must at times come in upon and overwhelm the mind of every thinking creature. . . . Then came one of those financial fluctuations . . . For two days I went about racking my brains for a plot of any sort; and on the second night I dreamed the scene at the window, and a scene afterwards split in two, in which Hyde, pursued for some crime, took the powder and underwent the change in the presence of his pursuers. All the rest was made awake, and consciously."

One of the most mysterious, lyrical, and richly symbolic works in English poetry is Coleridge's *Kubla Khan*, which was also dream-inspired. In the preface to an edition of his poems, Coleridge gave an account of how he came to write this fragment of a long poem after sleeping for three hours one afternoon in his cottage. He had been reading a passage about the Khan before he fell asleep, which he did as a result of taking opium for "a slight indisposition." When he woke up he had the complete poem in his head, but he had only managed to get part of it down on paper when he was interrupted by a visitor. An hour later, when he tried to resume his composition, he found that he had only a dim recollection of the rest of it and could write no more. The dream vision, as so often happens, had eluded the effort of consciousness to pin it down, and had slipped back to wherever it had originated. The experience might well have suggested the poet's question about waking from a dream in which you plucked a strange flower, and finding that flower in your hand. For that, in a sense, is what Coleridge did. Yet the flower all but dematerialized and he only had a petal left—the fragment *Kubla Khan*—to show that the flower had really existed.

Coleridge was fortunate. Others have brought back what they fancied to be exotic blooms from the world of dreams only to see them die without flowering. The American psychologist and philosopher William James once dreamed that he had conceived an idea that solved the secret of the Universe. Highly excited but still half asleep, he jotted it down. What he read when he looked at his note-pad in the morning was:

Higamus, hogamus,
Women are monogamous;
Hogamus, higamus,
Men are polygamous!

The dreaming mind, it seems, can be as silly as it can be inventive. On the other hand, it could be that it has its own subtle ways of mocking the pretensions of waking consciousness.

Dream Visions— and Nonsense Rhymes!

Below: the poet Coleridge. To his great regret, he was interrupted while writing down the poem *Kubla Khan* which came to him complete in a dream and he could not remember the rest of the words when he got back to it. Only a fragment was recorded.

Chapter 12
The Modern Breakthrough
in Dream Research

Can the intensely private world of dreams be opened to the dream
researcher and his laboratory machines? What can we learn about
the make-up of our minds from the patterns of our sleep and our
apparently vital requirement for dreaming? How did researchers
first learn how to identify the dreaming state in sleep? What function
does dreaming play in maintaining a balanced and healthy mind
during the time we are awake? What is there to be learned about the
development and working of our brains from a study of the way in
which we dream? Why do the senile dream so little, and premature
babies dream so much?

In 1959 a New York disk jockey, Peter Tripp, attempted a publicity stunt that temporarily cost him his sanity. He announced
that he was going to stay awake and at the turntable for at least
200 hours. Major Harold Williams, a psychologist of the Walter
Reed Army Institute of Research in Washington, was in charge
of the experiment. He was interested because the Army had
recently conducted its own research into the psychological effects
of sleep deprivation. Also participating were Dr. Louis Jolyon
West, a psychiatrist, and Dr. William Dement, a dream
researcher. After three days the disk jockey started to behave
peculiarly. He would laugh immoderately at things that weren't
at all funny, and take offense at imaginary insults. Hallucinations
and delusions followed. He thought that specks of paint on the
turntable were insects, and imagined that a doctor's suit was
made of crawling worms. He became convinced that he was
broadcasting from a building elsewhere in town, and that he had
already completed his 200 hours and was being tricked into
carrying on. Tripp was suffering from "gross mental illness,"
Dr. West reported. This illness was diagnosed as resulting from
his being deprived not only of sleep but also of dreams. The
hallucinations he experienced were in fact dream imagery breaking through into waking consciousness. Dr. West noticed that
the hallucinations were most intense between midnight and eight
o'clock in the morning: the time when the disk jockey would
normally be asleep and dreaming.

Modern research has revealed that a person
deprived of dreams suffers as severely as a
person who has been starved.
Opposite: a detail from *Temptation of
Saint Anthony*. When this saint chose to
retreat to the desert, he mortified the flesh
in many ways, almost certainly in part by
refusing to sleep. The nightmarish
"temptations" he reported as being his
torments certainly bear a great similarity to
hallucinations suffered by those who have
been denied the opportunity to dream.

The Scientists Explore Sleep

When Tripp finally slept after just over 201 hours of wakefulness, he remained asleep for 13 hours. According to the electroencephalograph (EEG) recording his brain waves, he spent 28 percent of that time dreaming. Normally, about 20 percent of sleeping time is devoted to dreaming. It was as if his unconscious were trying to make up for lost dream time.

Modern research into sleep and dreaming have established beyond doubt that people need to dream, and that a nightly quota of dream activity is essential to life and health. They have also demonstrated that everyone, without exception, dreams regularly. Some people claim that they hardly ever dream, but this cannot be. They are simply poor dream recallers.

These and many other discoveries about sleep and dreaming have been made possible by modern technology. Until the 1950s knowledge of dreams was based on data obtained from introspection or subjective reports which for the most part were recalled or written down some time after the actual dream experience. This situation was changed by an accidental discovery made in the Department of Physiology at the University of Chicago in 1953—a discovery that made it possible for psychologists to retrieve dreams from the limbo of forgetfulness where they normally vanish, and to study them under experimental conditions.

Professor Nathaniel Kleitman, a world-renowned expert on sleep, was conducting experiments on the sleep of babies. Eugene Aserinsky, one of his student assistants, happened to notice that for short periods during sleep an infant's eyes moved about rapidly beneath the closed lids. He drew Kleitman's attention to his observation, and together they conducted some experiments to discover what these rapid eye movements, called REM, might signify in both infants and adults. To monitor and record the occurrence of the rapid eye movements they used an EEG machine, which can record the electrical activity of the brain through electrodes attached to the scalp. These electrodes pick up electrical impulses from the brain, and the machine then amplifies these impulses and translates them into a written record by means of pens on a moving roll of paper. Aserinsky and Kleitman attached electrodes around their subjects' eyes to obtain a simultaneous record of brain activity and eye movements. This was the breakthrough experiment that enabled the whole field of sleep and dream research to become scientific.

It was accepted for many years that sleep is of two kinds, deep and light; that we go into a deep sleep soon after dropping off at night and gradually surface toward morning; and that we tend to have dreams prior to waking up. Such a conception of sleep lies behind the old idea that one hour of sleep before midnight is worth two after midnight. Another old idea of sleep is that a day spent industriously and virtuously will be rewarded by a profound and dreamless sleep. Both of these commonly held views of sleep have been disproved by modern discoveries.

For a start, there are not just two stages of sleep, but no less than four. After falling deeply asleep, we do not surface only once in the course of a normal night's sleep, but four or five times. Dreams normally occur in these surfacing periods of light sleep. The dreams we remember are usually those of the last such period

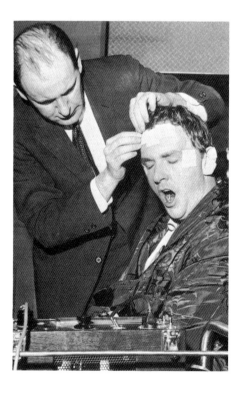

Below: disk jockey Peter Tripp getting a checkup after he had slept 13 hours straight. This long sleep followed his marathon of staying awake for 201 hours. Tripp suffered hallucinations during this period and a three-month depression afterward.

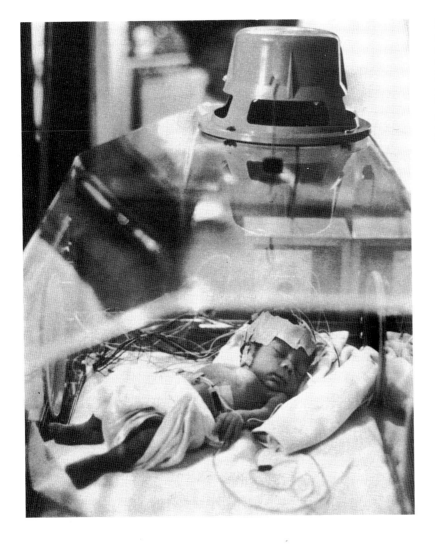

Left: a premature baby peacefully asleep in a New York City hospital, unaware of the electronic gear recording his brain waves. It was in studying the sleep of babies that Dr. Nathaniel Kleitman discovered the phenomenon of REM sleep. Premature babies, like this one, have been found to spend up to 80 percent of their sleep periods in the REM phase of sleep, during which time dreams occur.

Below: Dr. Kleitman checking the record of a graduate student, Bruce Richardson, during a month-long experiment in Mammoth Cave in which they tried to change to a 28-hour day. Richardson, in his twenties at the time, managed the change much more easily than did Kleitman, who was then 43.

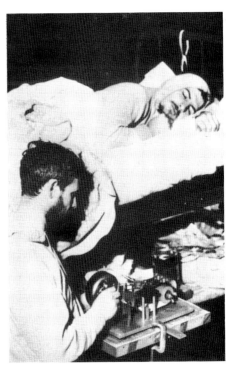

only because those of earlier dream periods in the night have been erased by the intervening periods of deep sleep.

Each of the four stages of sleep has its distinct pattern of brain activity, which is recorded on the EEG as wavy zigzag lines. A person falling asleep shows an increasingly steady pattern of alpha waves. These signify relaxation and are accompanied by deep and regular breathing, slow pulse rate, and a drop in body temperature. Then the alpha rhythms break up and a person enters what researchers term the Initial Stage 1 sleep. In this stage there might be dreamlike reveries, but nothing so organized as a dream. The sleeper continues down through Stages 2 and 3— each with their distinct pattern of brain activity—to Stage 4, or deep sleep. This stage is marked by delta waves, occurring about one per second. Normally a person reaches Stage 4 within about 15 minutes of closing his eyes. About 80 to 90 minutes after falling asleep comes a return through Stages 3 and 2 to Stage 1. This is a period of REMs and dreaming which lasts about 10 minutes. The process of descent and ascent through the stages of sleep is repeated four or five times a night, and each time the period of deep sleep becomes shorter while the period of light sleep becomes longer.

As long ago as 1892 the American psychologist George

Phases of Sleep

Trumbull Ladd had observed rapid eye movements in sleepers, and had put forward a theory that the brain has a mechanism for producing its own visual images even when it has ceased to interpret signals from the optic nerve. In the 1930s another American, the physiologist Edmund Jacobson, made the same observation. He wrote: "Watch the sleeper whose eyes move under his closed lids . . . Awaken him . . . you are likely to find . . . that he had seen something in a dream." But both Ladd and Jacobson lacked the equipment to follow up the clue and conduct a systematic investigation of dreaming. In the 1950s Aserinsky and Kleitman had the EEG and other machines. When a subject was wired to an EEG machine, with an extra channel added to monitor eye movements, it became possible for all the fluctuations of the sleep cycle to be minutely observed. The correlation between REM activity and dreaming was ascertained with a high degree of accuracy by waking the subject when the EEG showed the characteristic pattern.

Many psychologists took up sleep and dream research in the 1950s and 1960s. Prominent among them was Dr. Dement, who had worked with Kleitman at the University of Chicago. In 1960 he went to Mount Sinai Hospital in New York City where he carried out the first systematic series of dream deprivation experiments. Over a period of successive nights Dement awakened volunteer subjects every time they entered REM sleep. He observed that the REM periods steadily increased in number night after night until by about the tenth night subjects fell immediately back into REM sleep every time they were awakened. When they were allowed a night of undisturbed sleep they spent a larger proportion of it than normal in the REM stage. Dement also noticed that dream deprivation affected waking behavior. During the days following the experiments subjects showed signs of fatigue, irritability, and memory loss. They also had difficulty in concentrating. It became clear that dreams performed a function essential to psychological and physical health.

Contributions from several researchers in the field gradually built up a detailed picture of REM sleep. The term "paradoxical sleep" was sometimes used as an alternative description for REM sleep. This phrase comes from the paradox that, although a

Below: the phases of sleep during an adult's typical night. At first the sleeper sinks into a deep Stage 4 sleep, but rises to the REM or dreaming phase (as indicated by the thick black line) after about 80-90 minutes of sleep. The REM periods grow longer as the night progresses, and the sleeper sleeps more and more lightly toward the morning.

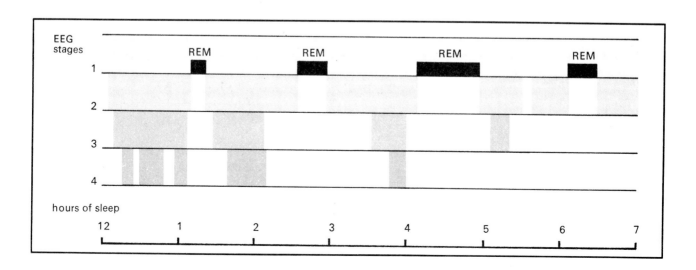

Right: this chart shows the brain waves during sleep, as recorded by the EEG machine.

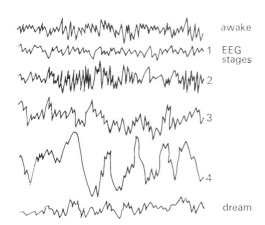

Below: a volunteer in a dream research laboratory. Electrodes are pasted to her head and body to monitor the course of her sleep.

Bottom: a researcher recording the brain waves of the same volunteer on an electroencephalograph, or EEG. It is said that one of the main requirements for a scientist interested in dream research is the ability to remain awake and alert all night while monitoring the peaceful sleep of others.

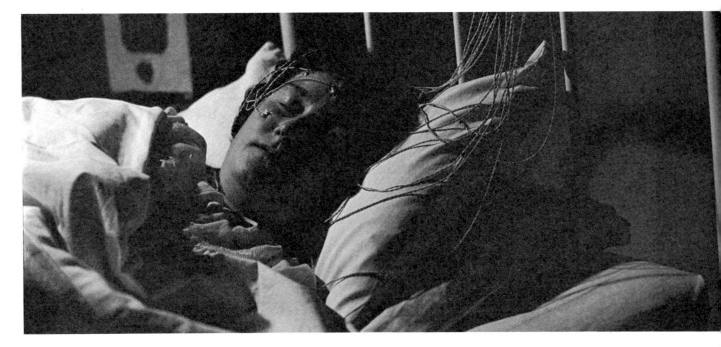

Modern Dream Investigation

person is asleep during a REM period, brain activity follows a pattern similar to the pattern during alert wakefulness. Sometimes this activity is more intense than when a person is awake. Other remarkable physical and physiological changes accompany REM sleep. Men have erections during the REM periods, sometimes of an intensity that can cause them acute discomfort on awakening. This has happened even when the content of their dreams is not apparently erotic. Adrenaline pours into the bloodstream, oxygen consumption in the brain increases, and breathing becomes irregular.

Before a sleeper enters the REM state he tends to twist and turn, but when REM sleep begins body movements stop abruptly and voluntary muscles relax. It is almost as if he were taking his seat in a theater and settling down to watch the show. Though most of the sleeper's muscles are relaxed in REM sleep, however, slight muscular activity does take place, and has been found to be related to the content of the dreams. In one case, for example, electrical impulses were recorded first from the subject's right hand, then from his left, and finally from his legs. When he was awakened he reported dreaming that he lifted a bucket with his right hand, transferred it to his left, and then began to walk. In other cases, subjects have reported hearing something in their dreams after patterns of electrical activity in the muscles of the inner ear had been recorded while they slept.

In one series of experiments Dr. Dement discovered a direct correspondence between sleeper's eye movements and the images that occurred in their dreams. The tracings from the EEG machine record both vertical and horizontal eye movement. A sleeper who was awakened from a dream in which his eyes had been making very rapid horizontal movements said that he had been watching two people throwing tomatoes at each other. Vertical movements occurred when the dream content involved climbing ladders or stairs. On being awakened from a REM period, one young woman reported dreaming that she walked up some stairs, glancing down at each one in turn, and on reaching the top had

Below: a volunteer subject in a dream experiment sleeps soundly, electrodes wired to his head.

Below center: soon after his brain waves indicate he is in an REM phase, the monitoring researcher rings a buzzer, and, still half-asleep, the subject reaches out groggily for his bedside phone. At that moment a light goes on.

Below far right: he reports his dream while the memory is still fresh. A track star himself, he had been dreaming of a discussion about a track meet. "I just found out that the two runners from Hunter weren't good at all."

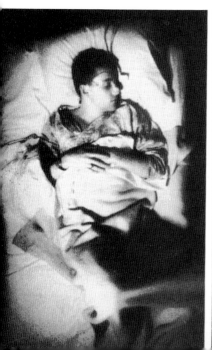
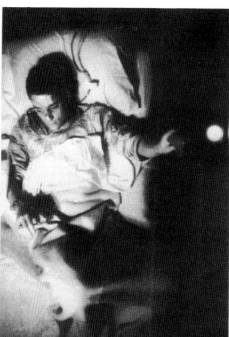
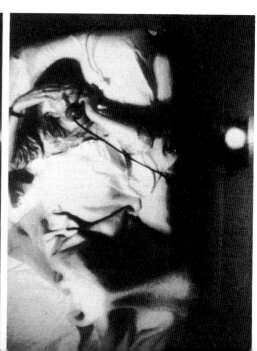

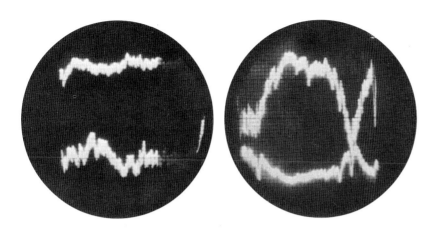

Far left: an oscilloscope registers virtually no eye movement while the sleeper is deeply asleep with no apparent dream activity.

Left: during lighter sleep, the track on the oscilloscope shows rapid eye movement, which is now recognized as a sign of dreaming.

walked over to a group of people. The experimenter hadn't seen the EEG tracings at the time, but he predicted on the basis of the dream report that they would show a series of vertical upward movements followed by a horizontal movement. The tracings proved him right. Such observations suggest that the brain does not distinguish between the visual imagery of the dream and that of waking life. We really do "see" events and images in our dreams in much the same way that we see events and objects in the real world. The same seems to apply to our other senses. We can hear, touch, and sometimes even taste and smell things in our dreams. But though the brain reacts in the same way to information coming in from the dream world and from the real world, it does not normally produce the same response to the different sets of signals. It appears to have a mechanism that inhibits motor response, that tells the body, "this is just a dream, so no action is necessary." But this mechanism does not always work properly, and when it fails, the dreamer may twitch and turn or even talk and walk in his sleep.

Dream experience has often prompted people with a philosophical turn of mind, particularly in the East, to ask such questions as, "What is reality?" and "May not the world we call real be a kind of dream, which seems substantial only because a majority of people agree that it is?" Chuang-Tzu, a Chinese philosopher of the 3rd century B.C., wrote: "One night I dreamed I was a butterfly, fluttering hither and thither, content with my lot. Suddenly I awoke and I was Chuang-tzu again. Who am I in reality? A butterfly dreaming that I am Chuang-tzu or Chuang-tzu imagining he was a butterfly?" The question has survived more than two millennia because it is unanswerable. But it draws attention to a type of dream experience that has fascinated some modern researchers: the so-called "lucid" dream. This is a dream in which the person is aware that he is dreaming. Such dreams are usually extremely vivid and accurate imitations of waking life, but they will contain some peculiarity—for example, a bird flying through a wall—that makes the dreamer realize the experience is imaginary.

Celia Green of the Institute of Psychophysical Research in Oxford, England, has collected and discussed a large number of these experiences in her book *Lucid Dreams*. Lucid dreams, she explains, differ from normal dreams in that they do not have the same elements of irrationality and discontinuity with waking

"Lucid Dreams"

experience. The lucid dreamer may be aware that he is dreaming, may to an extent control the development of his dream, even experiment with it. He may also retain all the memories and functions that he possesses in his normal waking state.

Some of these characteristics of the lucid dream are illustrated in the following example: "I dreamt that I stood at a table before a window. On the table were different objects. I was perfectly well aware that I was dreaming and I considered what sorts of experiments I could make. I began by trying to break a glass, by beating it with a stone. I put a small tablet of glass on two stones and struck it with another stone. Yet it would not break. Then I took a fine claret-glass from the table and struck it with my fist, with all my might, at the same time reflecting how dangerous it would be to do this in waking life; yet the glass remained whole. But lo; when I looked at it again after some time, it was broken. It broke all right, but a little too late, like an actor who misses his cue. This gave me a very curious impression of being in a *fake world* cleverly imitated, but with small failures."

Fascinated by the apparent reality of the "fake world" of his dream, the dreamer went on to make further experiments. "I took the broken glass and threw it out of the window, in order to observe whether I could hear the *tinkling*. I heard the noise all right and I even saw two dogs run away from it quite naturally. I thought what a good imitation this comedy-world was. Then I saw a decanter with claret and tasted it, and noted with perfect clearness of mind: 'Well, we can also have voluntary impressions of taste in this dream-world; this has quite the taste of wine.'"

Sometimes the lucid dream is preceded by a false awakening, resulting in a confusion of the worlds of dream and reality. In the following example the dreamer showed considerable courage in putting his belief that he was dreaming to the test: "I dreamed that my wife and I awoke, got up, and dressed. On pulling up the blind, we made the amazing discovery that the row of houses opposite had vanished and in their place were bare fields. I said to my wife, 'This means I am dreaming, though everything seems so real and I feel perfectly awake. Those houses could not disappear in the night, and look at all that grass!' But though my wife was greatly puzzled, I could not convince her it was a dream. 'Well,' I continued, 'I am prepared to stand by my reason and put it to the test. I will jump out of the window, and I shall take no harm.' Ruthlessly ignoring her pleading and objecting, I opened the window and climbed out on to the sill. I then jumped, and floated gently down into the street. When my feet touched the pavement I awoke . . . As a matter of fact, I was very nervous about jumping; for the atmosphere inside our bedroom seemed so absolutely real that it nearly made me accept the manifest absurdity of things outside."

A point to note here is that the scene outside the window was only absurd because the dreamer carried over from his waking state a memory of what it should be like. The dream world was perfectly normal and continuous with the real world in all ways but one, and it was the fact that the dreamer's mental faculties were functioning as in his waking state that he saw its flaw.

Broadly speaking, mankind's perennial interest in dreams has been of two kinds: a fascination with the hidden contents and

Below: Celia Elizabeth Green, a British dream researcher. She has had a particular interest in the lucid dream, in which the dreamer is aware that he is dreaming.

potentialities of the mind, and a fascination with the question of the relation between the world of dreams and the real world. No theory of the origin or function of dreams is all-embracing, and the lucid dream is a phenomenon particularly difficult to explain in terms of a theory like Freud's that regards dreams as a disguised expression of unconscious mental processes. Its subject matter is rarely bizarre or symbolic, and it does not appear to answer any psychological needs such as wish-fulfillment. If it suggests anything it is the ambiguity of reality and the tenuousness of our hold on it. If it leads anywhere it is into the thickets of speculative philosophy and parapsychology, where most scientists are reluctant to tread for fear of losing their heads, their way, and their reputation. Most scientists investigating the dream phenomenon are more concerned with such matters as the relationship between dreams and external stimuli. Dr. Dement's work has produced some interesting results in this area.

After plotting the pattern of the sleep cycle and demonstrating the human need for dreaming, Dement and his colleagues investigated whether the content of dreams can be influenced by the application of sensory stimuli. What would happen in a dream, they asked, if during REM sleep a dreamer's arms and legs were lightly sprayed with water, or if a bright light were shone directly in his face for a short time, or if a musical note sounded for a few seconds? They found that frequently the sensory stimulus was incorporated into the dream in some way. One sleeper who was sprayed dreamed that it was raining, another that a roof was leaking. The sudden light stimulated dreams of fire or lightning flashes, and the musical note of an earthquake and of the roaring waters of Niagara Falls.

Such experiments may suggest that the dream is a rather arbitrary phenomenon composed of images suggested by immediate sensory stimuli, the residue of the day's impressions and emotions, and a collection of the dreamer's memories. Another series of Dement's experiments showed, however, that this is not the case. Though external stimuli can be incorporated into the dream scenario, they are only incidental features, and it is the dreamer who plots the scenario and dictates its themes. When sleepers are wakened several times throughout a night to obtain dream reports in modern experiments, a continuity of theme often emerges, as in the following example:

"In the first dream, the dreamer was attending a lecture. He asked a question of the professor, who rebuffed him with a sneering remark. He became very angry, but managed to control himself. In the second dream, he was talking to a male acquaintance. He made some remark to which his friend took exception. Again he became very angry, and this time he called his friend a few uncomplimentary names before walking away. In the third dream he was working in a hospital and a nurse began to criticize him severely for some minor ineptitude in his work. Again, he experienced anger, but controlled it and confined himself to thinking: 'What an old hag she is!' The fourth and final dream found the dreamer eating dinner with his family. His mother wanted him to eat some leg of lamb, which he refused. She began pleading with him and he began to get angry. Then: 'She kept kissing me like a little kid and fishing for compliments on her

The Flying Messenger

Mary Arnold-Forster dreamed constantly about flying. Celia Green, author of *Lucid Dreams*, says in it that "many of Mrs. Arnold-Forster's dreams had considerable narrative interest." Here is one such dream:

Mary Arnold-Forster was in an office awaiting a dispatch from the British War Office. She had volunteered to fly it to World War I army headquarters in Belgium. While waiting she flew around near the ceiling, partly to test her flying powers and partly to see if she should leave from a window. She circled the room in flight and looked at the pictures hung high on the wall. An old engraving of the Second Earl Grey caught her eye because it hung crooked, and as she tried to straighten it, it came away in her hand.

Just then the person she was to see came in, and she flew down. She still held the engraving. The official turned out to be pleased that she had removed the picture of Earl Grey because, he said, it "will introduce you at once and be a guarantee of your good faith; you must take it with you."

The idea did not appeal to Mary Arnold-Forster. "Fancy having to carry this framed picture on my flight," she thought. However, she dutifully fastened it around her waist as best she could.

Right: Dr. William Dement gives a drink to
17-year-old Randy Gardner, who managed
to stay awake for 264 hours—a full 11 days.
He then slept for nearly 15 hours straight.

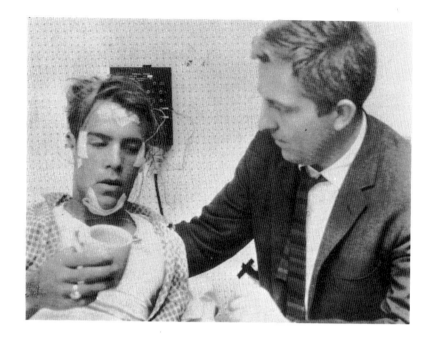

Below: *Sleep* by Salvador Dali. According
to the artist, the crutches supporting the
head are symbolic of "psychic balance,"
which makes sleep possible. Knock one of
them away, he says, and the result would be
insomnia.

cooking. I got absolutely burned up, and walked out of the house.'"

Modern techniques enabled this dream sequence to be recorded, but if we seek its significance we must go back to the theories of Freud and Jung. A Freudian analyst would probe the dreamer's associations to the professor, the friend, the nurse, the mother, and the theme of meat eating, and would regard the dreams as fulfilling the secret wish of an inhibited man to give vent to his anger. A Jungian would regard the dreams as compensatory, as an experience that would serve to bring equilibrium to the psyche by giving expression to a neglected aspect of it. The point is that Freud and Jung have not been superseded by the modern developments in dream research. Laboratory experiments have not been in the area of dream interpretation or analysis, but in techniques for recording dreams immediately after they have occurred.

The new techniques have, however, brought in their wake several new theories about the purposes of dreams and the functioning of the brain during dreaming. Sleep cycles with alternating REM and non-REM periods have been observed in mammals. Psychologists, physiologists, and even computer experts have put forward suggestions as to why these regular alternations should occur.

Common to most of these theories is the idea that REM and non-REM sleep must serve different purposes. Dr. Ian Oswald of the University of Edinburgh has suggested that non-REM sleep assists the process of growth and renewal of body tissues, while REM sleep facilitates a similar process in the brain. During Stages 3 and 4 of the sleep cycle the glands pour growth hormone into the blood, and the work of repairing and renewing body tissue is accomplished. But this process halts abruptly with the beginning of REM sleep. Furthermore, a predominance of periods of REM sleep has been found in patients recovering from overdoses of drugs, and in premature babies in the weeks before the time they should have been born. This suggests that both repair of brain damage and the process of brain growth are functions that take place during REM sleep. This hypothesis is also supported by evidence that senile people and mental defectives, in whom brain functions are atrophied or curtailed, have

Tests in Sleep Deprivation

Below: sleep stages of the first recovery night after a subject had been deprived of dreams for more than two weeks. Most of the night was spent in REM sleep, as the subject apparently made up for the period of REM deprivation.

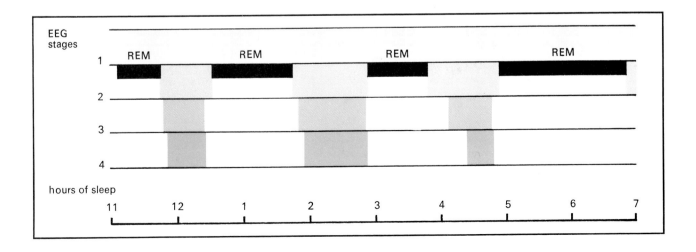

Dreams in the Laboratory

Right: Dr. Dement is shown recording the brain waves of a sleep-deprived cat. Cats make particularly good subjects for sleep research because they will sleep almost anywhere. Cats have been deprived of REM sleep for periods as long as 70 days, and it has been shown that they suffer definite personality changes: some become restless; others give up washing and sleep in their litter boxes. Deprived long enough of dreams, the cats die.

very little REM sleep. Furthermore, REM sleep increases when a person is in a situation that places great demands on learning abilities. For instance, a substantial increase was recorded in a group of subjects who, for the purpose of the experiment, had to learn to adjust to wearing glasses that made the world appear upside down. Such an accumulation of evidence lends strong support to Oswald's theory that REM sleep is essential to the health, growth, and performance of the brain.

Another theory that relates REM sleep and dreams to learning processes has been put forward by the British psychologist Dr. Christopher Evans. His theory involves a comparison between the functions of the brain and those of a computer. The brain and the computer perform similar operations in processing, storing, and retrieving information. An essential process in computer operations is the regular scanning and sorting of programs, and the rejection or "cleaning off" of information that is not needed for the task that the computer is currently engaged in. To effect this cleaning off process the computer is temporarily taken "off-

Far left: Dr. Ian Oswald questioning a subject wakened from REM sleep, with the EEG machine that has traced her sleep pattern.

Left: Dr. Christopher Evans, British dream researcher. He has developed a theory of dreams involving an analogy with computer function. He believes that dreaming represents the same kind of activity for the brain as "off-line" work on the computer, when programs are scanned and sorted, and those not required rejected.

Below: a painting of one of Dr. Evans' dreams. In it he was in his laboratory cafeteria, which was full of fish marvelously quick-frozen to allow study of the levels at which the fish were swimming. As is often possible, Evans could identify some trivial elements of the previous day: eating fish for lunch in the cafeteria, cleaning his home fish tank and watching the fish descend as he siphoned out the water, and seeing a TV ad for frozen fish sticks.

line"—that is, all its other functions are suspended. Evans suggests that a similar process takes place in the brain, that sleep is the brain's "off-line period," and that dreams serve the purpose of scanning and sorting all the impressions and memories accumulated in the course of the day and of rejecting those that are useless. This useless information may not be totally rejected but, as it were, relegated to a strange area in the brain and sealed off. In this way the main channels of the brain are left uncluttered and essential programs can function with maximum speed and efficiency.

The essential programs in the human brain are those that control basic routines: walking, eating, driving a car, doing simple jobs. More complex programs control decision making, patterns

of social and sexual relations, and the formulation of ideas and attitudes. As the programs become more complex they have to be more adaptable to changed circumstances, and more able to assimilate new material. Dreaming, according to the Evans theory, enables the brain to perform this daily task of adaptation, assimilation, and rejection by a computerlike process of updating the programs to ensure that the organism is competent to deal with the demands and challenges of changed situations in the waking world. When the cleaning off process is neglected or delayed in a computer, functional breakdowns and loss of speed and efficiency of operation occur. REM sleep deprivation experiments have shown that similar breakdowns and impairments occur in human beings who are prevented from dreaming.

Common characteristics of dreams that seem to support the comparison with computers are the elusiveness of dreams and their tendency to be composed of trivia. If the purpose of the process is to reject the unnecessary surplus of the day's experiences, it is to be expected that dreams would be quickly forgotten. And since the surplus will be the leftovers of the day's trivial, pointless experiences, it is not surprising that most dreams are apparently nonsensical.

Not all dreams are nonsensical, however, any more than all dreams are sexually symbolic. In a passage attacking critics of his theories, Freud wrote that the theories must be true "otherwise—and this seems highly improbable—there would have to be two quite different kinds of dreaming, one of which has come only under *my* observation and the other only under that of the earlier authorities." But what seemed to Freud "highly improbable" is known today to be true. There are many kinds of dreaming, not just two. Any dream theorist is likely to be able to find evidence for his theory without much difficulty. This is not to disparage theory or the theorist. Every theory casts a little more light on the world of dreams, though there are still some dreams that can't be explained in terms of any present theory. These are the dreams that enable the dreamer to transcend the limitations of time and space, and to gain information not available through normal channels. Discovering the secret behind these paranormal dreams is the remaining great challenge for explorers of the dreaming mind.

The Evans Theory

Left: a painting of one of his dreams by Swiss artist Erhard Jacoby. The sign is a normal European roadsign that indicates animals may be crossing. But in a muddled association of ideas common in dreams, the animals are too wildly fantastic to be seen on a road in Europe—they even include a brontosaurus.

Chapter 13
Dream Clairvoyance
and Telepathy

From what most of us remember when we waken, our dreams are sometimes amusing, sometimes frightening jumbles of nonsense and fragmentary bits of experience. But what about those dreams in which the dreamer apparently obtains information which could not be acquired through any normal means? Is it possible for a woman to see a body underwater, half buried in mud, from four miles away? Can a sleeping boy see all the details of an accident happening hundreds of miles from his bed? Is it possible for experimenters to interrupt a dream with an image transferred telepathically? The evidence is here.

Bertha Huse left her home in the early morning of October 31, 1898, and disappeared. When the alarm was raised, 150 men from her home town of Enfield, Vermont, searched the woods and shores around nearby Muscova Lake. The only clue they had was a report from a woman that she had seen a young person who might have been Bertha on Shaker Bridge, which crossed the lake. But the first day's search was fruitless. On the second and third days a diver was brought in to search the lake, but he found no sign of Bertha either. A Mrs. Titus lived in a village some four miles away. During the evening of the second day of the search she dozed off in her rocking chair. When her husband woke her up she said, "George, why didn't you let me be? In the morning I could have told you where the girl lies and all about it." Later that night and during the following night her husband heard her talking about the missing girl in her sleep. Once she seemed to be giving instructions to a diver, saying, "She's not down there but over here to the left." When she awoke on the morning of the fourth day, she told her husband that she had seen where Bertha was, and that they must go to the bridge at Enfield.

A local mill owner who had sponsored the search was so impressed by Mrs. Titus' conviction that he called out the diver again. When Mrs. Titus led him to a spot on the bridge and said, "This looks like the place that I saw last night," the diver protested that he had already searched there. "No," said Mrs.

Opposite: the assassination of the Archduke Franz Ferdinand in Sarajevo in 1914. The grim event was foreseen in a dream by the Archduke's tutor, Bishop Joseph Lanyi, who tried vainly to get a message to his old pupil warning of danger.

The Precognitive Dream: Examples

Below: the battle of Borodino—a small village near Moscow—in 1812 when Napoleon's army was invading Russia. The Countess Toutschkoff dreamed three months earlier that her husband was killed in Borodino. Anxiously searching maps when she awoke, she was immensely relieved to find no such name anywhere. But on September 7, the two armies locked in combat in the tiny town—so insignificant that no one had considered it worth putting on the map. General Toutschkoff was among the dead.

Titus, pointing to two other spots, "you have been down there and there, but not *there*. She is head down in the mud, one foot sticking up and a new rubber on it." The diver reluctantly went down at the spot she indicated. A crowd of villagers watched and waited. After about a minute a woman's hat bobbed to the surface. The anxious crowd surged forward to the rail and nearly knocked the diver's assistant off the bridge. When the diver surfaced some time later, he reported that he had found the body in exactly the position that Mrs. Titus had described.

The diver later reported how he had felt when, in the murky water 18 feet below the surface of the lake, he had first laid his hand upon the corpse. "I stopped short where I was," he said, "It is my business to recover bodies in the water and I am not afraid of them, but in this instance I was afraid of the woman on the bridge. I thought to myself, 'How can any woman come from four miles away and tell me or any other man where I would find the body?'" The psychologist William James, who investigated the case and interviewed and obtained signed statements from all the people involved, could not answer that question. He was as puzzled as the diver, but he committed himself to the statement that "the Titus case . . . is a decidedly solid document in favor of the admission of the supernormal faculty of seership."

"Seership," generally called clairvoyance, is a phenomenon often associated with dreams. There are many recorded cases of people apparently obtaining through dreams information they could not have obtained through any normal means. A skeptic

may be able to think up arguments that cast doubt on the authenticity of any individual case. But when the mass of evidence from many different sources is reviewed, it is difficult to avoid the conclusion that some minds possess a faculty for "seeing" objects and events paranormally, and that this faculty sometimes operates through dreams.

Another well-known tale of dream clairvoyance that solved a mystery is the Red Barn Murder case. In 1827 Maria Marten ran away from her village in Suffolk, England with William Corder, a farmer. Corder got involved with another woman, murdered Maria, and buried her under the floor of a barn. He wrote to the girl's parents, saying that he and Maria were married and keeping well, and for a year nobody had reason to suspect the crime. Then one night Maria's mother had a dream in which she saw the murder and the burial. The experience was so vivid, unexpected, and alarming that her husband decided to investigate. He found the barn that his wife had seen in her dream, broke up the floor, and discovered the decayed body of his daughter in a sack. Corder was arrested, confessed to the crime in prison, and was executed.

Fortunately, most clairvoyant dreams are not so gruesome, and some are even beneficial. If it had not been for a dream of the son of the poet Dante, one of the supreme works of world literature, the *Divine Comedy*, might have remained incomplete forever.

After Dante's death, his friends, followers, and family searched for months for the concluding cantos of the *Paradiso*, the last part of the *Divine Comedy*, but to no avail. They decided that he must not have had time to complete his great work. His two sons Jacopo and Piero, who were poets in a modest way, were persuaded by friends to try to complete the poem. Then one night Jacopo had a dream which, according to another great poet, Boccaccio, "not only induced him to abandon such presumptuous folly but showed him where the 13 cantos were which were wanting to the *Divine Commedia*." Jacopo awoke from his dream, and in the middle of the night rushed to the home of an old friend of his father's, Pier Giardino. In his dream, said Jacopo, his father had taken him by the hand, led him to a room in a house where they had lived and, touching one of the walls, had said, "What you have sought for so much is here." Jacopo's story so excited Giardino that he immediately dressed, and the two went to the house where Dante had died. They roused its owner even though it was still before dawn, and went to the room Jacopo had seen in his dream. There they found a small mat on the wall at the point where the dream-apparition had indicated. Lifting it, they discovered a window alcove in which lay some papers, moldy from the damp. When they were cleaned, these papers turned out to be the 13 missing cantos of the *Divine Comedy*.

Skeptics who seek to explain away dream clairvoyance tend to rest their case on one of two main arguments: the possibility of coincidence, or the probability that the unconscious contains more knowledge and is much more perceptive than we normally suppose. One of the basic principles of Western philosophy is that it is a profitless and futile exercise to multiply hypotheses.

Bismarck's Dream

Bismarck, the Prussian statesman who unified the German states into an empire, fought three major wars to achieve his goal of unification. He became the chancellor of the German empire after the third of these, and King Frederick William IV of Prussia became Emperor Wilhelm I of Germany. Bismarck tells about one of his premonitory dreams of eventual victory in his book *Thoughts and Memories*.

In the dream he was riding on a narrow path in the Alps. On the right was a precipice, and on the left was smooth rock. The path got so narrow that his horse refused to go forward any further. Bismarck could neither dismount nor turn around in the space.

In this moment of trial, Bismarck struck the mountainside with his whip, and called upon God. Miraculously, the whip grew in length without end, and the "rocky wall dropped like a piece of stage scenery." A broad path opened out, giving a view of hills and forests that looked like the landscape of Bohemia. Prussian troops carrying banners dotted the area. They appeared to be victors of a bloody battle.

Three years later Bismarck was at war with Austria, and his troops marched through Bohemia on the way. They won—as in his dream.

A Severed Head

"I dreamed that I had in my hands a small paper with an order printed in red ink, for the execution of the bearer, a woman . . . The woman appeared to have voluntarily brought the order, and she expressed herself as willing to die, if only I would hold her *hand*."

The dreamer, Dr. Walter Franklin Prince, was an American psychical researcher. In his own account of his dream he wrote that the woman was "slender of the willowy type, had blonde hair, small girlish features, and was rather pretty. She sat down to die without any appearance of reluctance. . . .

"Then the light went out and it was dark. I could not tell how she was put to death, but soon I felt her hand grip mine . . . and knew that the deed was being done. Then I felt one *hand* (of mine) on the hair of her head, which was loose and severed from the body, and felt the moisture of blood. Then the fingers of my other *hand* were caught in her teeth, and the mouth opened and shut several times as the teeth refastened on my *hand*, and I was filled with the horror of the thought of a severed but living head."

On the night after Dr. Prince had his harrowing nightmare, a young mentally disturbed woman left her home on Long Island to pay a visit to her sister. The police later found her body near a Long Island railroad station. Her head had been cut off by a train. Near the body lay a note in which the woman stated that she was seeking decapitation in order to prove a theory that her body and head could live independently of each other. Her name was Sarah *Hand*.

On investigation Dr. Prince learned that Sarah Hand, like the woman in his dream, was pretty, slender, and fair.

According to this principle, the interests of knowledge are best served when, confronted with a problem, we settle for the solution that does least violence to reason. In the case of apparently clairvoyant dreams, the principle would hold that coincidence, unconscious reasoning or knowledge, or even cynical lying or fraud, would be more acceptable explanations than clairvoyance. Yet sometimes these acceptable explanations are even more unlikely than the paranormal explanation. The Titus case offers fairly sound evidence for the paranormal hypothesis. Moreover it was investigated by William James, the leading psychologist of his age. He was a researcher of unimpeachable integrity, well aware of all the arguments and alternative explanations that the skeptics could muster.

Another strong case for dream clairvoyance is related in William Oliver Stevens' book *The Mystery of Dreams*. The testimony here is first-hand from the author's son.

The young man was late to breakfast one morning and did not respond to a call, so his mother went to his room to see what was wrong. She found him "sitting up in bed, his eyes staring with the air of being shaken by some horror that he had just witnessed." He said he had had a "terrible" dream, unlike any that he had ever had before. In it he had seemed to be in the air about 20 feet above a car traveling along a dirt road. A young man and a young woman were in the car, which suddenly swerved off the road to the left and crashed into a tall pole. The man, who was tall and thin and looked "like a foreigner," got out of the car clutching his stomach. He lay down on the grass and tried to smoke a cigarette, but apparently was in too great pain because the cigarette dropped from his mouth. The dreamer's attention was focused on the man, but he was aware of the girl standing by and knew that she wasn't badly hurt. When he saw the man exhale a puff of vapor he thought of tales he had heard about the soul being seen to leave the body at the moment of death. Although he realized that the exhalation was probably only cigarette smoke, he knew for certain that the man was doomed.

The Stevens family was then staying in their summer home on Nantucket Island. They had no radio contact with the mainland, but did receive the daily newspaper every afternoon. On this particular day the paper's front page had a photograph of a dark-haired man, whom Stevens' son immediately recognized as the man he had seen in his dream. The accompanying report related the circumstances of the death of the Count of Covadonga, former heir to the Spanish throne, in an automobile accident in Florida. The Count had been in the company of a young woman, a cigarette seller in a Miami night club. She had suffered only bruises in the accident. She said that the steering had failed when she swerved to avoid a truck, and that the car had gone off the road on the left side and struck a pole. The Count had been severely injured, but might have survived if his bleeding could have been staunched at the time. He later died in the hospital of haemophilia, and the woman was charged with manslaughter.

The correspondences between the dream and the external event in this case are obvious. One interesting difference was

The Mystery of Precognition

Left: the automobile in which Spanish ex-crown prince Count Covadonga was killed in Florida in 1938. Early that morning a young boy on Nantucket Island dreamed of the crash, apparently seeing the accident almost as it happened over 1000 miles away.

Below: the Swiss scientist Louis Agassiz trying to work out the structure of a fossil fish. He had a recurrent dream in which he saw the complete fish. The third time, still half-asleep, he copied down what he saw in the dream. The next day, he compared it with the fish, and classified it easily.

that the truck claimed to have caused the accident did not appear in the dream.

There are many recorded cases of telepathy—direct mind-to-mind communication—in dreams. One of the earliest was written down by Saint Augustine, a man who was disinclined to believe in any marvel that was not demonstrably the work of God. Here is Augustine's account of the story.

"A certain gentleman named Prestantius had been entreating a philosopher to solve him a doubt, which he absolutely refused to do. The night following, although Prestantius was broad awake, he saw the philosopher standing full before him, who just explained his doubts to him, and went away the moment after he had done. When Prestantius met this philosopher the next day, he asked him why, since no entreaties could prevail with him the day before to answer his question, he came unasked, and at an unseasonable time of night, and opened every point to his satisfaction. 'Upon my word it was not me that came to you; but in a dream I thought my own self that I was doing you such a service.'"

In this case, a kind of reciprocal telepathy seemed to be operating. The philosopher was aware, in his dream, of appearing to Prestantius, while the latter, while awake, experienced a tele-

Dream Telepathy in the Laboratory

Right: *The Descent from the Cross* by Max Beckman, which shows Christ as a brown and emaciated figure. This painting was one of the target pictures in a study of dream telepathy at the Maimonides Dream Laboratory. The researchers worked out a series of experiments in which a good telepathic subject would sleep while an agent tried to transmit ideas and images selected for him by the research team, and handed out in a random pattern.

pathic apparition of the philosopher. In other cases, the telepathic link occurs when both parties are asleep and dreaming. One such case of reciprocal dreaming occurred between two friends in Elmira, New York in 1892.

Dr. Adele Gleason dreamed that she was in a deserted spot in the midst of very dark woods. She was suddenly terribly afraid that a man she knew well might arrive unexpectedly and shake the tree next to her, causing the leaves to fall and burst into flames. Dr. Gleason awoke and wrote down the time of her dream and the initials of John R. Joslyn, the friend who had appeared in it. When she met Joslyn some days later she said, "I had a strange dream on Tuesday night." He replied that he had also had a strange dream that night and had written it down on awakening. "Let me tell you mine first," he said, and he proceeded to describe the identical dream from a different angle.

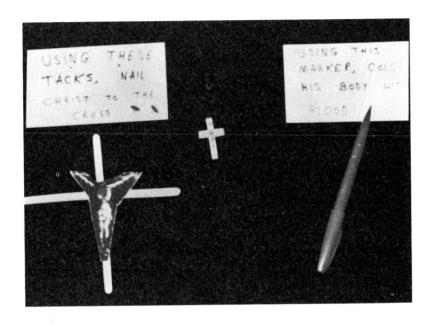

USING THESE TACKS, NAIL CHRIST TO THE CROSS

USING THIS MARKER, COLO HIS BODY WIT BLOOD

Left: for the particular series of experiments at the Maimonides Dream Laboratory, there was a box of multisensory material to intensify the agent's emotional involvement. These are the box contents for the Beckman picture shown opposite. The subject dreamed of a birthday party attended by an old emaciated Churchill, and a native ceremonial sacrifice. A dark-skinned chief was like a "totem pole god." The dream was given a very high correspondence rating to the target, including as it did the theme of sacrifice and rebirth (the birthday party) and the image of Churchill, the leader of his people, as emaciated as the figure in the target painting.

His written account of the dream was as follows: "I dreamed that I was walking at night in a remote spot where I sometimes go shooting. Soon I saw in the bushes, about 12 yards from the road, one of my women friends apparently paralyzed with fear of something that I did not see, rooted to the spot by the feeling of imminent danger. I came to her and shook the bush, upon which the leaves that fell from it burst into flames." The two dreams had occurred at the same time.

A Freudian analyst would no doubt revel in the symbolic significance of *tree* and *flames* and discover disguised sexual desire in the shared dream, but he would be at a loss to explain how the dreams could occur at the same time and contain the same strange imagery. The case seems a clear demonstration of the possibility of communication between minds in sleep independently of any channel of sense.

Such startling cases of shared dreams are fairly rare in the records of dream research, though they may occur more often than we know. People generally don't make a point of telling their dreams to the people who have figured in them. In any case these dreams, like others, are often forgotten by the time the dreamer wakes up.

People undergoing psychoanalysis often dream about their analyst—sometimes as himself, sometimes disguised as another person. This is not surprising because in the course of analysis a close relationship builds up between the two people. What has surprised some analysts is the occasional dream in which a patient somehow zeroes in on the analyst's own thoughts or on an event in the analyst's life of which the patient could not possibly be aware. In the book *Dream Telepathy*, which he co-authored with Dr. Stanley Krippner and Alan Vaughan, Dr. Montague Ullman describes several cases of telepathy between analyst and patient. One such case, which he calls the "Chromium Soap Dish Caper," involved Ullman himself.

The patient was a salesman for children's clothes. The book quoted him as follows: " 'I was wrapping up a few of the samples that had been on exhibit and was preparing to leave. Someone gave me, or I took, a chromium soap dish. I held it in my hand and I offered it to him. He took it. I was surprised. I asked him, are you a collector, too? Then I sort of smirked and said, knowingly, well, you're building a house. He blushed. He smirked and kept on smoking his cigar.'"

This trivial dream had little apparent meaning for the patient, but it did mean something to the doctor. On the day of the patient's dream, Ullman had been telling a friend about work he was having done on his house to correct a defect in the original structure. Although Ullman did not mention it to his friend, he was at the time thinking of an incident involving a chromium soap dish. This object was lying unused in the basement, and was spotted by one of the workmen. Ullman explained that it had been delivered by mistake during the building of the house a year and a half earlier. Annoyed by the rising costs of building his home, he had simply kept the dish "in a spirit of belligerent dishonesty." When the workman made a crack about his having gotten away with it, Ullman had been slightly embarrassed and had, he wrote, "managed a sheepish smirk."

The patient, it seemed, had unconsciously discovered a way to

Right: H. Rider Haggard had a vivid dream of his dog's death—in particular that the dying dog was trying desperately to speak to him, or at the very least communicate that it was dying. The next day it was discovered that the dog was killed by a train at just about the time of Haggard's dream about the animal.

strike back at the analyst, whose intrusions into his own psyche he resented. But apart from its analytic significance, the dream demonstrates the extreme subtlety of the telepathic process. Although there existed a strong relationship between the two minds, the subject matter that was transmitted was extremely trivial. This was no life-and-death matter, or even an emotionally charged event—unless Dr. Ullman was more affected by the discovery of his dishonesty than he admitted. In fact, the sender of this particular telepathic message seems to have played a relatively passive role. Instead, in some mysterious way the patient's mind apparently established contact with the mind of his analyst and ferreted out a fragment of thought that—although insignificant in itself—gratified his own subconscious wishes to get a step ahead of the analyst.

If the subtlety of such human-to-human telepathy is surprising, even more surprising is telepathic communication between human and animal. The novelist Rider Haggard had a dream in which he believed that he received a crisis telepathic communication from his dog. In his dream he saw the dog lying on its side in rough growth on the edge of water. It was clearly in pain and seemed to be struggling to speak to him. "My own personality," Rider Haggard wrote, "in some mysterious way seemed to me to be rising from the body of the dog, which I knew quite surely to be Bob and no other . . . In my vision the dog was trying to speak to me in words, and, failing, transmitted to my mind in an unidentified fashion the knowledge that it was dying. Then everything vanished and I woke to hear my wife asking why on earth I was making those horrible and weird noises."

The next day he told his dream to five others at the breakfast table. In the afternoon it was discovered that the dog was missing. They all remembered the dream, and a search was organized. Four days later the body of the dog was found against the weir in a nearby river. Inquiries among local people produced the information that a dog had been hit by a train crossing a bridge over the river at 11 o'clock the previous Saturday night. Signs of the accident—some blood and a broken dog collar identified as Bob's—were found on the bridge. It appeared that the dog had for a time lain in the reeds along the river bank, and had later been carried downstream by the current. It was not possible to ascertain the precise moment of death, but it could well have coincided with Rider Haggard's dream, which occurred at one o'clock in the morning about two hours after the accident. Reflecting on the implications of this domestic tragedy, the novelist wrote: "Of the remarkable issues opened by this occurrence I cannot venture to speak further than to say that . . . it does seem to suggest that there is a more intimate ghostly connection between all members of the animal world, including men, than has hitherto been believed, at any rate by Western peoples; that they may be, in short, all of them different manifestations of some central, informing life, though inhabiting the universe in such various shapes."

Statements like this greatly annoy the rational and scientific. Moreover, most scientists are even reluctant to accept spontaneous cases of clairvoyance and telepathy as evidence that these phenomena exist. If such phenomena exist, they argue,

Telepathy from Dog to Master?

Below: Dr. Wilfrid Daim, a well-knowm psychologist from Vienna. He first developed a method of controlled experimentation to study the phenomenon of dream telepathy, using modern techniques for monitoring sleep and dreams. During the 1940s he pioneered methods of using target symbols transmitted by an agent to a sleeping subject, who were on occasion separated by as much as four miles during the tests.

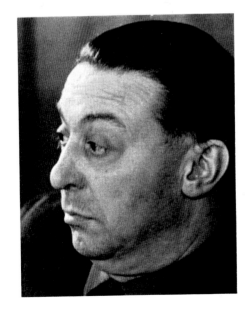

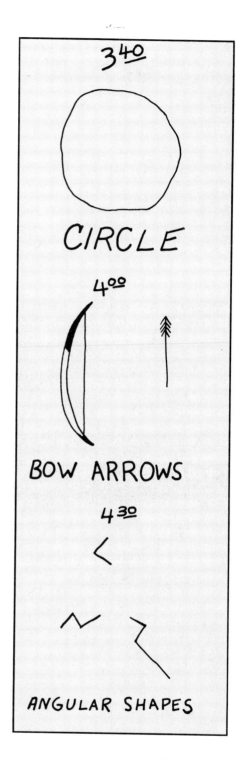

Above: some of the symbols used during the experiments with dream telepathy at the Maimonides Medical Center in New York. The times indicated are those when the symbols were transmitted by the agent to the sleeping subject.

they should be capable of being studied under controlled conditions, and of being produced at will. However, telepathy and clairvoyance appear to depend either on a strong personal attachment between the receiver of the message and the sender, on the intrinsic importance of the material conveyed, or on a combination of these two factors. So it does not seem likely that their occurrence in dreams can be regulated and observed in any systematic way. In recent years, however, the situation has changed. Controlled experiments in dream telepathy have been carried out that satisfy exacting standards of scientific proof. These experiments make use of sophisticated modern techniques for monitoring sleep and dreams, and they have received a good deal of publicity. The credit for devising and first putting into practice the basic method such experiments employ belongs to a Viennese psychologist, Dr. Wilfrid Daim. In the 1940s he independently conducted a series of experiments which he reported in the February 1949 issue of the *Parapsychological Bulletin* of Duke University.

Daim conducted his experiments in the early morning hours and participated in them himself, sometimes as sender and sometimes as receiver. The material to be transmitted was a colored geometric shape, selected at random from a pile of envelopes containing various colored shapes. The sender concentrated on the image with the object of projecting it into the dream consciousness of the receiver. Sender and receiver were sometimes located as far as four miles apart. On one occasion Daim concentrated on a red equilateral triangle on a black background. After a few minutes of concentration, he felt that he had been successful in transmitting the image, and he willed the receiver to wake up. The time he began the experiment was 6:30 a.m.

The receiver later reported that he had awakened at 6:35 a.m. He remembered a dream involving music and soldiers. Suddenly, in the midst of the soldiers, appeared "a three-cornered, glaring-red fir tree . . . ." It "pushes through the whole . . . and remains unmoved for seconds amid all the former dream contents. It is not a fir tree out of nature but such a one as one finds in children's primers, the trunk is black, color distinct, while all the other dream contents are of a colorless gray." In other words, the shape of a red equilateral triangle with a black background interrupted his ongoing dream at the time Daim was attempting to project such a pattern.

Similar experiments were carried out in the 1960s by Dr. Ullman and his colleagues at the Maimonides Medical Center. Their domain at the Medical Center later became known as the "dream laboratory." With machines that could monitor mental activity during sleep, these researchers began a systematic large-scale series of experiments designed to test the hypothesis that information can be communicated to sleeping subjects by extrasensory means. The first experiments used simple geometric shapes as targets. For instance, at 4:30 a.m. on one occasion the experimenter drew three angular shapes as shown on this page. At 6:30 a.m. the subject was awakened from a REM sleep period. He reported a series of dream impressions in the course of which he said: "some people were standing around, and they had in their hands *canes* shaped like hockey sticks, used upside down, the curved part up. But they were shaped more like *free form* than plain hockey sticks." In another session the experimenter drew a circle, and this same subject again produced a report of dream activity that incorporated the image. "I had an image of a . . . it was sort of like being on a round, like the bottom half of a large tube, such as if you would be going into the Holland Tunnel or something . . . I was on a road shaped like the curve of a trough."

More complex target materials were used and thousands of dreams that contained significant correspondences with the targets were recorded by the Maimonides researchers. This extensive work, conducted for more than a decade, has established without doubt and to the satisfaction of many scientists that dream telepathy is a reality.

Testing Dream Telepathy Today

Below: Charles Honorton, one of the Maimonides researchers, concentrating on a reproduction of *Zapatistas* by the Mexican artist José Orozco. It was used as a target in some of the dream telepathy tests because, like most target pictures chosen, it is vivid, simple, and emotional.

Chapter 14
Dreaming the Future

Do dreams offer some sort of strange preview of the future? After terrible disasters, people often come forward with tales of terrifying dreams which foretold the event. In our ordinary view of time as a comfortable progression in which the future follows the present, it is difficult to account for these dreams in which the future is seen to unfold itself now. Do we perhaps have to alter our concept of what time is to explain the eerie phenomenon of an effect preceding the cause in an upside down world in which the sequence of time seems to be mysteriously confused?

On Friday October 21, 1966 the people of Britain were stunned by news of an appalling tragedy. At 9:15 that morning in the little Welsh mining village of Aberfan, a mountain of coal waste had avalanched and buried the school. The waste weighed half a million tons, and had been loosened by two days of heavy rain. More than 140 people, most of them children who had just assembled for classes, died under the black landslide.

One of the children who died, nine-year-old Eryl Mai Jones, had told her mother the day before that she had dreamed she had gone to school "and there was no school there. Something black had come down all over it." During that night of the 19th when Eryl Mai had her dream, and also during the night of the 20th, several other people in various parts of England had disturbing dreams that seemed to contain premonitions of the disaster. One woman dreamed of a mountain flowing downward and a child running and screaming. Another saw a screaming child in a telephone booth and another child being followed by a "black billowing mass." A third saw in her dream a school and children dressed in Welsh national costume ascending to heaven. An elderly man dreamed of the word ABERFAN spelled out in bright light, though at the time he didn't know of the existence of the Welsh village and the word meant nothing to him.

After the tragedy, the press launched a survey to gather information on premonitions of the disaster. It revealed that many other people had had apparent dream premonitions of the

Opposite: the village of Aberfan, Wales, after a mountain of coal waste had buried part of it in 1966. Numerous precognitive dreams of the disaster were reported, including one in which a man who had never heard of the village saw the word "Aberfan" spelled out. Another person saw black horses drawing hearses down a hill in a dream, and still another dreamed of screaming children buried under coal slag.

Above: the plane crash in which the former heavyweight world boxing champion Rocky Marciano died. A complete stranger, Thomas Casas, who lived in New York, dreamed three months earlier that he saw a Piper-type plane with a blue rudder and a number like "N 129 N, N 429 N, or N 29 N" nose into a crash. He registered his premonition with the Central Premonitions Registry, set up in New York after the Aberfan tragedy like the British Premonitions Board established in London.

event for a period of some two weeks before it happened. One woman had had a dream of "screaming children buried by an avalanche of coal in a mining village." Another dreamed of "hundreds of black horses thundering down a hillside dragging hearses." A young man in Kent woke on October 17 with a vague sense of approaching catastrophe that remained with him the rest of the week. He told a girl in his office that "On Friday something terrible connected with death is going to happen." A Mr. Alexander Venn told his wife the same thing. He found that for days his thoughts kept turning to the subject of coal dust, and he drew a sketch of a head surrounded by a black cloud. A psychic in Plymouth, Mrs. Milden, had a precise trance vision of the tragedy the day before it happened. She saw a schoolhouse in a valley and an avalanche of coal pouring down a mountainside. At the bottom of the mountain people were digging in the slag for bodies. One of the workers wore a strange peaked cap, and there was a terrified little boy whose hair was cut in long bangs standing by. Watching a television report of rescue operations three days later, Mrs. Milden saw the very scene she had previewed, including the man with the strange cap and the boy with bangs.

A London psychiatrist, Dr. J. C. Barker, conducted the post-tragedy survey. He rejected many of the premonitions reported as too vague or inadequately substantiated, but he found 60 that satisfied him as being authentic and relevant. Of these, 36 were dream premonitions. Barker concluded that the question of whether or not precognitive dreams occurred required no further proof, and said that it was time an attempt was made to employ this strange human faculty to prevent future disasters. He suggested that people send their premonitions in to a central clearing house where a computer would be used to detect peaks or patterns in the flow of information. In this way an early warning system might be devised that could avert or minimize the effects of another misfortune like Aberfan. As a result of Dr. Barker's initiative, the British Premonitions Bureau was set up in London in 1967 and the Central Premonitions Registry in New York the following year. The existence of these bureaus is not yet widely enough known to attract the flood of information that Dr. Barker envisaged. They do, however, have on their files many impressive records of premonitions that have been fulfilled in recent years. The practical application of the erratic human faculty for seeing the future in dreams and visions may one day come about, especially as more evidence for the existence of this faculty accumulates.

There is no lack of such evidence from the past, most of it concerning premonitions of disaster for someone closely connected with the dreamer. Such a case is related in the biography of Nicholas Wotton, English Ambassador to France in the reign of Mary Tudor. He dreamed that his nephew, Thomas Wotton, "was inclined to be a party in such a project as, if he were not suddenly prevented would turn both to the loss of his life, and ruin of his family." According to his biographer, Wotton "did well know that common dreams are but a senseless paraphrase

Can We Really Dream the Future?

Left: Robert D. Nelson, who is the director of the Central Premonitions Registry. With a background of psychology and interest in the paranormal, Nelson is now a newspaperman.

Above: pictures of the baby son of airman hero Charles Lindbergh from a home movie. A few days after the boy was kidnapped in 1932, two Harvard researchers made a newspaper appeal for premonitory dreams about the event. About 1300 people in the United States and Canada responded before the baby's murdered body was found naked in a ditch. Only seven of the reported dreams involved the critical elements of death, nakedness, and a ditch.

on our waking thoughts, or of the business of the day past, or are the result of our over-engaged affection, when we betake ourselves to rest." However, when he had the same dream the following night, Wotton decided that this might not belong to the category of common dreams, and resolved to do something about it. Acting with all the cunning typical of a 16th-century diplomat, he wrote to the Queen and requested her to send for his nephew, have him interrogated, charge him with some minor offense, and commit him "into a favorable prison." He added that he would explain his reasons when he "should next become so happy as to see and speak to her Majesty." While young Thomas Wotton languished in prison as arranged, a plot to overthrow the Queen was discovered. Several of the plotters, known to be close friends of Wotton's nephew, were executed. When Nicholas Wotton visited his nephew some time later, Thomas admitted that he had known about the plot and would have been involved in it if his relative "had not so happily dreamed him into a prison."

Nicholas Wotton could easily have had some idea of his nephew's political persuasions, in which case the dream could have been a message from his unconscious rather than a paranormal glimpse of the future. But the same cannot be said of the precognitive dream that the writer Mark Twain told his biographer Albert Paine.

At the time of this experience Mark Twain had not yet adopted his pen name and was plain Sam Clemens, aged 23, working as an apprentice pilot on the Mississippi steamboat Pennsylvania. His 20-year-old brother Henry worked on the same boat as a clerk. One night Sam had a vivid dream vision of a metal coffin resting on two chairs. In it lay the body of his brother, and on his chest lay a bouquet of white flowers with a crimson one in the middle. Sam was staying in his sister's house in St. Louis at the time, and in the morning he told her about the dream. Then he put it out of his mind.

Some days later there was a fracas between Sam and the chief pilot on the Pennsylvania. This resulted in Sam's being transferred to the Lacey, which was following the Pennsylvania up river two days behind. Henry remained with the Pennsylvania. Several days later, when the Lacey landed at the town of Greenville, Mississippi, Sam learned that the Pennsylvania had blown up just before reaching Memphis, with the loss of 150 lives. He learned to his relief that his brother was not among the dead, though he was among those who had been severely scalded in the accident. When Sam arrived in Memphis, he found Henry lying unconscious in an improvised hospital with about 30 other critical cases. He stayed by him day and night, scarcely sleeping, and when Henry died on the sixth night after the accident, Sam fell into a long and heavy sleep of exhaustion. On waking he went to find his brother's body. He found it lying in a metal coffin which rested on two chairs. The scene was exactly like his dream vision, with one detail lacking. But while Sam was standing there gazing at his brother's body an elderly lady came into the room and placed on Henry's breast a bouquet of white flowers with a crimson rose in the middle. With this act, Sam's dream had come true to the last detail.

In the records of precognitive dreams death is the most recurrent theme. Many of these cases might dispose us to believe, with Prince Hamlet, that "There's a divinity that shapes our ends, Rough-hew them how we will." Such was the case of Robert Morris, a distinguished 18th-century American. He dreamed one night that he would be killed during the firing of a salute in his honor from a foreign ship. Morris was due to attend such a ceremony the following day, so this could have been an anxiety dream. He was so worried that he tried to have the salute called off, but the captain of the ship told him that to do so would upset his crew. Morris agreed to go ahead on condition that the firing of the salute be delayed until he was out of range of the guns. The captain said he would accompany Morris from the ship and himself raise his hand as the signal to the gunners when they were a good distance away. When Morris and the captain were rowed away from the ship toward the shore, the captain inadvertently raised his hand to brush a fly off his nose, before they got clear of the guns. The gunners thought this was the signal to fire the salvo, and they did so. Morris was wounded in the arm, the wound became infected, and he died some days later. He had been unable to avoid the fate of which he had dreamed.

A sailor whom the 19th-century English writer George Borrow met during a voyage to Lisbon didn't have any time to

Examining the Evidence

Below: the sinking of the *Titanic* on April 14, 1912. The ship was considered unsinkable, and therefore equipped with few lifeboats. This contributed to the heavy loss of life when the great ship struck an iceberg and sank. Survivors spoke of a sense of doom, which is not uncommon in hindsight, but there were several dreams in which the disaster was foreseen. In one of them, a young woman saw her mother in a crowded lifeboat that was in danger of capsizing. This was before she knew either of the sinking of the *Titanic*, or of her mother's presence on board in a surprise move to visit her. Later she learned that the scene had occurred just as she had seen it in her dream.

make plans to cheat fate. One day during a rough sea Borrow was standing on the forecastle of the ship talking to two sailors, one of whom had just come up on deck. This sailor told the writer that he had just dreamed that he fell into the sea from the cross-trees (poles attached to the mast). "A moment after," wrote Borrow, "the captain of the vessel, perceiving the squall was increasing, ordered the top sails to be taken in, whereupon this man with several others ran aloft; the yard was in the act of being hauled down, when a sudden gust of wind whirled it with violence, and a man was struck down from the cross-trees into the sea, which was working like yeast below. In a few moments he emerged; I saw his head on the crest of a billow, and instantaneously recognized in the unfortunate man the sailor who, a few moments before, had related his dream. I shall never forget the look of agony he cast whilst the steamer hurried past him." An attempt was made to rescue the sailor, but the sea was too rough and he drowned.

Dreams that come true are not always so dramatic. Dreams of disasters that subsequently occur are for obvious reasons more likely to be remembered and recorded than dreams of trivial events that later materialize. But foresights of commonplace matters are in a way more mysterious, for they are not associated with anxiety, memory, or any identifiable contents of the dreamer's subconscious. They seem to be evidence of the mind's ability to sometimes make sudden and arbitrary jumps in time.

Frederick Greenwood, in an Appendix to his book *Imagination in Dreams*, tells the following story: "One night I dreamt that, making a call on some matter of business, I was shown into a fine great drawing-room and asked to wait. Accordingly, I went over to the fire-place in the usual English way, proposing to wait there. And there, after the same fashion, I lounged with my arm upon the mantel-piece; but only for a few moments. For feeling that my fingers had rested on something strangely cold, I looked, and saw that they lay on a dead hand: a woman's hand newly cut from the wrist. Though I woke in horror on the instant, this dream was quite forgotten—at any rate for the time—when I did next make a call on some unimportant matter of business, was shown into a pretty little room adorned with various knick-knacks, and was then asked to wait. Glancing by chance toward the mantel-piece (the dream of the previous night still forgotten), what should I see upon it than the hand of a mummy, broken from the wrist. It was a very little hand, and on it was a ring . . . Wherefore I concluded that it was a woman's hand."

Greenwood conceded that the similarity between the dream and the trivial event of the next day might have been pure coincidence. However he felt that it was an unsatisfactory explanation because severed hands on mantelpieces are rarely encountered either in dreams or in reality. He was frankly puzzled, and he might well have expressed his puzzlement in Kipling's words: "How, or why, had I been shown an unreleased roll of my life film?"

Behind this question there is an assumption about the nature of time that some philosophically inclined people who have thought about dream precognition consider to be wrong. The

The Face of Death

A foreboding dream saved Lord Dufferin ,who was once the British ambassador to France, from possible death.

His dream was related by Camille Flammarion, French astronomer and psychical researcher.

Lord Dufferin dreamed that he went to the window of his room and looked out, compelled to do so by an overpowering apprehension. On looking down he saw someone walking by and carrying something. The figure looked up, and Lord Dufferin saw a hideous face. At the same moment he realized that the figure was carrying a coffin.

Years later during his service as ambassador, Lord Dufferin attended a public dinner in Paris. A staff member led him to the elevator that would take him up to the dining room. When he saw the elevator operator's face, Lord Dufferin gasped in alarm. It was the face of his dream.

Instead of getting into the elevator, Lord Dufferin went away to try to find out the operator's name. He had not gone far when he heard a crash, followed by screams and moans. The elevator had fallen down the shaft. Everyone in it was killed or seriously injured. But the ambassador had been saved by his fear of the face he had seen in his dream.

assumption is that when people are born they enter a time continuum that unrolls like a film in one direction and at an even speed. According to this notion all events take place "in time." Our consciousness, fed with information by our senses, registers these events as they occur, and then files them away as memories. According to this view, we can have knowledge of time present and time past, but never of time future. For the person who finds this idea of time unsatisfactory and incompatible with experience, there are two alternative approaches. The first approach starts with the proposition, "time is not like that," and the second with the proposition, "consciousness is not like that."

Prominent among the "time is not like that" theories is J. W. Dunne's theory of "serial time." Dunne, an engineer, developed an interest in dreams and precognition after he had had a dream prevision of the eruption of Mount Pelée on Martinique in 1902. He believed that there was "some extraordinary fault" in his relation to reality, something, he wrote, "so uniquely wrong that it compelled me to perceive, at rare intervals, large blocks of otherwise perfectly normal personal experience displaced from their proper positions in time." Investigations led him to the conclusion that he was not unique in having these experiences of the displacement of events in time, and taking a lead from Einstein's relativity theory, he suggested that there was a dimension of reality in which space and time were compounded. Under certain circumstances events could be observed as occupying space, spread out so that parts of the past and future were accessible to consciousness as well as the present. This fourth dimension of space-time could not be penetrated by the conscious mind according to Dunne; but the unconscious

Dunne's Theory of "Serial Time"

Below: a scene from a 1955 British movie based on the experience of Air Marshal Sir Victor Goddard. The Air Marshal overheard someone telling about a dream of a plane crash—and the plane was the one Goddard was taking the next day from Shanghai to Tokyo. Goddard was relieved to find that the number of passengers was six instead of seven as in the possibly precognitive dream. But a seventh passenger turned up. The plane crashed too, but the passengers survived.

"Foreknowledge"

Right: the eruption of Mount Pelée on Martinique in 1902. J. W. Dunne, who wrote about precognitive dreams and time, dreamed about it beforehand. He also dreamed that 4000 people would be killed in the disaster. A newspaper story he saw later gave a figure of 40,000 dead. As the final figure turned out to be nothing like either 4000 or 40,000, Dunne might have foreseen not the disaster itself, but the newspaper account, which in his dream became vividly dramatized.

could on certain occasions, and particularly in dreams, temporarily enter it.

A theory of precognition starting from the "consciousness is not like that" approach was put forward by H. F. Saltmarsh in his book *Foreknowledge*. Observing that our experience of time at the level of conscious awareness is not uniform—that sometimes "time flies" and at other times "time drags"—Saltmarsh concluded that different kinds of time are accessible to different states of consciousness. In our normal state of consciousness we are ruled by clock time. We are living in what he called the "specious present," and the time we perceive is of short duration. But for our subconscious the "now," the present moment, is stretched out to a longer duration so that it includes a part of the future. This accords to an extent with everyone's experience of time. It also agrees with the recent discoveries of neuropsychologists regarding the functions of the two halves of the brain. They have found that the left hemisphere of the cortex processes information in a sequential, logical, linear manner, whereas the right hemisphere processes information simultaneously and has little conception of linear time. If the right

Below: Tippu Sahib, one of the fiercest opponents of the British in India in the 18th century. When at last he was defeated and killed in Seringapatam in 1799, the British found a book in which he had carefully recorded his dreams. It became clear that much of Tippu Sahib's military planning and strategy was the result of dream interpretation, and that he fully accepted the Muslim tradition that "the power of prophecy has passed away, yet revelation by dreams still remains."

hemisphere is damaged, perception of sequence is unaffected, but damage to the left hemisphere can disrupt such perception. These discoveries suggest that it is the right hemisphere of the brain that is involved in dreaming, and that combines information coming in from many sources—perhaps including the future—into a "patterned whole." It is the left hemisphere that arranges the dream material into a linear sequence.

This is but a brief sampling of the types of theories that redefine either the concept of time or the concept of consciousness. But none of these theories has been proved conclusively. In the meantime, more and more evidence accumulates to support the idea that dreaming the future is possible—however it operates.

The collection of the evidence on precognitive dreaming has generally been haphazard, but in recent years some researchers have taken a more systematic approach. Among these is the German parapsychologist Dr. Hans Bender of the University of Freiburg, who has produced two detailed studies of precognitive dreams. One of the studies is based on people's experiences during World War II. The other deals with the

Mrs Hellström's Dream

Eva Hellström, a Swedish physical researcher, once dreamed that she and her husband were flying over Stockholm and saw a traffic accident. She wrote the vivid dream down.

"I looked down and thought we were somewhere in the neighborhood of the Kungsträdgarden . . . I said to myself, 'The green [train] ran into [the tram] from the back . . . I saw an ordinary blue tram of the Number 4 type, and a green train . . . run into the tram."

Eva Hellström also made a sketch of the accident as it had appeared in her dream. At the time there were no green railroad cars in service. But when some months later a few green cars were introduced, she was sure her dream was accurate. She then wrote in her diary: "The accident will happen when the train from Djursholm [a suburb of Stockholm] and the Number 4 trolley meet at Valhallavägen [a Stockholm street.] This is a place where there have been accidents between autos and trains but so far as I know, *never with a trolley . . .*"

On March 4, 1956, nearly two years after her dream, a collision occurred at Valhallavägen between a Number 4 trolley and a green Djursholm train. The positions of the vehicles were exactly as in Mrs. Hellström's sketch.

Above: actress Christine Mylius, who has been sending details of her dreams—many of which are apparently precognitive—to the noted German parapsychologist Dr. Hans Bender for his study over the course of 20 years.

Right: sketch of an accident between a train and a streetcar as seen in the dream of Eva Hellström, a Swedish psychical researcher. Nearly two years later, the accident happened almost exactly as she had dreamed it.

remarkable dreams about her future that actress Christine Mylius recorded over a period of 20 years.

One of the strangest of Dr. Bender's World War II cases concerns a recurrent precognitive dream that was fulfilled 27 years after it was first dreamed. Two weeks after her son was born in 1919 a German mother had a vivid dream in which she saw herself walking along an unfamiliar beach looking for the child. She dug in the samd with her fingers knowing he was buried somewhere there. While dreaming she screamed so frantically that her husband tried to wake her. Before she was fully awake she shouted, "You must help me look for our Hans. He is lying by the sea under the sand." This nightmare was dismissed the first time, but it kept recurring. Over the years as her son grew up the mother dreamed over and over of desperately searching for his body among the sand dunes of an unfamiliar beach.

The war came, and the son served in the German army throughout. When it ended he was interned in a French prison camp, where he died in 1946. The mother's attempts to find out where he was buried finally brought a letter from two comrades who had been with him when he died. The letter informed her that "Hans' grave lies in the dunes near Fort Mahon, 800 meters from the sea."

Consistent precognitive dreamers are rare, but Dr. Bender discovered one in Christine Mylius. Over the years she has filed more than 2000 dreams with his Institute, and many of these have proved to be precognitive. In 1957 and 1958 she had a series of dreams that seemed to be pieces of a story involving the sea. In one she was swimming with several women and their babies. One of the babies swam beneath the water, and she feared it would drown. In another a cameraman was trying to

(Green carriage)

Grön vagn

(Ordinary blue tram)

vanlig blå spårvagn

Kan ij rita det.
(can't draw it)

film her as she swam but she told him, "It's not worth it." In a third she dreamed about a gigantic lobster being eaten at a party attended by many people. She sent these dream incidents in her report to Dr. Bender every two weeks, and then forgot them.

In 1959 Christine Mylius was engaged to play a part in the film *Night Fell upon Gotenhafen*. In the film a ship carrying refugee women and children was torpedoed in the Baltic, resulting in the loss of many lives. Her earlier dream of the drowned baby corresponded to a scene in the film in which she played a mother who lost her baby after the torpedoing. The dream about the cameraman in which she said, "It's not worth it," also came to mind during this film. It happened that after three exhausting takes of a scene in which she was filmed by an underwater camera as she sank beneath the surface, the particular scene was cut from the film. It had not been worth the effort. Finally, the dream of the party at which an immense lobster was the main dish came true during the filming. Some of the divers came up with a 12-pound lobster, and the cast and crew had a dinner of it. These and many other dream details relating to the film and its production were locked away in the Mylius file in Dr. Bender's Institute a year before the script was written and two years before the first scenes of the film were shot.

Another consistent precognitive dreamer is Mrs. Eva Hellström, founder of the Swedish Society for Psychical Research. One night in 1954 Eva Hellström had a vivid dream in which she and her husband Bo were flying over Stockholm. As she looked down on the streets and buildings, she suddenly saw a collision between a streetcar and a train.

When she awoke, Mrs. Hellström wrote down the details of her dream. She noticed the curious fact that, whereas all trains at that time were painted brown, the one in her dream had been green. She was certain nonetheless that the dream was genuinely precognitive because it had a realistic quality typical of previous dreams that had come true. She had her account witnessed, a measure she always took, and she included a sketch of the accident as she had seen it.

The following year several new green trains were brought into service. The year after that, an accident between one of these green cars and a Stockholm streetcar occurred exactly as Eva Hellström had predicted.

Scientists are never satisfied with descriptive evidence of paranormal phenomena, however well-authenticated they may be. But some carefully controlled experiments in recent years have brought dream precognition into the laboratory. At the Maimonides Medical Center, Dr. Montague Ullman and Dr. Stanley Krippner ran a series of tests in which the experimenter would concentrate on a picture to see if he could convey its content telepathically to the sleeping subject. The subject's dream would be recorded when he or she entered REM sleep. Many of the dreams contained elements from the target pictures. Occasionally, however, the researchers found that a subject would incorporate material that had similarities not with the target picture for that particular evening, but with one used on a later occasion. The Maimonides team carried out several series of experiments designed to test the English sensitive

Consistent Precognitive Dreaming

Below: Eva Hellström. Her dream about a traffic accident was precognitive.

Dreaming the Future to Order!

Opposite: Van Gogh's *Hospital Corridor at Saint Remy*, chosen as a target picture for the first experiment involving Malcolm Bessent, a British psychic, at the Maimonides Dream Laboratory. The multisensory experience had many elements of hospitalization and specifically mental illness. Four times during the night *before* this experience, Bessent dreamed of a mental hospital, and a patient trying to escape down a corridor toward an archway.

Below: the actress Mrs. Patrick Campbell. Late in her life when her fame had dimmed and she was sick, she was tenderly nursed by actress Sara Allgood. As thanks, she gave Miss Allgood a framed watercolor of a heron. She then went to France, and Miss Allgood went to Hollywood. There her first dream in a new house was of Mrs. Campbell, who asked her, "Have you found my gift from the grave? Look behind the picture." Behind the heron she found a Max Beerbohm caricature of Mrs. Campbell, worth $2000. She was puzzled because she thought Mrs. Campbell was still alive. She later found that she had died the day she had dreamed about her.

Malcolm Bessent for precognition. The procedure was a complex one, worked out to eliminate the possibility of any other form of extrasensory perception such as telepathy or clairvoyance.

The targets in these experiments were not known by anybody at the time Bessent recorded his dreams. They were determined on the following morning by a random method in which a key word was selected. The experimenters then devised a "special waking experience" based on the key word. The idea behind this was that the dreamer might more successfully foresee a future event if it had some potential impact on the emotions, as in spontaneous cases.

The first experiment was an unqualified success. Wired to an EEG that monitored his brain rhythms and eye movements, Bessent was awakened four times from dreams in which there occurred images of a mental hospital, a large concrete building, doctors and psychologists in white coats, and the theme of a female patient disguised as a doctor trying to escape down a corridor toward an archway. The dreams were all characterized by a general feeling of hostility.

Each of the dreams was recorded by the experimenter monitoring Bessent's sleep, and its contents kept secret. In the morning Dr. Krippner got the key word around which to construct the waking experience by an elaborate method that ensured randomness of selection. The word, one of 1200 possible ones, was "corridor." Guided by this, Krippner selected from his picture files Van Gogh's painting *Hospital Corridor at Saint Remy*. He and his assistants then worked out a multisensory experience to which they would subject Bessent.

When all was ready, two men dressed in white hospital uniforms entered Bessent's room, forced him into a tight-fitting jacket, and led him out into a darkened corridor. There he could hear the eerie music from the movie *Spellbound* and the sound of distant hysterical laughter. He was taken into a room where Krippner, seated at a desk, continued to laugh wildly, then made him swallow a pill and dabbed acetone on his face to "disinfect" him. On the wall was Van Gogh's painting, which seemed to Bessent to reproduce a scene from his dream. Then Dr. Krippner turned off the light and showed Bessent slides of weird drawings which he said had been done by mental patients. Throughout this whole performance Krippner had no idea how closely the little drama he had just devised corresponded with the themes and images that had occurred in Bessent's dreams some hours before. But when the dream records were compared with the special waking experience that had been devised around the key word "corridor," the correspondences were unmistakable. It seemed unlikely that such striking similarities could be mere coincidence. Moreover, similar patterns of close correspondence emerged in subsequent experiments with Malcolm Bessent. Incredibly, a repeatable laboratory experiment had been devised that upset one of the basic laws accepted by science and common sense: that effects cannot precede causes. Here was a man who could dream the future to order—and under the most ingeniously designed and strictly controlled conditions. Wouldn't the numerous tales of people who had dreamed of future events now have to be regarded in a new light?

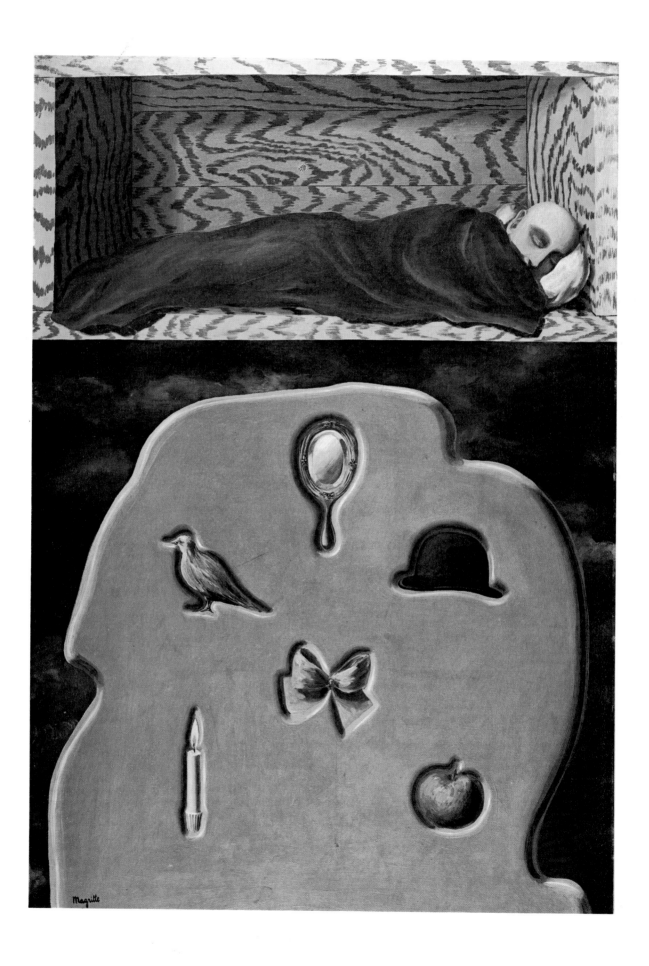

Chapter 15
Dream Interpretation Today

If dreams are, as Freud believed, the most direct way to understanding the subconscious, in which most of the trouble and unhappiness of his patients lay, then the interpretation of dreams is vitally important. But modern analytical practice suggests that understanding what the dream means is only part of the job. What else can we learn from dreams? How can understanding our dreams guide us to a fuller knowledge of ourselves and our needs and desires? In what directions are dream researchers going now in an attempt to use the dreaming mind to open the horizons for the waking self?

A quiet young schoolteacher named Jean sits among a group of people interested in what they call "dreamwork" and tells them about an overtly sexual dream she had had the previous night. She dreamed that she was in a car driven by a girlfriend. Her friend violated some traffic law, and was seen to do so by a state trooper. She stopped the car, but before the state trooper reached them, Jean changed places with her friend so that she was in the driver's seat. The trooper said nothing about the switch, but told the two that he would have to take them in. They followed him into a building in which there was a long table covered with papers. Several policemen were interviewing people at this table. Instead of interrogating them there as Jean expected, the trooper, who "was tall and had boots and the whole bit," took the girls into a plush office and seduced them. "I didn't care," Jean said, because it was "better than being arrested."

Any Freudian analyst would recognize this as a wish-fulfillment dream, a projection from the unconscious of repressed sexual desires. But what then? What do you do with such recognition? Traditional psychiatry holds that you need do nothing, that the recognition is enough, and that the dream itself has already served to channel off the potentially disruptive psychic forces by giving expression to them. But Jean is not undergoing psychoanalysis. She is participating in a Gestalt dreamwork seminar. Gestalt psychology takes its name from the German word meaning "figure" or "structure," and is mainly

Opposite: *The Reckless Sleeper* by René Magritte—a curious early work with an enigmatic sleeping figure and a group of objects, or perhaps dream images, embedded in a slab. The irrational juxtapositions and Freudian symbolism of some of the objects are obvious. And indeed the insights of Freud and Jung are still relevant to the modern understanding of dream symbols.

Gestalt Group Therapy Methods

concerned with perception, learning, and problem-solving. Gestalt therapy, which is related to Gestalt psychology, holds that dreams are pointers to "unfinished business" in the personality. They are a gift of material from the unconscious that the person can use to achieve a fuller personality integration, and a release of tied-up energies.

Gestalt dreamwork is done in a group so that the dreamer gets feedback from the rest of the group when he or she acts out situations suggested by the dream material. The session is conducted by a therapist, who doesn't so much interpret the dream as direct the dreamwork—somewhat like a theater director. "My function as a therapist," wrote the late Fritz Perls, who developed Gestalt therapy, "is to help you to the awareness of the here and now, and to frustrate you in any attempt to break out of this." The Freudian approach to dreams, he said, "barks up the wrong tree." It involves too much verbalizing and analyzing, which only serve to keep real experience at a distance. Even the physical setup for Freudian analysis, with the patient lying on a couch and the therapist seated out of sight behind him, creates an artificial situation. It emphasizes the therapist's possession of special knowledge and skills, and relegates the patient to the passive role of producing material for the therapist to analyze and interpret.

By contrast, Gestalt dreamwork creates a real-life situation in which the therapist, the subject, and a group of interested participants work together on the dream. "I believe," Perls said, "that in a dream we have a clear existential message of what's missing in our lives, what we avoid doing and living, and we have

Below: a Gestalt group therapy session with Dr. Frederick A. Perls in the chair at the right. In psychiatry dreams are an indispensable tool in enabling the psychiatrist first to see and then to help his patient come to terms with subconscious desires and fears repressed in a person's waking existence.

plenty of material to reassimilate and reopen the alienated parts of ourselves." The function of the Gestalt therapist in this dreamwork is to help the subject to stay with and work through the material presented in the dream.

When Jean had related her dream fantasy of being seduced by the state trooper, she confessed that she felt nervous. Her legs were trembling. "Stay with your nervousness," said the therapist, Jack Downing. "Exaggerate the trembling." Blushing, the young woman did as he said, exaggerating the trembling movements in her thighs and pelvic area. Asked what she was feeling in her genitals, she answered, "Warm." Downing then told her to put the state trooper in the empty chair opposite her and speak to him. This is standard Gestalt technique. Fragments of the dream material are isolated, brought into focus, and worked with by being acted out. "You're very imposing. And handsome," Jean told the imaginary state trooper. She then had to pretend to be him. "How do you feel?" Downing asked her. "Very self-assured and confident. Towering," Jean said. As herself again, she had to say to the empty chair, "You excite me," and she added, "I'm not afraid of you." Again in the role of the state trooper, she said, "You know I'm not going to hurt you, we're just going to have fun together. No trouble with the law."

By directing this little exchange between the characters in Jean's dream, Downing brought out her masculine side, which her unconscious had personified as the state trooper. He had made her aware of an element of aggressive sexuality in her nature which her upbringing and social conditioning had made her feel guilty about. She had therefore suppressed it. Her unconscious had cunningly absolved her from guilt by making her seducer the embodiment of the law.

This understanding was not the end of the dreamwork. The purpose of Gestalt therapy is to complete "unfinished business" in the personality. To do so in this case Downing decided to use a "bioenergetic" exercise "to help her melt her frozen sexual energy." Jean was instructed to lie on her back on the floor, draw up her knees, raise her bottom an inch or two and begin "belly breathing." "Allow each breath to go deeper until you feel the breathing all through your genitals," Downing told her. Following his directions Jean grew oblivious of the group watching her. She was led on to simulate the movements of sexual intercourse, and at the same time to moan and grunt. When he judged that her "frozen sexual assets" were unthawed, Downing told her to stop and asked, "How do you like your dream?" Jean answered, "I see why I wanted to be in the driver's seat when the trooper came." She was limp and happy after five orgasms.

After a dreamwork experience of this intensity, Downing says, most people report that they have changed for the better and that the change has a lasting effect on their lives. Because Jean now had "her sexual function ... more fully available to her," he surmised that she would "probably enjoy her husband more," and would at least be enriched by being "aware of herself in a way she was not before."

The method Downing used in working with Jean's dream would no doubt shock some people and seem unnecessarily sensational to others. But it is based on a coherent theory of

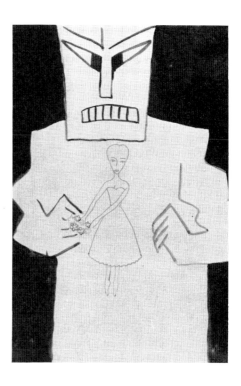

Above: a drawing by a mental patient of her relationship with her psychiatrist. Her caption read, "All I want to do is give him flowers, but look at him!"

Above: a drawing by a patient under analysis by Jung reveals his conflicting sides and layers of consciousness. He shows a black monster on the emotional (red) side and a gentle woman on the spiritual (blue) side. The green flower, according to Jung, acts as a link between the two parts of his personality.

personality developed by Perls. According to this theory there are five layers of the personality that a person has to work through before he can live fully. The first is the cliché layer, where we deal with life and relationships with meaningless formulas and exchanges of clichés without making any contact at all. The second is the synthetic layer, where we play out our roles as husband, wife, lover, parent, child, boss, or employee with a minimum of contact and no real life. The third is the impulse layer, the first level of real awareness, where genuine feelings—love, anger, joy—are bottled up and denied expression, resulting in perplexity and neurosis. The fourth is the implosive or death layer, a layer of crisis, where the denied life energies contract inward and seize up, forming a hard knot. Then comes the fifth, the explosive or life layer, where the knotted energies are released and exploded, leaving the person free, fulfilled, capable of genuine and uncluttered feeling, able to live and respond directly and vitally without needing defensive stratagems like clichés and role-playing. According to Perls there are four kinds of explosion: grief, anger, orgasm, and joy. The skill of the Gestalt therapist lies partly in the ability to diagnose a neurosis from the symptoms afforded by the dream, and partly in the ability to guide a person through the several personality layers to the explosive layer. There the unfinished business, or incomplete gestalt, of the personality is finally rounded off.

Here is an example of Perls' own dreamwork therapy recorded during one of his workshops at the Esalen Institute in California. A participant named Carl told the group about a recurrent dream he had, as follows:

"The scene is a ridge of mountains out here, and a flat desert with white sand. The sky is almost a black-blue—very dark sky, with the moon casting a very pale light over everything. And there's a train track crossing the desert in a perfectly straight line. And the train is coming along. And the sound that I hear is not the sound of a train whistle but rather a very high-pitched sort of electrical frequency whine or whistle-like sound but very steady . . . And I feel that I am in the sand—not directly in front of the train, but in the sand. I feel my head level is in the sand. I can see. And it's quite rich and often quite frightening, mainly because of the sound which is sort of infinite. And it starts and never ends. It just is there. And it drives very heavily on me. And the train sort of never ends. And I'm pretty sure it's death of some sort that's being represented in there . . . But the fear . . . It's much more of a very deep penetrating fear that's steadier. And as I think back on my life I think that those dreams are the only real feelings of fright I've ever had."

Perls regarded this as "a very typical dream of the death layer or implosive layer, where people contract and nothing happens." The desert was death, as Carl had realized, but the most significant image in the dream was that of the train, a symbol of driving energy. Instructed to be the train, Carl said: "I'm a train and I'm going somewhere, but it's nowhere . . . I have enormous direction, straight on a track. But there's no home, no resting place at the end. There's always a straight track and a direction of power . . ." Then he had to speak as if he were the tracks, and he said, "I am the tracks. I'm lying on my back and life is running over me."

Five layers of Human Personality

Left: a painting based on the one described in *The Picture of Dorian Gray*, a short story by Oscar Wilde. It tells about a youth driven to self-destruction by forces within himself. As the suppressed part of his personality gains to make his character deteriorate, his portrait also physically disintegrates. Jung viewed the suppressed part of the personality as the "shadow"— the negative and unacceptable aspects of themselves that individuals try to conceal from the world.

Above: the typical concept of the
traditional analyst-patient relationship—in
which the analyst interprets the patient's
dreams—is summed up by the psychiatrist's
couch. In this case, the couch is the one
Freud himself used during his practice of
analysis in Vienna at the end of the 19th
century.

Perls picked up the word "life" as a positive sign, and told Carl
to imagine a conversation between the train and the track. This
imaginary dialogue led to the realization that the tracks represented his mother, who controlled and directed his life force.
Here, then, was the root cause of Carl's neurosis, the knot of
resentment that was keeping his energies locked up on the
implosive or death layer.

Working with the material that his unconscious had thrown
up, Carl had to try to break through to the explosive or life layer.
Perls had him dramatize a conversation between himself and his
mother. An increasingly outspoken altercation led to Carl's
saying to his mother: "you've gotta try to pick up on where *I* am,
or who I am, and let me lead my life and not try to control it."
This was a breakthrough, an angry assertion of independence.
But now Perls took a different approach. Throughout the session
he had been observing Carl's movements and posture. He moved
only his hands and he leaned forward, leading with his head like
someone making a football tackle. "Let's finish with some discussion between your head and the rest of your body," Perls
said. The discussion revealed that Carl kept his head and body
functions completely separate, in opposition, unintegrated.
Perls advised him to work at integrating these functions by
practicing expressive dancing, and also by getting some treatment in "structural integration" of the body.

Perls claimed that with his method he can get to the heart of a
personality in half an hour, whereas psychoanalysis takes months
to get as far. The examples of Gestalt therapy presented here
clearly illustrate the correspondences and the differences between
it and the Freudian approach to dreams. Both start from the

belief that the symbolism of dreams gives a clue to a real-life situation. But whereas psychoanalysis stops with the interpretation of the symbolism and the understanding of the dream, Gestalt therapy works through the symbolism. The person has to relive the dream and exaggerate its important features in order to complete the "unfinished business" in the personality that the symbolism indicates. Gestalt therapy does not depend on interpretation by an analyst, but revolves around the dreamer's own discovery, through dramatization, of the significance of dreams. This makes it more flexible than psychoanalysis. Unlike the Freudian school of therapy, the Gestalt approach is not limited to a sexual interpretation of the meaning of dreams. It can enhance positive and pleasant dream experiences as well as interpret the bizarre and nightmarish. Its emphasis on the importance of dreams as the road to personality integration derives from Jung. While retaining many of the most important insights of both Freud and Jung, the Gestalt approach includes an emphasis typical of the 1970s on uninhibited, physical expression of the life needs indicated by a dream.

Today there is a steadily growing realization that health, happiness, and ultimately even survival—both of the individual and of society—depend on gaining an understanding of and a degree of control over our unconscious mental processes. Wars, racial antagonisms, and the compulsive pursuit of affluence can be regarded as symptoms of collective neuroses that constitute a serious threat to human survival. In this situation, all attempts to understand the many layers of human consciousness are quests for knowledge of vital importance. The widespread dissatisfaction with Freudian psychoanalysis is partly due to the fact that

Above: the new experiments in mental therapy are far more informal. This photograph is from a film made at the Esalen Institute, Big Sur, California, and shows a session of one of the Encounter groups held there. Dr. Perls has conducted several workshops using dreamwork therapy at the California Institute.

Above: Sigmund Freud, the first doctor to use psychoanalysis in the treatment of mental distress or illness. His work on dreams and their meanings has had a deep influence on modern thinking.

this kind of therapy aims to reconcile patients to a society that is itself sick. Although anyone who works with dreams today must acknowledge a debt to Freud, there are very few contemporary psychologists who dwell as exclusively as orthodox Freudians have on the pathology of the unconscious. To psychologists of the various schools that make up the "Human Potentials Movement," the unconscious is the source of health as well as of sickness, and dreams can be used as an aid to promoting the growth and development of the personality as well as a tool for diagnosing its ills.

Back in the 1940s the American psychologist Calvin Hall undertook a systematic study of dreams and developed principles for interpreting them that departed radically from psychoanalytic theory and method. Dissatisfied with the dream sample on which psychoanalysis based its theories, and which was drawn from patients undergoing treatment, Hall started by collecting and analyzing 10,000 dreams of normal people. He found that the majority of dreams are concerned with everyday situations and problems, and no elaborate theoretical framework is needed to discover their meaning. "A dream," he wrote, "is a personal document, a letter to oneself," and "the meaning of a dream will not be found in some theory about dreams; it is right there in the dream itself." Dreams, he believed, furnish us with valuable knowledge of ourselves and others, and our conception of our situation in the world. This knowledge is not readily available to consciousness because in our waking life we are continually busy and distracted from ourselves. Our waking consciousness also tends to think in the abstract terms of language, which—unless we are especially vigilant and critical— can distort or disguise reality rather than portray it. But dreams, Hall wrote, "are pictures of what the mind is thinking," and "anyone who can look at a picture and say what it means ought to be able to look at his dream pictures and say what they mean."

Of course, the ability to look at a picture and say what it means requires a certain training, a grasp of the principles of composition, draftsmanship, color, harmony, and symbolism. A rule that applies in life as in art is that what we gain from an experience depends on the knowledge, understanding, and effort we invest in it. The same applies to the understanding of dreams. At first sight they present us with a chaotic jumble of information, and we need some working principles to go by if we are to make sense of them. We might make a start, Hall suggests, by relating the dream material to one or another of five systems of ideas that the mind uses in its attempts to find order in reality and experience. These are:

1. The system that organizes the individual's self-conceptions.
2. The system that defines his or her views of other people.
3. The system that contains his views of the world, his values, ideals, and his relation to his environment.
4. The system that includes his conception of his own impulses or driving forces, how they are gratified or frustrated, and what penalties are incurred if the rules that control them are broken.
5. The system that defines his inner conflicts and organizes his attempts to solve them.

The interpretation of dreams, according to Hall, should start with examining the dream material in the light of these five questions: How do I see myself? How do I see others? How do I see the world? How do I see my impulses? How do I see my conflicts? Because many dreams are concerned with conflicts, Hall further suggests five kinds of conflict that might be found in the dream: difficulties in parent-child relationships; conflicting desires for security and freedom; sexual conflicts; the struggle to reconcile the demands of nature and impulse with the restrictions imposed by society; and finally, the basically biological conflict between the forces of life, creativity, and synthesis and those that lead to death and disintegration.

These categories will aid the person who seeks self-knowledge by examining the contents of his dreams. Further points that the person must bear in mind are:

1. The dream represents the immediate situation, the way the dreamer sees things at a particular time. He usually, however, has more than one conception of himself, others, and the world.

2. Everything that appears or occurs in the dream is the dreamer's own creation and is significant, however bizarre or foolish it may seem.

3. An isolated dream gives little reliable information. Dreams should be studied in series and over a period of time, and the information contained in them should be continually compared and consolidated.

The importance of both Perls' and Hall's approach to dreams is that they retrieve a rich vein of experience for us to use either for therapy or for self-knowledge. This mine of experience, common to all people, has generally been regarded by Western society as an inaccessible and worthless residue of personality factors discarded by our consciousness. Hall's book *The Meaning of Dreams* was, coincidentally, published in 1953, the year of the breakthrough discovery of sleep cycles and the development of REM monitoring techniques. In this way the discovery that everyone dreams regularly, and in fact needs to dream, was complemented by a systematic down-to-earth method of dealing with the wealth of material that the new techniques uncovered. Until that time one method of dream interpretation—Freud's— had predominated, and it had been employed almost exclusively for the diagnosis and treatment of patients undergoing psycho-analysis. Freud had so ruled dream interpretation that he could even get away with dismissing the evidence for clairvoyant dreams with the following words: "A dream without condensation, distortion, dramatization, above all, without wish-fulfillment surely hardly deserves the name." Such a narrow view of one of the richest, most varied, and most mysterious phenomena of the human mind is hard to excuse. By 1953, however, when the work of such individuals as Aserinsky, Kleitman, and Hall had opened up new doors to the unconscious, the grip of Freudian dogma had relaxed. Modern psychoanalysis accommodates a variety of ideas about dreams. The most influential of these, apart from Freud's, are those of C. G. Jung. Both Hall and Perls learned a great deal from Jung. But perhaps the most important thing they learned was to regard the dream not as a wish fulfillment but as a *need* fulfillment—a function that the uncon-

"A Dream is a Personal Document"

Ann Faraday's Recurring Dream

In her book *Dream Power*, Ann Faraday recounts a recurring dream she had during her second pregnancy, which she put down to her struggle to reconcile herself to motherhood.

Night after night in her dreams she was pursued by a wild cat, dog, or wolf. Sometimes she simply tried to run away, but often she fought the animal. She always won the fight either by beating her pursuer with a stick or by killing it with a knife.

Right at the end of her pregnancy, Ann Faraday's dream took a new more frightening turn. This time she met a wolf-like dog which attacked her. She beat it with a stick until it was past doing her harm, but she continued to beat it to death. As it died, its face became a woman's face and its eyes turned golden and dangerous. She realized that this woman had been "called up" to avenge the dog. At that point she awoke crying "Ecube" or something like that.

She went to Greek history and myth to look up Hecuba and Hecate as possible sources of "Ecube." What she found was disquieting: Hecuba had been such a nag that she was turned into a bitch and driven into the sea. Hecate had three animal heads—of which one was a dog.

Prospects of "Dream Power"

scious employs to achieve health, wholeness, balance, integration, and self-knowledge. They themselves made an important contribution in ridding dream interpretation of its elements of mystique. They showed that it was not a special skill possessed by the secular priesthood of psychoanalysts, but one that ordinary people could learn and apply to enrich their own lives.

In her recent book *Dream Power*, the British psychologist Dr. Ann Faraday shows how the interpretation and use of dreams can be used to enhance personal relationships, to revitalize religion, and to improve human relations in education and industry as well as to diagnose and treat both physical and mental illnesses. Until recently the only recognized practical value of dreams has been diagnostic and therapeutic. To a society like ours, Dr. Faraday's vision of a greatly extended application of "dream power" may seem utopian. But the growth of Transcendental Meditation in recent years shows that there is a widely recognized need to tap psychic forces our culture has long neglected. "Getting and spending we lay waste our powers," wrote the poet Wordsworth, a man who knew and celebrated the life-enhancing value of dreaming. There are many signs today that young people are disenchanted with a society whose primary activities and values are based on getting and spending, and that they are not prepared to lay waste their psychic powers on such pursuits. Perhaps the day when "dream power" will be applied in all the ways that Dr. Faraday envisages is not so far distant.

As the chemist Kekulé said to his colleague, "Let us learn to dream, gentlemen, and then we may perhaps find the truth." Today we know that we do not need to learn to dream, for it is an activity we all engage in every night of our lives. But we do need to learn how to pay attention to and work with our dreams. Few of us have access to EEG and REM sleep monitoring apparatus, but we do know about the common pattern of sleep cycles. Those who want to collect their dreams to better understand their subconscious can greatly increase their supply of dream data by having a gentle alarm awaken them at two-hour intervals throughout the night. A dim bedside light and a notepad and pen or a tape recorder beside the bed are the only other items needed for a systematic exploration of the world of dreams. The dreamer should observe these few basic techniques: 1. don't awaken too abruptly; 2. stay with the dream, dwell on it, and make note of any associations to particular features of it that consciousness immediately furnishes; 3. collect dreams in series and relate them to each other. The dreams obtained in this way may be worked with by the Gestalt method or examined according to the principles suggested by Hall. Different dreams will require different methods of work and interpretation, for in dealing with this most fertile area of the mind there can be no rules, only guidelines.

One thing alone is certain. Anybody who takes dreams seriously and works with them consistently and intelligently must certainly gain in knowledge and in power. And the attentive fisher for dreams may one day be rewarded by catching one of the big ones—what Jung called the "great" dreams—which glide elusively among the intricate coral reefs of the mind.

Opposite: Mr. Sandman bends over a child's bed in this painting entitled *Dream Land*. Visions of delightful fairies and castles mingle casually with the scary nightmares lurking under the bed. Little does the child who cries "There's a dream in my bed!" realize how complicated it all is, or that he will continue taking his nightly journeys into a strange but eerily familiar land through all the rest of his life.

Index

Picture Credits